The Act of Writing
COMM 170

Custom Publication for Professors
Dan Gaze and Susan Whitzman
Centennial College

MCGRAW-HILL RYERSON LIMITED

Toronto Montréal Boston Burr Ridge, IL Dubuque, IA Madison, WI New York San Francisco
St. Louis Bangkok Bogotá Caracas Kuala Lumpur Lisbon London Madrid Mexico City Milan
New Delhi Santiago Seoul Singapore Sydney Taipei

The Act of Writing: Canadian Essays for Composition, Eighth Edition, by Ronald Conrad.
Published by McGraw-Hill Ryerson Limited, a Subsidiary of The McGraw-Hill Companies, Inc., 1221 Avenue of the Americas, New York, NY, 10020.

ISBN-10: 0-07-069663-2
ISBN-13: 978-0-07-069663-1

Printed and bound in Canada

Contents

***The Act of Writing: Canadian Essays for Composition,* Eighth Edition,**
by Ronald Conrad.

Contents by Subject

Outsiders

The City

The Environment

Work

Violence in Society

Science and Technology

Business and Industry

The Arts

Laughs

Peoples and Places

Mainly Canadian

Introduction: The Act of Writing

Writing is one of the most misunderstood of human activities. It is strange that after all the years we've spent in school, after all the hours we've spent reading other people's writing and producing our own, most of us can't say what really happens when we write. We can describe other complex tasks—driving a car, producing a spreadsheet, casting for trout, or searching the Web. But to many people the act of writing is a mystery. Not that we don't have theories, either those told us in school or those we have arrived at ourselves. But many of these theories are misconceptions that actually hinder our efforts to write. Let's look at some of them.

MISCONCEPTION: ***Writing is like following a blueprint: I figure it all out in advance and then just fill in the details.*** Of course an outline, used sensibly, will help. But a generation or two ago, many students were taught that their best thinking should go into a logical and detailed outline—and that the writing itself was secondary. Thus they were reduced to carpenters or plumbers of the written word, who merely sawed, cut and fit pieces in place once the master plan was established. The problem with this reassuringly logical approach (which even today is taught in some places) is that it views writing as a technology, not as the art that all our practical experience tells us it is. How many of us have given up on a required outline, done our thinking mostly as we wrote the essay itself, then later produced the outline by seeing what we wrote? Or how many of us have painfully constructed a detailed outline in advance, only to find while writing the essay that our real message does not fit the plan?

Writing is exploring! We know which way we are headed and the main landmarks we hope to pass, but not every twist and turn of the path. What a dull trip that would be! Let's leave room for discovery, because our best ideas may occur in the act of writing. The Quebec poet Hector de St.-Denys Garneau actually said, "I cannot think except when writing." Some teachers reflect this fact of writing as discovery by calling a first version the *discovery draft.*

But while avoiding the rigor mortis of overplanning, let's not go to the opposite extreme, like Stephen Leacock's famous horseman who "rode madly off in all directions." We do work best with an outline, five or ten or fifteen lines that define the main point and how we intend to support it. But the outline should be a compass on a journey, not the blueprint of a construction project.

MISCONCEPTION: ***If I don't hit it right the first time, I've failed.*** It's not hard to see where this idea came from: in school we write so many essays and tests within the limits of one class period that writing in a hurry begins to seem normal. But under such conditions, merely producing enough is hard; seriously revising it is even harder. Few people can "hit it right the first time." Professional writers know this; most of them take longer to write than we do. They tinker with words and sentences, they delete and replace sections, they go through two or three or even five or ten versions—and sometimes they throw the whole thing out and start over. These writers know by experience that writing is not a hit-or-miss affair with only one try allowed, but a *process.* They know that revision can yield amazing results.

MISCONCEPTION: ***When I write, I am speaking on paper.*** If you've heard a recording of yourself speaking, you were no doubt surprised at all the filler words you used. "Uh," "um," "well" and "hmmm" may fill the gaps between your thoughts very conveniently, but they hardly help to carry the message. And if you listened closely, you may have been surprised at the number of incomplete statements—fragments that by themselves made little or no sense. Fillers and fragments are accepted in speech because, after all, we're making up our message on the spot. There is no chance to plan, revise, edit or proofread.

But in writing there is, and this fact increases the expectations of your reader far beyond those of your listener. Language in written form can be planned. It is complete. It is precise and concise. It uses standard words. It has punctuation. It follows the rules. In short, it is a product of the time that its written form allows you to give it, not a spur-of-the-moment, hope-for-the-best effort like the speech that comes so easily from your mouth.

MISCONCEPTION: ***The best words are the biggest words.*** Variations on this theme are *If my writing looks scholarly it will impress the reader,* and even *If I make my essay so difficult that no one knows what I'm saying, everyone will believe me.* At the roots of these widespread ideas is a notion that writing is a kind of competition between writer and reader. A writer who is obscure enough will make the reader feel like a dummy and will thus win the game. But ask yourself: In real life do you *ambulate* or *walk*? *Expectorate* or *spit*? *Interdigitate* or *hold hands*? *Cogitate* or *think*?

Avoiding this game of writer vs. reader is not easy when so many leaders in business, education and government play it. The first step toward open communication, though, is to think of your reader not as an opponent but as a teammate. You are both moving toward the same goal, which is the reader's clear understanding of your ideas.

Another step is to admit that words small in size can be large in meaning. The best-loved writings in our language (think of the lines from Shakespeare you may have memorized for school) are filled with short words. Writing made of them is more concise, more vivid, and usually more profound than writing made of the elephantine words that some of us ransack the dictionary or thesaurus for. If a long word—like "elephantine" above—conveys your meaning best, by all means use it. But often the writer, like the architect, finds that *less is more.*

MISCONCEPTION: ***I don't like to write.*** For some unfortunate people this statement is true. But for most who say it, the truth is really "I don't like to *begin* writing." Who does? Staring at that blank page or screen is like staring from a diving board at the cold water below. But a swimmer and a writer both gather the courage to plunge in, and soon they both feel a new sensation: they don't want to come out. Teachers whose students write journals in class see the process at work every day. As class begins, the writers are filled with stress: they chew their pens and frown as they stare at the page to be filled. But in a while they are scribbling furiously, recording in an almost trance-like state their latest experiences, feelings and insights. When the teacher asks them to stop, in order to begin the next activity, they are annoyed: they sigh and *keep on writing* till asked a second or third time to stop.

Let's admit that most writers—and that includes professionals—dread the beginning. Let's also admit that most writers can enjoy the rest of it, hard work though it may be.

With some of the most widespread misconceptions behind us now, let's take a fresh look at the act of writing. First, allow for personal differences. *Know yourself.* If you are a person whose desk is piled high with papers and books, whose closet is an avalanche waiting to happen, and whose shoes have not been shined in two years, you may write best by planning little and relying on your spontaneity. But if you are a person who plans an August holiday in January, keeps a budget right down to the penny, and washes the car every Wednesday and Saturday whether it needs it or not, you may write best by planning fully.

On the other hand, your natural tendencies may have caused you problems and so may need to be controlled. If your spontaneity has produced writings that wander off topic, plan more: make a careful outline. If overorganizing has sucked the life out of your writing, free yourself up: leave more room for discovery as you write. Whatever the case, try to determine and use the approach that works for *you.*

Let's allow also for differences in writing tasks. If you are dashing off a short personal sketch, your planning may be no more than an idea and a few moments of thought. If you are writing a long research paper, the product of days in the library, you may need an outline two pages long. No single approach works for every person and every assignment. Keep in mind, then, that the process we are about to examine is a *starting point*, a basis but not a blueprint, for your own writing.

BEFORE YOU START THE ESSAY, TRY ANSWERING THESE QUESTIONS:

1. WHY AM I WRITING? Today most of us are writing more than ever before. In Margaret Wente's essay "Busy, Busy, Busy" (Chapter 2), someone says: "I took three days off and when I got back to the office I had six hundred e-mails." Another person replies: "That's nothing.... I had two thousand...." Mobile communication devices add to the flurry, with text messaging throughout the day. Even while in school, we exchange written digital messages to plan our social events, organize our activities or just to entertain each other with our comments. We know why we are writing. But in an academic sense, when we begin to imagine and write an essay, do we know why we are writing? This basic question too often goes unasked. If the answer is "to fill up five pages," "to impress" or "to get an A," you begin with a severe handicap. The immediate reason to write may be a class assignment, but the real reason must be to communicate something of value. Otherwise your motivation is lost and so is your performance. So, from a list of topics, choose the one that means the most to you. If no topic seems significant, devise a way to *make* one significant. Probe the topic through the exercise of freewriting, explained later. Look at your topic from a new viewpoint or approach it in some unusual way.

If that fails, and if your teacher is approachable, voice your concern and ask for an alternative topic. One teacher always made students analyze the relative merits of chocolate and vanilla ice cream, on the theory that a dull subject will not distract a writer from the real goals: grammar and style. He was wrong. Research shows motivation to be the single greatest factor in writing performance—and motivation comes from writing about things that matter.

When you write on your own, as in a personal journal, you may still need to answer the question *Why am I writing?* Just recording events may not be enough. Add your feelings, your perceptions and your conclusions about those events. If you have problems, as most people do, confront them on the page. The more you discover yourself and your world through writing, the more important the writing becomes.

2. WHO IS MY AUDIENCE? Do you talk the same way to a friend and a stranger? To an old person and a child? Probably not. Neither would you write the same way to all readers. In a personal journal you can write as freely as you think, for you are your own reader: omissions and excesses of all kinds will be understood and forgiven. In messages to a close friend you are nearly as free, because the reader knows you well enough to supply missing explanations or interpret remarks in the light of your personality. But your freedom shrinks when you write for others: a business person, a public official, a teacher. Now you must fight a misconception shared by many people: *Everyone is like me.*

This idea is seldom articulated but may lurk as a natural assumption in the back of our minds. It is a form of egotism. If you assume everyone is like you, many readers will not accept or even understand your message—because they are *not* like you. They did not grow up in your family, neighbourhood or even country. They are older or younger, or of the opposite sex. They have had different life experiences, so now they have different knowledge and temperaments and values.

Accept these differences as you write. You will never prove your point by quoting Marx to a banker, the Bible to an atheist, or Margaret Atwood to a male supremacist. Any argument built on a partisan foundation will collapse if the reader does not accept that foundation. Instead, build from facts or ideas that your reader probably *does* accept: killing is bad, government is necessary, women are human beings, and so on. Is your subject controversial? Then avoid an open display of bias. Calling police "pigs" or intellectuals "eggheads" or abortionists "hired killers" will appeal only to those who shared your view in the first place. (For more on these matters, read the introduction to Chapter 9, "Argumentation and Persuasion.")

Does the reader know what you know? If you write about statistics for a statistics teacher, use any technical terms customary to the field, and avoid the insult of explaining elementary points. But if you write on the same subject for a class exercise in English or a letter to the editor of your hometown newspaper, your reader will be very different: avoid most technical terms, define those you do use, and explain more fully each step of your argument.

The more open you become to the individuality of your reader, the more open your reader becomes to your message. It's a matter of mutual respect.

3. HOW BIG IS MY TOPIC? Classroom essays are shorter than most people realize. A book may contain 100,000 words; a magazine article 2000 or 5000; a classroom essay as few as 500 or even 250. So narrowing the essay topic is more important than most people realize.

One student, who had been a political prisoner before coming to Canada, chose to write about economic systems. He knew the subject well, as his teacher found out talking with him, and he was committed to it. But what he attempted was an analysis of communism, socialism and capitalism, all in two pages! A lack of focus spread his very short essay so thin that it approached the state of saying nothing about everything. It was the barest scratching of the surface, a summary of basic facts everyone already knows.

If the same person had focussed on his arrest and imprisonment—or even on one day in his cell—he might have said far more about the system he opposed. He could have told his readers about the rotten food, the noise, the open bucket latrine, the insulting guards, and the patriotic slogans on the walls. He could have described the other prisoners who had been arrested for showing up at political protests. It is in specifics that we best see generalities. Think of writing as photography. Putting aside the wide-angle view that includes too much at a distance, let the zoom bring you up close to a small part of the subject. Select the part most meaningful to you, the part most characteristic of the whole, then take the picture.

Nearly all the essays in this book are closeups: they explore one situation, one incident, one person or one process. Yet many of them are longer than the essays you will write. So when you choose a topic, judge its size. And if you have to, *change* its size to fit your writing task.

4. WHAT MESSAGE AM I SENDING? ***(Or: What is my* THESIS STATEMENT*?)*** You may know your topic well. But unless you send a message concerning it, your reader will think *What's the point?* A message is often a value judgement: Are robots dangerous? Will they take away our jobs or someday even rule over us? Or do they help us? Will they free us at last from the dehumanizing tyranny of manual labour? Most of the essays in this book take such a stance, either pro or con, toward their subjects. Some avoid judging their subjects directly, but send other messages: what it's like to be homeless, or what it's like to operate on someone's brain.

If you have chosen a topic because it seems meaningful, you will probably have a message to send. So what do you most feel like saying about the topic? Try the techniques of brainstorming and freewriting described in the next section, "Prewriting," to help you find out. Once you know, get your message down in writing. This **THESIS STATEMENT**, as it is called, is normally a single sentence that occurs at or near the beginning of an essay. But it doesn't just announce the subject; it also clearly conveys the writer's message, the writer's *opinion,* about some aspect of that subject.

For example, the sentence "*Many people have credit cards*" does announce an overall subject, but could never be a thesis statement because it is too general. It tells us something we already know. How could we spend several pages arguing that many people have credit cards? But certainly there are other messages about this important subject that could be sent. Let's look at some potential thesis statements. Which ones focus their subject down to a closeup? Which ones take into account their audience? Which ones announce a message, a point of view, that is worth supporting?

- *Many students have credit cards.* (Forget it: this is almost as general as "Many people have credit cards.")
- *I once lost my credit card.* (This is more specific, but how could it be argued when it's merely an incident? Where is the opinion we need?)

- *The fastest way to gain control over your finances is to cut up your credit card.* (Now we're getting somewhere: the topic is very specific, and the statement is an opinion that needs support so that readers will accept it. All kinds of evidence might be given: the high credit card interest rates, the risk of identity theft and other fraud, the ease of spending more with a card, etc.)
- *In order to keep the working class enslaved in debt, the greedy masters of our capitalist system promote more and more use of credit cards.* (This writer forgot to ask "Who is my audience?" Any reader who does like our economic system will probably reject the argument that follows. That argument might still succeed, though, with more tactful language and with enough factual examples (such as the interest rate of many cards nearing 20% annually).
- *A credit card is a good financial tool if the balance is paid off each month.* (Here again is a worthwhile potential thesis statement: it is well focussed, and it has an idea that requires support so the reader will accept it.)

PREWRITING

So how do we begin the act of writing? By putting those first words on a page? The philosopher Lao-Tze said, "A journey of a thousand miles begins with a single step." In a way he was right: if we never take that official first step, we'll certainly never arrive at our destination. But how much daydreaming and planning do we do beforehand? Do we set out on a journey without consulting the map or the calendar or the tourist brochure or the travel guide—not to mention our wallet? And do we write an essay without somehow answering the questions we have just asked:

Why am I writing?
Who is my audience?
How big is my topic?
What message am I sending?

The process of writing, then, begins in thought. But thoughts do not come on command. Like the person on the diving board, we look down at the cold water and dread the plunge. Some writers like to break the ice by manipulating their environment: finding a quiet spot, going to a favourite chair with good lighting, or listening to music. Others fortify themselves with a good night's sleep, junk food or coffee. Any of these tricks may help, but they all skirt the real issue: How do we begin to *think*?

One direct approach, a variation on the old technique of outlining, is ***brainstorming***. Once you have roughly identified your subject, just write down words or phrases that relate in any way to it, in a list going down a page. Put down anything that comes, letting one thought lead to another. Some entries will seem off-topic, trivial or even crazy, but others may be just what you need: the keys to your essay. Circle them. Put them in order. As crude as this primitive outline may seem, it has served a purpose: your thoughts have begun to arrive. The process is in motion. You have taken that first "step" before even starting the first draft.

A similar but even more powerful icebreaker is ***freewriting***. Put a blank page on the desk with your watch beside it. Think of your topic. Now write! Put down anything that comes: sentences, phrases, words—logical thoughts, hasty impressions, even pure garbage. Do not cease the physical act of writing, do not even lift the pen from the page, or your fingers from the keyboard, for at least five minutes. If your next thought doesn't come, write the last one over and over till the next one does come. What emerges may surprise you.

Like brainstorming, freewriting is an exercise in free association: the flow of your thoughts, the sudden leaps of your intuition, will break the ice so you can write. They may do even more: as in brainstorming, you may end up with a page of scribbling that contains the main points of your essay. Try to find them. Circle them. Put them in order. See if your intuition has led the way in answering the questions: *Why am I writing? Who is my audience? How big is my topic? What message am I sending?* If all goes well, you have already begun your journey.

THE FIRST WORDS

Once your thoughts are flowing comes the next step, the opening passage of your essay. In a very short composition your THESIS STATEMENT may serve also as the first words. But in most essays of medium to long length, it comes at the end of an introduction. Only about one-fourth of the selections in this book start right off with what could be called a thesis statement. What do the others start with?

BACKGROUND INFORMATION: About half the essays in this book lead off by telling the circumstances in which the topic is set. For examples, see the beginnings of our selections by Gabori (p. 26), Simic (p. 84), Wiebe (p. 101), Garneau (p. 138), McQuaig (p. 154), Hocking (p. 354), Dobbs (p. 361), Schindler (p. 404), Atwood (p. 392) and Christy (p. 409).

ANECDOTE: A brief story, usually of a humorous or dramatic incident, can lead into the topic. See Wente (p. 61), Pearson (p. 133), Callwood (p. 161), Pigott (p. 196), Taylor (p. 216), Bernstein (p. 311) and Leacock (p. 338).

QUOTATION OR ALLUSION: The words of a philosopher, of a news report, of a recognized specialist in the subject, or of anyone with close experience of it can be used to break the ice. See Pearson (p. 133), Taylor (p. 216), Dobbs (p. 361) and Kogawa (p. 373).

SENSE IMAGES: Vivid description can attract a reader's interest to the topic. See Lane (p. 37), Geddes (p. 45), Fiorito (p. 77), McLaren (p. 96), Wiebe (p. 101), Harrison (p. 108), Mackintosh (p. 270), Klein (p. 398) and Dallaire (p. 414).

A STRIKING COMPARISON OR CONTRAST: Showing how things are like or unlike each other is a dramatic way to introduce a topic. See Shields (p. 31), Gabori (p. 26), Rosenthal (p. 71), Garneau (p. 138), Anderson (p. 191), Nolen (p. 202), Pigott (p. 196), Koehl (p. 318) and Hocking (p. 354).

NARRATIVE: Several selections in this book begin by telling a story upon which the essay is based. See Carr (p. 117), D'Angelo (p. 144), Pigott (p. 196), Dobbs (p. 361), Klein (p. 398) and Dallaire (p. 414).

AN UNUSUAL OR PUZZLING STATEMENT: Such an opening appeals to the reader's curiosity. See Simic (p. 84), Carr (p. 117), Pearson (p. 133) and Evans (p. 238).

FIGURES OF SPEECH: A striking METAPHOR, SIMILE or PERSONIFICATION can spark the opening. See Hill (p. 228) and Bennett (p. 264).

Most of these introductions are short: a couple of sentences or a paragraph or two at the most. And all are designed to *interest* the reader, for a bored reader may not even finish the essay, let alone like or understand it. Writing is fishing. You throw in the line. Your reader tastes the bait (your introduction), bites, is pulled through the stream of your argument, and—if the line of thought doesn't break—lands in your net.

You, the writer, may also be hooked. Once you have hit upon a strong introduction, one that shows off the drama or importance of your topic, the beginning may carry you along. And once you get going, the idea embodied in your thesis statement may pull you through the essay, enabling you to write freely as one page leads to another. You may become less and less aware of your surroundings as you become more and more immersed in your subject. By the time you develop a good beginning, you may experience the act of writing the way one student described it: "At first I couldn't start, but then I couldn't stop."

THE BODY

An introduction to an essay is like your head: it may decide to go somewhere but it needs your body to take it there. The "body" of your essay has the main work to do: following the direction set by your introduction, and especially by your thesis statement, the body explains, illustrates and sometimes attempts to prove your point. But if it ever ignores the direction set by the head, it ceases to do its job. Even the best of explanations, without a purpose, is like one of those unfortunate football players who completes a spectacular run to the wrong goal. On the other hand, we know that writing is discovery. The acts of writing and revising will sometimes take us in a direction better than the old one decided by the introduction. When that happens, correct not the body but the head—so the two can move together in the new direction.

One of the easiest ways to keep a direction is to choose a pattern for your essay—and that is what much of this book is about. As you read and discuss the essays that follow, and as you write your own essays, trying out the patterns other writers use, you will explore a range of choices:

NARRATION: In simple time order, from the first event to the last event, tell a story that illustrates the point. (See pages 26 to 52.)

EXAMPLE: Give one in-depth example that explains the point, or a number of shorter examples. (See pages 61 to 87.)

DESCRIPTION: Recreate for your reader, through vivid language, your own or someone else's experience with the subject. (See pages 96 to 124.)

CAUSE AND EFFECT: Explain by showing how one situation or event causes another. (See pages 133 to 182.)

COMPARISON AND CONTRAST: Explain by showing how two things are like or unlike each other. (See pages 191 to 244.)

ANALOGY AND RELATED DEVICES: In comparing two things, use the one to explain the other. (See pages 253 to 275.)

CLASSIFICATION: Make a point by dividing your subject into parts, then explaining each in turn. (See pages 284 to 302.)

PROCESS ANALYSIS: Show how something is done or how something happens. (See pages 311 to 341.)

ARGUMENTATION AND PERSUASION: Using any pattern that works, make your point through logic and/or emotion. (See pages 354 to 421.)

Seldom does one of these methods appear alone. A *process analysis,* for example, is usually told as a *narrative.* Here and there it may use *examples, description* or any of the other patterns to help make its point, but these combinations occur naturally, often without the writer's knowing it. In most cases the only form actually chosen by a writer is the main one that organizes the whole essay.

How do you choose the right form? Let the subject be your guide. In architecture, form follows function. Rather than cram an office into a preselected structure, a designer likes to begin with the function of that office. How much space does it need? What shape? What barriers and passageways between one section and another? What front to present to the world?

An essay is much the same: the needs of its subject, if you are open to them, can suggest a form. If the main idea is to explain what something is like, you will tend to choose *examples* and *description.* If the subject is unusual or little known, you may *compare or contrast,* or make an *analogy* with something the reader does know. If its parts seem important, you may examine them one by one through *classification.* When some other need is greater, you may use still another form. If you stay open to the subject, whatever it is, this process can be so natural that you *recognize* a form rather than *choose* it.

If the process is natural, then why study these forms at all? Well, architecture students certainly study different kinds of building design, so their future condominiums or shopping centres don't collapse and kill people. Fortunately, readers are not killed by poorly organized essays, but the idea is similar: if the writer has a conscious knowledge of all the possibilities, his or her arguments will be easier to build and will be less likely to collapse.

Consider the longer essay—say, a major report or research paper. A jumble of notes sits on your desk. They are in chaos. Even with brainstorming or freewriting, knowing your purpose, having the facts and completing a thesis statement, you don't know how to coordinate all those facts. First give the natural process its best chance: *sort all your notes into groups of related material,* using a pair of scissors if necessary to divide unrelated points. When everything is in two stacks, or three stacks or five, let your mind work freely. How do these groups relate to each other? Does one contradict another? Are they all steps in a process or parts of a whole? Now add your conscious knowledge of the forms: Do you see *narration, example, description, cause and effect, comparison and contrast, analogy, classification* or *process analysis*? It is the rare case when one of these forms cannot supply a structure to support your argument.

Right now you are practising them one by one, as the students in architecture school study different structures one by one—so that in all your future writing you will have choices. And for now, you may be using the topics at the end of the readings, or the larger list of Topics for Writing on the Online Learning Centre at www.mcgrawhill.ca/olc/conrad, because they are coordinated to go with the form you have just read and discussed. But in your future writing you will go a step further, making the match yourself between topic and form.

Yet, even when you are looking over 30 options, you are exercising choice: spend a good long time to pick the topic that strikes you as most interesting, most significant—and therefore most motivating. It is writing about things that matter that will most increase your performance—now and always.

TRANSITIONS

We have mentioned the passageways inside a building. Without them an office would be useless: no one could move from one room to another to have meetings. Yet some essays are built without passageways. One point ends where another begins, without even a "then" or "therefore" or "however" or "finally" to join them. Readers then have to break down walls to follow thoughts from one room to the next.

Help your readers. *You* know why one point follows another, but do *they*? Make sure by supplying plenty of transition words. They come in many kinds: to show *contrast* say "although" or "but" or "on the other hand" or "instead." To show *causality* say "because" or "therefore" or "as a result" or "since." To show *progression in time*, say "first" or "next" or "finally" or "last" or "in conclusion." And when you are moving readers from one main part of your essay to the next, devote a full sentence or even a paragraph of transition to the job (one good example is paragraph 10 of Doris Anderson's essay).

It is a little-known fact that one of the quickest and easiest ways for most students to make their writing stronger is to use many more of these transition words. Look for places where they are needed. In fact, when you are proofing and checking, devote one complete read-through of your manuscript to adding transition words. Make sure they are the right ones, too, so that each will help convey the logic of the passage.

Your overall essay plan may already be the right one, arranging your points in their most logical order. But now let that logic show: through use of transitions, give your readers a door between every room.

THE CLOSING

A recent piece of e-mail humour says that a conclusion is "the place where you got tired of thinking." Well, if you got some sleep last night and had your coffee, that doesn't have to happen. Every essay does have an ending—the place where the writing stops. But just halting the words is not enough. A closing in some way has to be deliberate, has to achieve a worthwhile purpose, has to let your reader know that this is where you have chosen to stop. If you quit at just any convenient spot, without engineering an effect to fit your ending, the essay may trail off or even fall flat. But as preachers, composers, playwrights and film directors know, a good closing can be even stronger than a good opening. How do the essays in this book come to a close? They use a variety of devices:

REFERENCE TO THE OPENING: Repeating or restating something from the opening gives a sense of culmination, of having come full circle. See the openings and closings by Wente (pp. 61 and 63), Rosenthal (pp. 71 and 73), Fiorito (pp. 77 and 81), Simic (pp. 84 and 87), Nolen (pp. 202 and 207), Evans (pp. 238 and 244), Lam (pp. 285 and 287), Kogawa (pp. 374 and 377) and Christy (pp. 410 and 411).

CONTRAST OR REVERSAL: This ironic device exploits the dramatic potential of the closing. See the opening and closing by Wente (pp. 61 and 63), Fiorito (pp. 77 and 81) and Sampang (pp. 176 and 182).

QUESTION: A question and its answer, or a question calling for the reader's answer, is a common means of closing. See Leacock (p. 341) and Christy (p. 411).

QUOTATION: A good quotation, of either prose or poetry, can add authority and interest to a closing.

TRANSITION SIGNALS: Words, phrases or sentences of transition commonly signal the closing. See Gabori (p. 28), Sampang (p. 182), Pigott (p. 199), Evans (p. 244) and Johnston (p. 261).

REVEALING THE SIGNIFICANCE: Showing the implications or importance of the subject makes for a strong closing. See Gabori (p. 28), Shields (p. 34), Lane (p. 41), Garneau (p. 140), Petrowski (p. 172), Callwood (p. 165), Johnston (p. 261), Dobbs (p. 369), Atwood (p. 395) and Dallaire (p. 421).

SUMMARY: About a fourth of the essays in this book give a summary, either alone or in combination with other closing techniques, but one that is always short. See McQuaig (p. 158), Anderson (p. 193), Bennett (p. 267), Koehl (p. 320) and Hocking (p. 358).

CONCLUSION: Although "conclusion" is often a label for the closing in general, more accurately it is only one of many closing techniques—the drawing of a conclusion from the discussion in the essay. See Geddes (p. 52), Rosenthal (p. 73), Pearson (p. 135), Garneau (p. 140), Mustafa (p. 151), Callwood (p. 165), Traill (p. 225), Lam and Lee (p. 254), Ford (p. 325), Atwood (p. 395) and Klein (p. 401).

PREDICTION: A short look at the subject's future can very logically close a discussion of that subject's past or present. See Geddes (p. 52), Petrowski (p. 172), Evans (p. 244) and Savage (p. 389). Sometimes discussing the future takes the form of a call to action.

You have probably noticed that some authors are named here more than once; closings, like openings, can exploit more than one technique. In fact, the more the better. Stay open to techniques that appear while you write, even as you construct a closing using a technique you have deliberately chosen.

Any of these choices will be stronger, though, when used with the most fundamental technique of all: building your whole essay toward a high point or *climax*. Put your points in order from least important to most important, from least useful to most useful, or from least dramatic to most dramatic. (Sometimes you will not know this order till late in the writing. Just use your software to cut and paste.) When everything leads up to that climax, you have set the stage for a closing that applies all the dramatic power of the final position.

When you get there, apply the force of that closing to a real message. Techniques used just for their own sake are cheap tricks. Do not waste them. Instead, use them to underline your basic message, to impress upon your audience one last and most convincing time that what you have to say is significant. Your closing, more than any other part of your essay, can send the reader away disappointed—or moved.

THE PROCESS: HOW MUCH REVISION?

We have discussed the act of writing as a process in which, rather than trying to "hit it right the first time," we follow a number of steps in the journey toward a good essay. The rest of this book develops that approach. After each selection you'll find an assignment called "Process in Writing" that draws on the essay you've just read, suggesting a related topic for an essay of your own. The main steps of the process are given, individualized for each topic.

At the end of each chapter are sections called "Process in Writing: Guidelines" that give the steps of a process designed for the organizational form you've just studied. Also, in the online Topics for Writing at www.mcgrawhill.ca/olc/conrad, you'll find a whole page of essay topics designed for such practice. Whether you write on an end-of-essay or an online topic, remember that these steps are only *guidelines* to the process; choose the ones that seem best for each case.

Our process of writing is flexible; it is not a blueprint like the elaborate outlines students have in the past been made to construct.

Above all, the process is "recursive"—that is, while you may begin with brainstorming or freewriting, go on to a discovery draft, revise your argument in further versions, and finally edit for spelling and punctuation, you may also double back or jump ahead at any time. Studies show that professionals writing all kinds of documents in all kinds of fields do this. While generating their first version they may stop here and there to improve a word choice or fix punctuation—changes that normally are made later. Or, while they are in the middle of editing or even proofreading, a fine new idea may come thundering out of their mind; so they may back up a few steps, write it out, and add it to their argument, maybe dropping something else they had thought was good. All this is consistent with the reality that *we think while writing.*

Do feel free to transgress the process "guidelines" in these ways, but not so often that you undercut the advantages of the process itself. For example, in writing your first version you may detect some weak sentence structure. If you must, stop here to edit. But better yet, why not just mark the spot (at the keyboard, insert something easy to see, such as several asterisks), then come back to fix things later? For now, let the material keep rolling out uninterrupted. Then later on, while you are editing or even proofreading, a whole new idea may arrive. You could go back even now to fit it in—but this means work, maybe even reorganization. Proceed only if it is a real improvement and if you have the time.

WHEN YOU DO GET TO THE MAIN PROOFREADING, THE FINAL QUALITY CONTROL, TRY THESE TECHNIQUES:

- Whenever possible, leave some time between the writing and the checking, so that you can see text with new eyes, and more easily catch errors.
- Try reading your manuscript backwards, sentence by sentence. This will isolate each sentence from its context, so that you can more easily see if it makes sense on its own.
- Lay a straight edge, such as a ruler, under each line of print as you check it. This will prevent visual confusion.

- Read your manuscript aloud, slowly, because your ear will hear things that your eye will not see. For example, you may have used one word too many times in the same passage; when you hear this repetition, you will recognize it and can then look for replacement words.
- Keep in mind the tools of your computer, and their limitations. When using your thesaurus (digital or paper), don't choose and add any word whose meaning you don't really know. Use the paper dictionary to make sure. Spelling is another matter: of course your software will signal right away when you have misspelled a word. Make the corrections, either then or later, but keep in mind that computer spelling programs cannot detect a correctly spelled word that is in the wrong place (for example, "there" for "their," or "to" for "too.") So there is still work to do of your own. Don't trust your grammar checking program either. It is better to keep a book of usage and grammar on your desk, and consult it often.

Finally, how much revision is enough? Gone are the days when students would write on paper, insert a mass of corrections between the lines or in the margin, then copy the whole thing over into draft two, make more corrections, then go on to draft three or even four or five. This whole labour-intensive system has of course been changed by the computer. Now most of us compose our first version right onto the screen. Later we make changes—anything from adding a comma to seriously revising the whole argument. Then whenever we are done, for the moment, we save. Later we return as often as we want, making further improvements. Finally we apply proofing techniques such as those listed above, and save again. The important thing is not calculating how many "drafts" we are producing, but just getting down to work and spending serious time refining our argument, our organization, our style, our correctness.

When do you reach the journey's end? You will probably know when you get there. It is the point where your response to a significant topic has become so direct, so exact, so forceful, that at last you know exactly what you think. It is clear that you were writing for others, but at this moment it is even clearer that you were writing for yourself.

Geostock/Getty Images

"Her eyes are bright with a cold, steady patience. I have stared into them and tried to see into her arachnid mind but what stared back at me was nothing I knew or understood."

—Patrick Lane, "There Is a Season"

1 NARRATION

AND THEN....

Telling a story, or *narrating*, is an appealing and natural way to convey information. Every time you tell a joke, trade gossip, invent a ghost story or tell a friend what you did on the weekend, you are narrating. In both speech and writing, telling a story can also be the most direct way to make a point. If your idea or opinion was formed by an experience, a clear account of that experience can help others understand and believe your point.

For example, in this chapter George Gabori narrates his experience of a schoolyard fight. At age nine, the Jewish boy has just moved to a public school in his village in Hungary. A new friend, Tivadar, asks him one day whether it was the Jews who killed Jesus. They had not, young George's father informs him that night. But the next day when George relates this information to his friend, Tivadar hits him and bloodies his nose. A crowd gathers, shouting to "kill the Jew," but in fact it is young George who gets in a blow that sends Tivadar sprawling and helpless. Later, he assumes his father will be angry,

21

especially when the father muses, "Jews don't fight." George asks, outraged, "Then why did you put me in a Christian school?"

"That's why I put you there, my son," the father replies, then kisses him and adds, "You're learning fast; only next time don't hit him quite so hard."

So why did George Gabori, years later living in Canada and writing his autobiography, retell this event? Why, in fact, did he use it as the opening passage to his whole life's story? The answer is clear: this was the day he learned what racism is, and that knowledge would be central to his later life. It turned him into a scrapper who blew up German trains in the Resistance, and who survived both Nazi and communist concentration camps.

Notice that nowhere in this passage does Gabori editorialize on what it was he learned that day. There is no official thesis statement, as there normally is in the essays we write. But there is what could be called an *"implied" thesis statement.* It is simply the fact that this short reading, like all effective narratives, has a point.

In "There Is a Season," later in this chapter, Patrick Lane offers another kind of implied thesis statement. After reporting on the whole mating ceremony of the orb-weaver spider, after showing us the male strumming on the web, the female charging to make a meal of him, then his escaping as she tears off one of his legs, Lane ends the passage with his own resolve to give the food gift of a moth or a fly to "one of the great mothers of the garden." In this envisioned act, Lane "implies" his sense of respect and wonder at the lives of these spiders.

Of course narratives don't have to be violent or tragic or even dramatic. When Carol Shields in "Encounter" tells of her memorable walk in the rain, sharing an umbrella with a total stranger in Tokyo, we quickly grasp her underlying point that communication is a universal desire.

Narration is such an all-purpose tool that many authors in other chapters of this book use it too. Emily Carr narrates three painting expeditions to coastal native villages. Paul D'Angelo narrates a personal encounter in an elevator. Both Hugh MacLennan and Kildare Dobbs narrate the details of dramatic human-made explosions. Dr. Mark Bernstein narrates a brain operation, and General Roméo

Dallaire narrates an incident that, for him and for us, sums up the tragedy of genocide in Rwanda. (See below for page numbers.)

(By the way, the term "narration" can also refer to pieces of speech quoted in an essay or in fiction. In this chapter, though, we are using it mostly in its larger sense of telling a story.)

Many *examples* given by writers are really bits of *narrative.* To show how Canadians love risky water sports (in "This Boat Is My Boat," p. 216), Drew Hayden Taylor takes us out on the waves of the Georgian Bay, briefly narrating an experience that makes the point very clear.

In some ways narrating is easy. For example, the only research Shields required was her own experience; and her basic plan of organization was no more complicated than the chronological order in which the events occurred. (A flashback to the past or a glance at the future may intervene, but basically a narrative is the easiest of all writing to organize.) Yet a narrative, like any form of writing, is built on choices:

CHOICE OF SCOPE: Time stretches infinitely toward both the past and future—but where does your narrative most logically begin and end? Include only parts that develop your point. Do you need to dwell on getting dressed, eating breakfast, brushing your teeth and catching the bus, on the day you became a Canadian citizen? Or did the event really begin when you opened the courthouse door? When facts about the past or future are needed, sketch them in briefly so you interrupt the least you can.

Note that different narratives can have different time spans: while Shields shares maybe half an hour of her life story with us, Lane shares several hours, Gabori shares two days and Carole Geddes ("Growing Up Native") shares her whole lifetime so far. Of course the challenge increases with the span of time: Geddes is very careful to choose details that convey her main life experiences without consuming too many words.

CHOICE OF DETAILS: Which details count? Reject random or trivial ones and seek those that convey your main impression or idea. When on that school playground young Gabori experiences racist violence, he tells us how he tastes his own blood. What could more clearly convey his experience that day? Choose details that are vivid. Reject weak ones and select those that help the reader *see, hear, feel, smell* or *taste*—in other words those which, by appealing to the senses, help readers live the event.

CHOICE OF CONNECTIONS: Readers love to be "swept along" by narrative. How is this effect achieved? Partly just through a good story. Time signals, though, increase the impact of any narrative. Like road signs for the driver, terms like "at first," "next," "then," "immediately," "suddenly," "later," "finally" and "at last" show the way and encourage progress. Use these road signs, and others like them, at every curve. Choose carefully, so signals speed the reader to your chosen destination.

So far we have been discussing mostly the first-person narrative. There are many advantages to writing about yourself. You know your subject well (in fact, is there any subject you know better?), yet in writing about yourself you may better understand your own ideas and actions. Your vital interest in your subject will motivate the writing. And finally, readers appreciate the authenticity of a story told by the very person who lived the event.

But of course writing in third person opens up many more possibilities. Only by writing about others can one discuss past eras, places one has never visited, and events one has never experienced. Kildare Dobbs does this masterfully in his narrative "The Scar," in Chapter 9. He was not in Hiroshima the day it crumbled beneath an atomic blast, but his research and his imagination almost make it seem so; more importantly, reading his narrative almost makes us feel we were there too.

Note: Many authors in later chapters combine narration with other ways to develop their material. For more examples, see these selections:

Margaret Wente, "Busy, Busy, Busy," p. 61
Rudy Wiebe, "The Bull," p. 101
Emily Carr, "D'Sonoqua," p. 117
Charles Yale Harrison, "In the Trenches," p. 108

Paul D'Angelo, "The Step Not Taken," p. 144
Crisanta Sampang, "Trading Motherhood for Dollars," p. 176
Hugh MacLennan, "A Sound Beyond Hearing," p. 296
Dr. Mark Bernstein, "Yes, It Is Brain Surgery," p. 311
Kildare Dobbs, "The Scar," p. 361
Lt.-Gen. Roméo Dallaire, "*Cri de coeur*," p. 414

GEORGE GABORI

Coming of Age in Putnok

Translated from the Hungarian by Eric Johnson with George Faludy

For much of his life George Gabori (1924–1997) drove taxi and ran a cab company in Toronto. Like many immigrants to this country, though, he had a past he would never forget. Gabori (pronounced Gábori) was born to a Jewish family in the village of Putnok, Hungary. His childhood was happy but short, for when the Germans overran Hungary and threatened the existence of the Jews, he joined the resistance. He led daring sabotage raids, blowing up German trains, till the Gestapo sent him, still a teenager, to a concentration camp. When later the Russians drove out the Germans, Gabori was as troublesome for the communists as he had been for the Nazis: soon after his release from Dachau, he was breaking rocks in a notorious Soviet labour camp. Always outspoken in favour of democracy, Gabori played a part in the 1956 Revolution, then escaped from Hungary to Canada, a "decent land," where years later he wrote his memoirs in Hungarian. With the help of Hungarian poet George Faludy, Eric Johnson condensed and translated the enormous manuscript, and in 1981 it was published. Since then, When Evils Were Most Free *has become a minor Canadian classic and has been translated into many other languages. Our selection is its opening passage.*

1 When I was nine years old my father, victorious after a long argument with my grandfather, took me out of our town's only *cheder* and enrolled me in its only public school. Overnight I was transported from the world of Hebrew letters and

26

monotonously repeated texts to the still stranger world of Hungarian letters, patriotic slogans and walls covered with maps.

Grandfather rolled his eyes and predicted trouble, but it seemed 2
he was wrong. I sat beside a boy my own age named Tivadar, a gentile—everybody was a gentile in that school except me. Tivadar and I got along famously until, after two or three weeks, he approached me in the schoolyard one day and asked me if it was true what the others were saying, that "we" had murdered Jesus.

Strange to tell—for this was 1933 and we were in Hungary—I had 3
never heard about this historical episode, and I left Tivadar amicably enough, promising to ask my father about it. We met again the next morning and I told him what I had learned: that the Romans had killed Jesus, and that anyway Jesus had been a Jew, like me, so what did it matter to the Christians?

"That's not true," said Tivadar menacingly. 4

"My father does not lie," I replied. 5

By now a crowd had gathered around us and there was nothing 6
for it but to fight it out. There were cheers and laughter as Tivadar hit me in the nose before I got my jacket off. It was not the first time I had tasted my own blood, but it was the first time a Christian had made it flow. Tivadar was flushed with pleasure and excitement at the applause and not at all expecting it when I lashed out with my fist and sent him sprawling backward on the cobbles. The crowd of boys groaned and shouted to Tivadar to get up and kill the Jew, but poor Tivadar did not move. Frightened, I grabbed my jacket and shoved my way through the crowd stunned into silence by this overturning of the laws of nature.

They were silent at home too when I told them what had hap- 7
pened. My father sent for me from his office in the afternoon, and I entered cap in hand. He always wore a braided Slovak jacket at work and looked more like a peasant than a Jewish wine merchant.

"Well, who started it?" asked my father, wearing an expression I 8
had never seen on his face before. I was not at all frightened.

"He did. I told him what you said about Jesus and he challenged 9
me."

My father clamped his teeth on his cigar and nodded, looking 10
right through me.

11 "Jews don't fight," he finally said.

12 "Then why did you put me in a Christian school?" I asked in a loud, outraged whine.

13 "That's why I put you there, my son," he said at last, then swept me up and kissed me on the forehead. "You're learning fast; only next time don't hit him quite so hard."

14 Then he sent me out quickly and I stopped on the landing, startled to hear loud, whooping, solitary laughter coming out of my father's office.

EXPLORATIONS:

George Gabori, *When Evils Were Most Free*
George Faludy, *My Happy Days in Hell*
Adam Horvath, "Lives Lived: George Gabori," Toronto *Globe and Mail*, December 7, 1997
Anne Frank, *The Diary of Anne Frank*
Anne Michaels, *Fugitive Pieces*
Barbara Coloroso,
The Bully, the Bullied and the Bystander
Extraordinary Evil: A Brief History of Genocide
http://www.bullying.org
http://www.cyberbullying.org
http://en.wikipedia.org/wiki/1956_Hungarian_Revolution
http://ftp.nizkor.org/ftp.py?bibliographies/biblio.04

STRUCTURE:

1. What overall pattern organizes this selection?
2. Point out at least ten words or phrases in this *narrative* that signal the flow of time.
3. Scrutinize Gabori's opening paragraph: has he prepared us for the selection? Name every fact revealed about the setting and about the author.

STYLE:

1. How economical of words is this opening passage of Gabori's life story? How clearly does it reveal the author and his times? Would you predict with any confidence his character or fate as an adult? Do these pages tempt you to read the whole book? Why or why not?
2. *When Evils Were Most Free* is translated and condensed from the Hungarian original. Does this act separate us from Gabori's thoughts? How exact can translations be? If you are bilingual or multilingual, how precisely can you put sayings from one language into another? Can translator Eric Johnson even be seen as a co-author of these pages?
3. In paragraph 6 Gabori states, "It was not the first time I had tasted my own blood. . . ." What makes this image strong?

IDEAS FOR DISCUSSION AND WRITING:

1. What exactly is the "overturning of the laws of nature" at the end of paragraph 6?
2. Was Gabori's father right to move the boy from a Hebrew *cheder* to a public school? In disproving the STEREOTYPE that "Jews don't fight" (par. 11), has the boy learned a worthy lesson? Or does he merely copy the worst traits of his opponents, thereby becoming like them?
3. Every ethnic group in Canada—including English Canadians—is a minority. Has your minority been persecuted here? If you have been a victim, *narrate* an actual incident, including your own reaction. Like Gabori, give many specifics.
4. In taunting and hitting his Jewish classmate, Tivadar is a bully. Have you seen bullying in your own school years? Visit the http://www.bullying.org and http://www.cyberbullying.org websites above, and report to the class if these materials bring to mind experiences of your own.
5. What are autobiographies for? What do you think writing your own life story would do for you? For others?
6. **PROCESS IN WRITING:** *Write a chapter of your own autobiography. Select one key incident in your life, then freewrite on it for a few minutes. Look*

over what you have produced, keep the best of it, and from this write your first draft. Have you begun and ended at just the right places, narrating *the event itself but omitting parts that don't matter? Enrich the next draft with more* IMAGES *and* examples, *following Gabori's lead. Now share your* narrative *with a group of classmates, and adjust whatever does not communicate with this* AUDIENCE. *Finally, read your narrative aloud, with expression, to the whole class.*

Note: See also the Topics for Writing on the Online Learning Centre at www.mcgrawhill.ca/olc/conrad.

CAROL GEDDES

Growing Up Native

Since Carol Geddes tells her own life story in the narrative that follows, we will not repeat it all here. Born into the security of her Tlingit First Nations family in the wilds of the Yukon, she was six when she first knew her country's majority culture and began to see the problems it causes for Native people. Since then she has spent her life integrating these two worlds. She celebrates the current "renaissance" of interest in Native culture, yet also values the rest of North American life. "We need our culture," she writes, "but there's no reason why we can't preserve it and have an automatic washing machine and a holiday in Mexico, as well." Hers is a success story. Despite the obstacles, she completed a university degree in English and philosophy (Carleton, 1978), did graduate studies in communications at McGill, and is today a successful filmmaker and spokesperson for her people. In addition to her films Place for Our People *(1981),* Doctor, Lawyer, Indian Chief *(National Film Board, 1986) and* Picturing a People: George Johnston, Tlingit Photographer *(NFB, 1997), she has produced some 25 videos on the lives and culture of aboriginal people in Canada. Geddes is a producer at Studio One of the National Film Board, and has taught other filmmakers at the Banff Centre for the Arts. She has also been a Director of the Yukon Human Rights Commission, the Yukon Heritage Resources Board and the Women's Television Network Foundation, and is the first Northerner and first Native Person to be a Director of the Canada Council. In her spare time she does wilderness hiking and fishing in the Yukon, where she lives. Our selection, from* homemakers *magazine of October 1990, won the National Magazine Awards Foundation Silver Award.*

1 I remember it was cold. We were walking through a swamp near our home in the Yukon bush. Maybe it was fall and moose-hunting season. I don't know. I think I was about four years old at the time. The muskeg was too springy to walk on, so people were taking turns carrying me—passing me from one set of arms to another. The details about where we were are vague, but the memory of those arms and the feeling of acceptance I had is one of the most vivid memories of my childhood. It didn't matter who was carrying me—there was security in every pair of arms. That response to children is typical of the native community. It's the first thing I think of when I cast my mind back to the Yukon bush, where I was born and lived with my family.

2 I was six years old when we moved out of the bush, first to Teslin, where I had a hint of the problems native people face, then to Whitehorse, where there was unimaginable racism. Eventually I moved to Ottawa and Montreal, where I further discovered that to grow up native in Canada is to feel the sting of humiliation and the boot of discrimination. But it is also to experience the enviable security of an extended family and to learn to appreciate the richness of the heritage and traditions of a culture most North Americans have never been lucky enough to know. As a film-maker, I have tried to explore these contradictions, and our triumph over them, for the half-million aboriginals who are part of the tide of swelling independence of the First Nations today.

3 But I'm getting ahead of myself. If I'm to tell the story of what it's like to grow up native in northern Canada, I have to go back to the bush where I was born, because there's more to my story than the hurtful stereotyping that depicts Indian people as drunken welfare cases. Our area was known as 12-mile (it was 12 miles from another tiny village). There were about 40 people living there—including 25 kids, eight of them my brothers and sisters—in a sort of family compound. Each family had its own timber plank house for sleeping, and there was one large common kitchen area with gravel on the ground and a tent frame over it. Everybody would go there and cook meals together. In summer, my grandmother always had a smudge fire going to smoke fish and tan moose hides. I can remember the cosy warmth of the fire, the smell of good food, and always having

someone to talk to. We kids had built-in playmates and would spend hours running in the bush, picking berries, building rafts on the lake and playing in abandoned mink cages.

One of the people in my village tells a story about the day the old 4
lifestyle began to change. He had been away hunting in the bush for about a month. On his way back, he heard a strange sound coming from far away. He ran up to the crest of a hill, looked over the top of it and saw a bulldozer. He had never seen or heard of such a thing before and he couldn't imagine what it was. We didn't have magazines or newspapers in our village, and the people didn't know that the Alaska Highway was being built as a defence against a presumed Japanese invasion during the Second World War. That was the beginning of the end of the Teslin Tlingit people's way of life. From that moment on, nothing turned back to the way it was. Although there were employment opportunities for my father and uncles, who were young men at the time, the speed and force with which the Alaska Highway was rammed through the wilderness caused tremendous upheaval for Yukon native people.

It wasn't as though we'd never experienced change before. The 5
Tlingit Nation, which I belong to, arrived in the Yukon from the Alaskan coast around the turn of the century. They were the middlemen and women between the Russian traders and the Yukon inland Indians. The Tlingit gained power and prestige by trading European products such as metal goods and cloth for the rich and varied furs so much in fashion in Europe. The Tlingit controlled Yukon trading because they controlled the trading routes through the high mountain passes. When trading ceased to be an effective means of survival, my grandparents began raising wild mink in cages. Mink prices were really high before and during the war, but afterwards the prices went plunging down. So, although the mink pens were still there when I was a little girl, my father mainly worked on highway construction and hunted in the bush. The Yukon was then, and still is in some ways, in a transitional period—from living off the land to getting into a European wage-based economy.

As a young child, I didn't see the full extent of the upheaval. I 6
remember a lot of togetherness, a lot of happiness while we lived in the bush. There's a very strong sense of family in the native

community, and a fondness for children, especially young children. Even today, it's like a special form of entertainment if someone brings a baby to visit. That sense of family is the one thing that has survived all the incredible difficulties native people have had. Throughout a time of tremendous problems, the extended family system has somehow lasted, providing a strong circle for people to survive in. When parents were struggling with alcoholism or had to go away to find work, when one of the many epidemics swept through the community, or when a marriage broke up and one parent left, aunts, uncles and grandparents would try to fill those roles. It's been very important to me in terms of emotional support to be able to rely on my extended family. There are still times when such support keeps me going.

7 Life was much simpler when we lived in the bush. Although we were poor and wore the same clothes all year, we were warm enough and had plenty to eat. But even as a youngster, I began to be aware of some of the problems we would face later on. Travelling missionaries would come and impose themselves on us, for example. They'd sit at our campfire and read the Bible to us and lecture us about how we had to live a Christian life. I remember being very frightened by stories we heard about parents sending their kids away to live with white people who didn't have any children. We thought those people were mean and that if we were bad, we'd be sent away, too. Of course, that was when social workers were scooping up native children and adopting them out to white families in the south. The consequences were usually disastrous for the children who were taken away—alienation, alcoholism and suicide, among other things. I knew some of those kids. The survivors are still struggling to recover.

8 The residential schools were another source of misery for the kids. Although I didn't have to go, my brothers and sisters were there. They told stories about having their hair cut off in case they were carrying head lice, and of being forced to do hard chores without enough food to eat. They were told that the Indian culture was evil, that Indian people were bad, that their only hope was to be Christian. They had to stand up and say things like "I've found the Lord," when a teacher told them to speak. Sexual abuse was rampant in the residential school system.

By the time we moved to Whitehorse, I was excited about the idea 9
of living in what I thought of as a big town. I'd had a taste of the outside world from books at school in Teslin (a town of 250 people), and I was tremendously curious about what life was like. I was hungry for experiences such as going to the circus. In fact, for a while, I was obsessed with stories and pictures about the circus, but then when I was 12 and saw my first one, I was put off by the condition and treatment of the animals.

Going to school in Whitehorse was a shock. The clash of native and 10
white values was confusing and frightening. Let me tell you a story. The older boys in our community were already accomplished hunters and fishermen, but since they had to trap beaver in the spring and hunt moose in the fall, and go out trapping in the winter as well, they missed a lot of school. We were all in one classroom and some of my very large teenage cousins had to sit squeezed into little desks. These guys couldn't read very well. We girls had been in school all along, so, of course, we were better readers. One day the teacher was trying to get one of the older boys to read. She was typical of the teachers at that time, insensitive and ignorant of cultural complexities. In an increasingly loud voice, she kept commanding him to "Read it, read it." He couldn't. He sat there completely still, but I could see that he was breaking into a sweat. The teacher then said, "Look, she can read it," and she pointed to me, indicating that I should stand up and read. For a young child to try to show up an older boy is wrong and totally contrary to native cultural values, so I refused. She told me to stand up and I did. My hands were trembling as I held my reader. She yelled at me to read and when I didn't she smashed her pointing stick on the desk to frighten me. In terror, I wet my pants. As I stood there fighting my tears of shame, she said I was disgusting and sent me home. I had to walk a long distance through the bush by myself to get home. I remember feeling this tremendous confusion, on top of my humiliation. We were always told the white teachers knew best, and so we had to do whatever they said at school. And yet I had a really strong sense of receiving mixed messages about what I was supposed to do in the community and what I was supposed to do at school.

Pretty soon I hated school. Moving to a predominantly white high 11
school was even worse. We weren't allowed to join anything the white

kids started. We were the butt of jokes because of our secondhand clothes and moose meat sandwiches. We were constantly being rejected. The prevailing attitude was that Indians were stupid. When it was time to make course choices in class—between typing and science, for example—they didn't even ask the native kids, they just put us all in typing. You get a really bad image of yourself in a situation like that. I bought into it. I thought we were awful. The whole experience was terribly undermining. Once, my grandmother gave me a pretty little pencil box. I walked into the classroom one day to find the word "squaw" carved on it. That night I burned it in the wood stove. I joined the tough crowd and by the time I was 15 years old, I was more likely to be leaning against the school smoking a cigarette than trying to join in. I was burned out from trying to join the system. The principal told my father there was no point in sending me back to school so, with a Grade 9 education, I started to work at a series of menial jobs.

12 Seven years later something happened to me that would change my life forever. I had moved to Ottawa with a man and was working as a waitress in a restaurant. One day, a friend invited me to her place for coffee. While I was there, she told me she was going to university in the fall and showed me her reading list. I'll never forget the minutes that followed. I was feeling vaguely envious of her and, once again, inferior. I remember taking the paper in my hand, seeing the books on it and realizing, Oh, my God, I've read these books! It hit me like a thunderclap. I was stunned that books I had read were being read in university. University was for white kids, not native kids. We were too stupid, we didn't have the kind of mind it took to do those things. My eyes moved down the list, and my heart started beating faster and faster as I suddenly realized I could go to university, too!

13 My partner at the time was a loving supportive man who helped me in every way. I applied to the university immediately as a mature student but when I had to write Grade 9 on the application, I was sure they'd turn me down. They didn't. I graduated five years later, earning a bachelor of arts in English and philosophy (with distinction).

14 It was while I was studying for a master's degree in communications at McGill a few years later that I was approached to direct my

second film (the first was a student film). *Doctor, Lawyer, Indian Chief* (a National Film Board production) depicts the struggle of a number of native women—one who began her adult life on welfare, a government minister, a chief, a fisherwoman and Canada's first native woman lawyer. The film is about overcoming obstacles and surviving. It's the story of most native people.

Today, there's a glimmer of hope that more of us native people will 15
overcome the obstacles that have tripped us up ever since we began sharing this land. Some say our cultures are going through a renaissance. Maybe that's true. Certainly there's a renewed interest in native dancing, acting and singing, and in other cultural traditions. Even indigenous forms of government are becoming strong again. But we can't forget that the majority of native people live in urban areas and continue to suffer from alcohol and drug abuse and the plagues of a people who have lost their culture and have become lost themselves. And the welfare system is the insidious glue that holds together the machine of oppression of native people.

Too many non-native people have refused to try to understand the 16
issues behind our land claims. They make complacent pronouncements such as "Go back to your bows and arrows and fish with spears if you want aboriginal rights. If not, give it up and assimilate into white Canadian culture." I don't agree with that. We need our culture, but there's no reason why we can't preserve it and have an automatic washing machine and a holiday in Mexico, as well.

The time has come for native people to make our own decisions. 17
We need to have self-government. I have no illusions that it will be smooth sailing—there will be trial and error and further struggle. And if that means crawling before we can stand up and walk, so be it. We'll have to learn through experience.

While we're learning, we have a lot to teach and give to the world— 18
a holistic philosophy, a way of living with the earth, not disposing of it. It is critical that we all learn from the elders that an individual is not more important than a forest; we know that we're here to live on and with the earth, not to subdue it.

The wheels are in motion for a revival, for change in the way 19
native people are taking their place in Canada. I can see that we're

equipped, we have the tools to do the work. We have an enormous number of smart, talented, moral Indian people. It's thrilling to be a part of this movement.

20 Someday, when I'm an elder, I'll tell the children the stories: about the bush, about the hard times, about the renaissance, and especially about the importance of knowing your place in your nation.

EXPLORATIONS:

Carol Geddes, *Doctor, Lawyer, Indian Chief* (NFB film, 29 min.)
Daniel David Moses and Terry Goldie, eds., *An Anthology of Canadian Native Writers in English*
Penny Petrone, ed., *First People, First Voices* (anthology of writings by First Nations people in Canada)
Julie Cruikshank, *Life Lived Like a Story* (interviews with Native Canadian women)
Brian Maracle, *Back on the Rez: Finding the Way Home* (memoir)
Basil Johnston, *Indian School Days* (memoir)
Hugh Brody, *Maps and Dreams* (anthropology)
Tomson Highway, *Kiss of the Fur Queen* (novel)
http://www.nfb.ca/portraits/carol_geddes/en
http://users.ap.net/~chenae/natlink.html
http://www.nativeweb.org
http://www.collectionscanada.ca/02/02012001_e.html

STRUCTURE:

1. "I remember it was cold," says Geddes in her opening sentence, and "Someday, when I'm an elder," she says in her closing sentence. Most *narratives* in this chapter relate one incident, but "Growing Up Native" tells the highs and lows of a whole life. Has Geddes attempted too much? Or has she got her message across by focussing on the right moments of her life? Cite examples to defend your answer.
2. Did you have the impression of being *told* a story, rather than reading it on the page? Cite passages where "Growing Up Native"

comes across as oral history, as a tale told in person. Why do you think Geddes may have taken this approach?

3. Does Geddes *narrate* in straight chronological order? Point out any flashbacks or other departures from the pattern.
4. Read paragraph 12 aloud. Analyze its power as a TRANSITION between Geddes' past and present.

STYLE:

1. Geddes' paragraphs are well organized: most begin with a topic sentence, then clearly develop it with examples. Identify five paragraphs that follow this pattern.
2. Why are paragraph 10 and several others so long? Why is paragraph 20 so short?
3. In paragraph 2 Geddes tells of "the sting of humiliation and the boot of discrimination." Find other good FIGURES OF SPEECH in paragraphs 9, 12 and 15.

IDEAS FOR DISCUSSION AND WRITING:

1. Despite the hardships of living in the bush, does Geddes' childhood sound like a good one? If so, why? Give *examples.*
2. Geddes exposes various ways in which First Nations people have been STEREOTYPED. Point out the worst of these.
3. The white high school of paragraph 11 routinely put native students in typing instead of science. How do the high schools of your province advise minority students as to course selection and career? Is a minority or working-class student shut out from opportunity, or encouraged to try? Give *examples* from your own observation.
4. Geddes envisions First Nations people keeping their culture, yet also having washing machines and holidays in Mexico (par. 16). Discuss techniques for achieving such goals in the urban setting where most Native people now live.
5. **PROCESS IN WRITING:** *Interview someone who either grew up long ago, or who is from a culture very different from yours, to hear her or his life story. Tape the interview, then at home play it back, taking notes. Now choose either one main event of this* narrative *(such as the scene in which Geddes realizes she too can go to university), OR choose to give the overall sweep*

of the story. Also choose whether to just assemble the best excerpts from the tape to put in writing, OR to summarize the key events in your own words. Load your first draft with the best examples *you have. Stay mainly in time order, but do use a flashback or flashforward if they enhance the story. Finally edit your version for things like spelling and punctuation. Read it aloud to the class. If there is time, also play the interview so the class can see how you chose and arranged the material of your* narrative.

Note: See also the Topics for Writing on the Online Learning Centre at www.mcgrawhill.ca/olc/conrad.

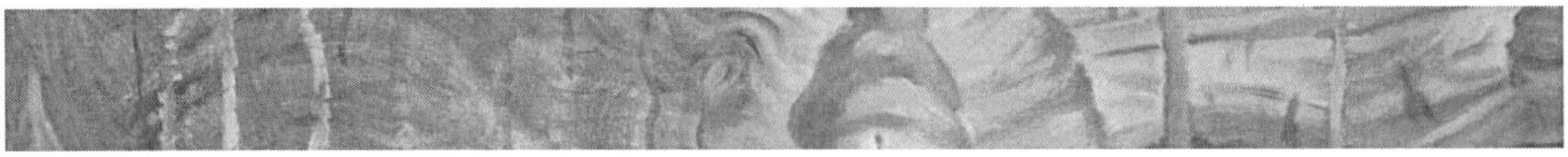

EXAMPLE 2

FOR EXAMPLE....

Many an audience, after struggling to grasp a speaker's message, has been saved from boredom or even sleep by the powerful words "*for example....*" Heads lift up, eyes return to the front, bodies shift in their chairs, and suddenly the message is clear to all.

Writers, like speakers, use examples. Do you enjoy reading pages of abstract reasoning, generalizations, theory without application? You have probably heard the Chinese proverb "A picture is worth a thousand words." When the writer's words never form "pictures," how can you "see" the point? Of course generalizations have their place. For example your thesis statement is one, and so are subpoints, summaries and conclusions. These and others are needed, but cannot do the job alone. If you do not "show" as well as "tell," your reader will be like the people in the audience sinking into their seats—until you, like the speaker, say "for example...."

Why not try for at least 50% example content in every essay, to avoid the hot-air approach to writing? This means, though, that you need to know the subject. Two suggestions:

- If you cannot think of examples, then you may have chosen the wrong topic. Try another, before investing too much time in a topic that will not work for you. The best essays are like icebergs: only a tenth of what you know shows above the surface, but it is supported by the other nine-tenths below.
- If examples do not come to mind, take action. Go to the library. Use the online catalogue and periodical indexes. Consult reference works such as the almanac or the encyclopedia. Check the more reliable sources on the Internet (ones belonging to well-known governmental or educational organizations). If you are quoting, make sure to use quotation marks and attribute each source.

Examples take many forms:

PERSONAL EXPERIENCE: To illustrate your point, narrate an incident you have experienced. Did an earthquake or tornado or ice storm or heat wave or flood or tsunami show you the power of nature? Did your car accident illustrate the dangers of drinking and driving, or did your fire show the dangers of smoking in bed? Did a major success or failure demonstrate the importance of your work or planning or persistence?

THE EXPERIENCE OF OTHERS: To illustrate the point, narrate an incident you saw in person or heard about from others. Did your neighbour's unloved child run away from home or rob a milk store or get married at age 16? Did your cousin lose her job because of automation or downsizing or outsourcing or a corporate merger? Did a famous person succeed despite a physical disability or a deprived childhood?

HYPOTHETICAL EXAMPLES: In a future-oriented society like ours, many arguments speculate about what might happen *if*.... Since the event or situation has not yet come to pass, use your best judgement to imagine the results. What would happen if street drugs were legalized? If the forests were all cut? If Quebec separated? If the national debt were paid off? If the polar ice cap melted? If our electricity came from wind turbines? If a world government were adopted?

QUOTATIONS: If the words of a poet, politician, scientist or other prominent person illustrate your point clearly and authoritatively, quote them (using quotation marks) and of course state who said them. What did Aristotle, Shakespeare, Marx, Einstein, Jane Jacobs, Warren Buffet, Nelson Mandela, Mordecai Richler or Margaret Atwood say about love or power or sex or money or old age or war? Start with the index of *Colombo's Canadian Quotations* or *Bartlett's Familiar Quotations* to find an apt statement on almost any important topic. Or go online to check out *Bartlett* at http://www.bartleby.com/100, entering keywords for a search. Another good source is *Wikiquote* at http://en.wikiquote.org/wiki/Main_Page.

STATISTICS: These numerical examples lend a scientific, objective quality to your argument. Tell what percentage of marriages will end in divorce or how many minutes each cigarette takes off one's life or how much energy a person consumes travelling by car as opposed to train, bus or airplane. Good places to find statistics are *The World Almanac and Book of Facts, Canada Year Book* and any good atlas. Be scrupulously honest, because everyone knows how statistics can lie (remember the statistician who drowned in the river that averaged two feet deep!).

OTHER DEVICES: Later chapters in this book discuss cause and effect, comparison and contrast, and analogy. These devices may be used not only to plan the structure of an entire essay, but also to construct short and vivid examples within the essay.

Almost all good writing has examples, but is there an upper limit? Some writers, such as Karen Von Hahn and Jeffrey Rosenthal in this chapter, go far beyond the 50% level suggested above. Von Hahn reaches probably 80% and Rosenthal 90% or more. Some readers of Rosenthal may tune out during his succession of poker hand examples, but probably more because of the mathematics involved than the sheer number of cases. As for Von Hahn, many of her examples are very short bits of narrative, which are easy to digest and have a high degree of human interest. So are those of

Margaret Wente, Joe Fiorito and Goran Simic, all in this chapter. Among the authors in other chapters who also make massive and skilful use of examples are Patricia Pearson in Chapter 4 and Doris Anderson in Chapter 5. You may want to look ahead and see their techniques and arguments now. Though it is very possible to disagree with the arguments of any of these prolific example users, it would be astonishing if you did not at least understand their views after "seeing" them so clearly in action.

Another way to use examples is to let one long one make the point. On page 170 of Chapter 4, Nathalie Petrowski develops one extended example of one young man who became a mass murderer. Yet through the single case of Marc Lépine, she helps us "see" the situation of many other Canadian youth who may also explode into violence if we do not reduce the pressures our society puts on them. Of course one example—or a hundred—will prove nothing. Statistics come close to proof, especially when based on a large and carefully designed study. But in general an example is not proof; it is a device of illustration and therefore an aid to both understanding and enjoyment.

Note: Authors in other chapters also use many examples, as well as other ways to develop their point. See especially these selections:

Patricia Pearson, "Avoiding the Big C: A Little Simple Advice," p. 133
June Callwood, "Forgiveness," p. 161
Doris Anderson, "The 51-Per-Cent Minority," p. 191
Drew Hayden Taylor, "This Boat Is My Boat," p. 216
Catharine Parr Trail, "Remarks of Security of Person and Property in Canada," p. 222
Lawrence Hill, "Black + White = Black," p. 228
Samantha Bennett, "It's Not Just the Weather That's Cooler in Canada," p. 264
Margaret Atwood, "Letter to America," p. 392

GORAN SIMIC

Goodbye Muse, Hello Prada

Born in Bosnia in 1952, Goran Simic had become a leading writer and intellectual of his country by the early 90s, when civil war broke out in Yugoslavia. With his Muslim wife and two young children, he spent a harrowing three years in the siege of Sarajevo, living the appalling events he would later describe so vividly in his poems. Then when in 1996 he and his family immigrated to this country, with the help of PEN Canada, he had a rude awakening: as he relates in this selection, what his new employers wanted was not his brain but his muscles. Yet despite the drudgery he so wittily depicts on these pages, Simic found time to resume his real career. In Yugoslavia he had edited several literary magazines, and published many books of short stories, plays, radio dramas and lyrics for opera. Then in 1997 Oxford Press published a collection of his powerful Sarajevo poems, Sprinting from the Graveyard, *translated by David Harsent. More poems followed:* Peace and War *in 1998,* Immigrant Blues *in 2003,* From Sarajevo with Sorrow *in 2005, and also in 2005 a book of short stories,* Yesterday's People. *By now Simic has published a dozen books, and has been translated into almost a dozen languages. He also writes essays, such as our lively and ironic selection from the February 24, 2000 Toronto* Globe and Mail.

1 "You shouldn't have gone to another continent just to be a slave. You could get a better job here in Bosnia," my father told me bitterly last month when we met.

2 It was his honest reaction to my honest need to inform him, which I'd avoided for three years, about my job in Canada. I hadn't

expected he'd easily swallow the fact that I was no longer a bookshop owner or a book columnist, as I'd been in Sarajevo, but just a worker in a Holt Renfrew warehouse.

But I hadn't bargained with the words "labourer" and "North 3
America" summoning to his mind historical images of black slaves in the American South toiling in the cotton fields, with me in the middle of them.

My brother was still a general in the army, my other brother was 4
still a professor, but I'd switched from being a respectable poet to being a slave. What a disgrace to the family!

That moment I realized how much I'd erred in being honest with 5
my father. At his age—almost 80—he accepted only good news. He'd had enough bad news the past few years. After having fought as a partisan during the Second World War and celebrated victory over fascism, he experienced the Bosnian war, which finished like a bad football game: 0-0, with 200,000 killed, and nothing to celebrate.

Instead of enjoying retirement in his own flat or in our family 6
house in Sarajevo, he lives in a rented house in the middle of a nowhere village because a rural refugee family squatted in his flat and because our family home was plundered and destroyed by his former neighbours.

"You know why our neighbours will never invite me again to their 7
homes?" he asked me sadly. "Because I would recognize some of my own furniture."

I didn't let him say all this happened just because he was a Serb, 8
since I don't think there's a difference between Muslim and Serb thieves. They all have the same religion: robbery.

Then I tried to make him smile by putting all my effort into 9
describing a Canada that is not the American South, and where there are no slaves.

After I came to Canada, it didn't take long to realize that poetry 10
would not pay my bills. Moreover, judging by the public attention it received, poetry seemed like an unwanted pregnancy in the marriage between publishers and readers. "You're a poet, fine, but what's your real job?" I heard.

In my first Canadian job, I came to realize that the load of ideas 11
and words I carried in my head was worth less than what I could lug

on my back. At first I didn't understand this, not because of vanity or the feeling that a job labouring in a warehouse could ruin my poet's image, but because it didn't dawn on me that for $1,100 a month my muscles were going to be rented along with just 10 per cent of my brain. With the rest I could do whatever I wanted—but only at lunch break and after 4 p.m. Good-bye, muse. Hello, boss. I now understood that I was a replaceable wheel in a machine someone else made.

12 I got precious advice on how to save my soul from my old friend Sasha Bukvic, one of the best sculptors in the former Yugoslavia, who now worked at a job like mine. "Since you have to spend three hours on the commute, don't sleep on the buses or subway cars," he told me. "This is the time for who you are."

13 It wasn't easy to keep my eyelids open, but soon my favoured travelling companions were Milan Kundera, Jung Chang and Joseph Brodsky—all of them writers who lived outside their homelands. But the books didn't keep me from noticing how, at 6 a.m., the bus driving to Mississauga carried almost entirely first-generation immigrants. Only the driver was Canadian-born.

14 Alone among the 20 workers who came from all over the world—India, Iraq, Ethiopia—and who mostly worked scanning or marking down prices, I was the one who moved merchandise from world-famous clothing designers. Loading trucks, moving suits from one line to another, carting boxes, I soon realized how closely the prices of coats matched their weights.

15 On the one hand, I felt some designers had good fun searching for the quickest way to get money out of rich people's pockets. (Once I saw a Jamaican employee staring in disgust at the price tag of a Prada suit. The price was higher than his entire year's earnings.) On the other hand, it was a pleasure to handle a wardrobe I imagined myself wearing.

16 After a while I could recognize designers by their styles, the same way I would notice the difference between French surrealism and German symbolism, but I avoided saying this. Somebody might wickedly note that the difference between poetry and haute couture amounted to quite a few more zeros on the price tag.

17 The painter Johnny Cadiz, who worked with me for almost two years, commented that our communication could be weirdly ambiguous:

18 "Where is Armani?"

19 "He's in the room with Donna Karan."

20 "Who hung up Calvin Klein on the rolling rack?"

21 "What's Prada doing in the same box as the Boss?"

22 I didn't spot any workers who weren't reading the horoscope in the morning and weren't certain that next Friday they'd be Lotto 649 millionaires. It was amusing to listen to what they'd do with the money, but at the top of everybody's wish list was always: Quit this job immediately. What they'd say as a farewell to the managers was not generally to be found in dictionaries. But I heard worse cursing before Christmas when the managers announced that everyone would be laid off till the first week of the New Year.

23 To be honest, I didn't learn as much about the job as I learned about my co-workers. You can learn quickly about a job, but you learn about people all your life. Some of them had lost everything, some had lost relatives, some held two jobs just to earn enough to bring their children here, or to feed their families. I asked myself who I was to think that my struggles were more important than theirs.

24 Once, at a PEN Canada° social gathering, I was introduced to Hilary Weston, a nice woman who is Lieutenant-Governor of Ontario and married to the man who owns Holt Renfrew and many other enterprises. When I told her I worked in the Holt Renfrew warehouse she said, "Great! I hope one day you'll be manager." I didn't tell her I wanted to remain a writer.

25 As it happened, I met her again, two years later, this time on Canada Book Day. After I told her I was quitting the job, she said, "Pity. But good luck."

26 I didn't tell my father any of this. He would have said, "What did I tell you. There are still slaves in America!"

°PEN Canada: The Canadian branch of International PEN, a world association of writers that defends freedom of opinion and "campaigns on behalf of writers around the world persecuted for the expression of their thoughts." See http://www.pencanada.ca.

EXPLORATIONS:

Goran Simic,

Sprinting from the Graveyard (poems, translated by David Harsent)

Immigrant Blues (poems, translated by Amela Simic)

Selected Sorrows (CD of his selected poems, set to music by Miro Brcic)

André Aciman, ed., *Letters of Transit: Reflections on Exile, Identity, Language, and Loss*

http://www.angelfire.com/poetry/goransimic

http://www.brickbooks.ca/BL-Simic.htm

http://www.sentinelpoetry.org.uk/online0805/index_files/page0002.htm

http://www.cbc.ca/wordsatlarge/blog/2007/10/goran_simic_interview.html

STRUCTURE:

1. A good opening attracts the reader's attention. Does this one? Point out every technique Simic uses in paragraph 1 to get us reading.
2. How far does the rest of Simic's introduction extend? What does the rest of it achieve?
3. Identify the THESIS STATEMENT.
4. The body of the argument (starting in par. 11) appears in *chronological* order. Point out several time signals that move us on to each new part of the author's Canadian experience.
5. It is *examples* that do the main work of supporting Simic's argument. Point out two or three of your favourites. Has Simic reached the recommended 50% of *example* content for effective essays? Have you? Calculate this percentage for your own most recent essay, and report it to the class.

STYLE:

1. When in paragraph 11 Simic says, "the load of ideas and words I carried in my head was worth less than what I could lug on my

back," he uses the power of IRONY. Point out five more strong ironies in this essay.
2. If the subject of "Goodbye Muse, Hello Prada" is loss and hard times, why does Simic use so much humour? Does this strengthen or weaken his message?
3. Read paragraphs 17 through 21 aloud. What is so weird about this conversation, and why?

IDEAS FOR DISCUSSION AND WRITING:

1. Why does society pay Goran Simic more for lugging suits and coats around a warehouse than for writing poetry? Which activity do you see as having more value? Defend your answer with reasons.
2. Have you or your family, like Simic, risked your profession by immigrating to Canada? Give every reason you can think of why a doctor, lawyer, teacher or writer would come here if it means going to work as a labourer, security guard or janitor.
3. Have you, like Simic, been a "slave" renting your muscles and 10% of your brain? Tell the techniques you have found for coping with such a job.
4. Simic reports that he earns $1100 a month. In your own town or city, how much must you make to rent housing? To buy a condo or house? To support a family? To buy the kinds of clothes our author lugs around the Holt Renfrew warehouse? Have you bought lottery tickets, like all Simic's co-workers, to solve these problems? Why or why not?
5. Like more and more employees, our author commutes three hours a day (par. 12). How long is your own trip to school or work? Tell what you do to make it more pleasant or productive. Sleep? Read? How serious a problem is traffic and commuting time in the place where you live? What can individuals do about it? What can government do?
6. **PROCESS IN WRITING:** *Close your eyes, and think of the worst job you have ever had. Now taking notes, fill a page with colourful* examples *of what it was like. Looking these over, put your overall point into a THESIS STATEMENT, then write a discovery draft, packing the argument with your* examples. *The next day, look again. Have you reached at least a* 50%

content of examples? *If not, add. Does each* example *support the overall point? If not, cut or revise. Is your* TONE *consistent (either humorous and ironic, like Simic's tone, or serious)? If not, revise. Finally, hone the spelling and punctuation before printing your best version to show the class.*

Note: See also the Topics for Writing on the Online Learning Centre at www.mcgrawhill.ca/olc/conrad.

Image PDP00903. Courtesy of Royal BC Museum, BC Archives

The eyes were two rounds of black, set in wider rounds of white, and placed in deep sockets under wide, black eyebrows. Their fixed stare bored into me as if the very life of the old cedar looked out....

—Emily Carr, "D'Sonoqua"

3 DESCRIPTION

IT'S LARGE AND PURPLE AND....

Consider the writer's tools: words in rows on a page. The writer cannot use gestures, facial expression or voice, as the public speaker does. The writer cannot use colour, shape, motion or sound, as the filmmaker does. Yet words on a page can be powerful. We've all seen readers so involved in the words of a book that they fail to hear their own name called for dinner, or pass their own stop on the bus. These people have entered another world, living at second hand what a writer has lived or at least imagined at first hand.

How does writing do this to us? How does it make experience come alive? There are many ways, and one of the best is description. In simulating real life, description makes frequent appeals to our senses:

sight **hearing** **touch** **smell** **taste**

In "D'Sonoqua," in this chapter, Emily Carr appeals to our senses of smell and sight together when she writes, "Smell and blurred light oozed thickly out of the engine room, and except for one lantern on the wharf everything else was dark." Then in the next paragraph she moves on to hearing and touch: "Every gasp of the engine shook us like a great sob."

In her first sentence alone, Christie McLaren shows us the "red hair and the purple dress" of her "Suitcase Lady" who sits "night after night" in the "harsh light of a 24-hour doughnut shop on Queen Street West." These details have already begun to "show" us one particular homeless person and her life.

In his selection, Rudy Wiebe makes sure we see, hear and even smell the escaped bull: the "body solid and thick as a steamer smoking across our yard," and the lips "twisting back above his gigantic teeth as he roared the smell [of manure] into the sky...." Wiebe makes it easy, indeed, for readers to share the terror of the three-year-old that Wiebe was when he witnessed this event.

Similarly, behind every descriptive choice you make, behind every image you give your reader, should be your own overall purpose. In a warmup exercise such as freewriting, or even as you begin a discovery draft, you may not yet know that purpose. But the act of writing should soon make it clear: Is your subject scary, inspiring, pitiful, exasperating, ugly, beautiful, calm or violent? Once you know, help your audience to know as well. In some pieces of descriptive writing, a thesis statement helps readers to grasp the point; other times, as is often the case in narratives, an "implied thesis statement" does the job (review the chapter introduction to "Narration," where this point is discussed).

Figures of speech—such as the similes and metaphors discussed in Chapter 6—are powerful tools of description. When Emily Carr writes that a person's face is "greeny-brown and wrinkled like a baked apple," we see old age clearly. In other places she uses onomatopoetic terms—words like "scuttled," "slithered," "grated" and "ooze"—that describe by sounding like what they mean. (See FIGURES OF SPEECH in the glossary.)

In a description some words are better than others. Use short and strong ones from everyday life, not the long and flabby ones that some would-be writers think are eloquent. Do we really "perspire" or do we "sweat"? "Ambulate" or "walk"? "Altercate" or "argue"?

"Masticate" or "chew"? "Expectorate" or "spit"? It is obvious that the second term in each case is stronger, more vivid, more descriptive. So why would we use the first?

Choose words that convey the right *feeling* as well as the right dictionary meaning. One student closed a pretty description of the ocean by saying "the water was as still as a pan full of oil." The image of water as oil may imply stillness, but this water is not exactly something we would want to dive into or even watch at sunset—we'd be too busy thinking of pollution! Another person described forest trees in autumn as being the colour of a fire engine. The colour may be right, but will the image of a large truck perched in the tree branches really give us that autumn feeling?

Take the time, then, to *feel*, as well as *think*, your words. Search drafts for weak or inexact or inappropriate terms, and replace them. If the right word doesn't come, find it in a dictionary or thesaurus. And realize that your electronic thesaurus may be fast, but a desk-size book version offers far more choices to help your overall idea or feeling, whatever it may be, come through clearly. One more thing: Do not let your search lead to wordiness. A paragraph of mostly small, strong, well-chosen words (what some writers have called "noun and verb language") can say more than a page of large and vague ones.

Note: Many authors in other chapters use description to help make their point. See especially these examples:

Patrick Lane, "There Is a Season," p. 37
Catherine Pigott, "Chicken-Hips," p. 196
Hugh MacLennan, "A Sound Beyond Hearing," p. 296
Dr. Mark Bernstein, "Yes, It Is Brain Surgery," p. 311
Candace Savage, "Stuck on the Prairies: Where Is Here?," p. 381
Joy Kogawa, "Grinning and Happy," p. 373
Lt.-Gen. Roméo Dallaire, "*Cri de coeur*," p. 414

CHRISTIE McLAREN

Suitcase Lady*

Christie McLaren lives in Canmore, Alberta, where she does freelance writing and editing. But it was in 1981, as a student at the University of Waterloo, that she spent a term reporting for the Toronto Globe and Mail *as part of her English co-op work experience: after spending several evenings with "the Vicomtesse," she heard the story that she reports in this selection. After graduating, McLaren spent a year and a half at the* Winnipeg Free Press, *then returned to the* Globe, *where she continued to report on many issues. An avid hiker, backpacker, skier and canoeist, McLaren channelled her love of the outdoors into several years of investigating forestry, energy and other environmental topics, as well as writing on national health policy and Ontario politics. Her articles have appeared also in* Nature Canada, Equinox *and* Explore Magazine. *Then in 2002 appeared her book on the Canadian forestry industry,* The Last Stand. *Though a professional journalist, McLaren says that "writing is nothing but pain while you're doing it and nothing but relief when it's done. Any joy or satisfaction, I think, is a bit of fleeting luck."*

1 Night after night, the woman with the red hair and the purple dress sits in the harsh light of a 24-hour doughnut shop on Queen Street West.

2 Somewhere in her bleary eyes and in the deep lines of her face is a story that probably no one will ever really know. She is taking pains to write something on a notepad and crying steadily.

*Editor's title.

She calls herself Vicomtesse Antonia The Linds'ays. She's the suit- 3
case lady of Queen Street.

No one knows how many women there are like her in Toronto. 4
They carry their belongings in shopping bags and spend their days and nights scrounging for food. They have no one and nowhere to go.

This night, in a warm corner with a pot of tea and a pack of 5
Player's, the Vicomtesse is in a mood to talk.

Out of her past come a few scraps: a mother named Savaria; the 6
child of a poor family in Montreal; a brief marriage when she was 20; a son in Toronto who is now 40. "We never got along well because I didn't bring him up. I was too poor. He never call me mama."

She looks out the window. She's 60 years old. 7

With her words she spins herself a cocoon. She talks about drapes 8
and carpets, castles and kings. She often lapses into French. She lets her tea get cold. Her hands are big, rough, farmer's hands. How she ended up in the doughnut shop remains a mystery, maybe even to her.

"Before, I had a kitchen and a room and my own furniture. I had 9
to leave everything and go."

It's two years that she's been on the go, since the rooming houses 10
stopped taking her. "I don't have no place to stay."

So she walks. A sturdy coat covers her dress and worn leather boots 11
are on her feet. But her big legs are bare and chapped and she has a ragged cough.

Yes, she says, her legs get tired. She has swollen ankles and, with 12
no socks in her boots, she has blisters. She says she has socks—in the suitcase—but they make her feet itch.

As for money, "I bum on the street. I don't like it, but I have to. 13
I have to survive. The only pleasure I got is my cigaret." She lights another one. "It's not a life."

She recalls the Saturday, a long time ago, when she made $27, and 14
laughs when she tells about how she had to make the money last through Sunday, too. Now she gets "maybe $7 or $8," and eats "very poor."

When she is asked how people treat her, the answer is very matter-of- 15
fact: "Some give money. Some are very polite and some are rude."

16 In warm weather, she passes her time at the big square in front of City Hall. When it's cold she takes her suitcase west to the doughnut shop.

17 The waitresses who bring food to the woman look upon her with compassion. They persuaded their boss that her sitting does no harm.

18 Where does she sleep? "Any place I can find a place to sleep. In the park, in stores—like here I stay and sit, on Yonge Street." She shrugs. Sometimes she goes into an underground parking garage.

19 She doesn't look like she knows what sleep is. "This week I sleep three hours in four days. I feel tired but I wash my face with cold water and I feel okay." Some questions make her eyes turn from the window and stare hard. Then they well over with tears. Like the one about loneliness. "I don't talk much to people," she answers. "Just the elderly, sometimes, in the park."

20 Her suitcase is full of dreams.

21 Carefully, she unzips it and pulls out a sheaf of papers—"my concertos."

22 Each page is crammed with neatly written musical notes—the careful writing she does on the doughnut shop table—but the bar lines are missing. Questions about missing bar lines she tosses aside. Each "concerto" has a French name—Tresor, La Tempete, Le Retour—and each one bears the signature of the Vicomtesse. She smiles and points to one. "A very lovely piece of music. I like it."

23 She digs in her suitcase again, almost shyly, and produces a round plastic box. Out of it emerges a tiara. Like a little girl, she smooths back her dirty hair and proudly puts it on. No one in the doughnut shop seems to notice.

24 She cares passionately about the young, the old and the ones who suffer. So who takes care of the suitcase lady?

25 "God takes care of me, that's for sure," she says, nodding thoughtfully. "But I'm not what you call crazy about religion. I believe always try to do the best to help people—the elderly, and kids, and my country, and my city of Toronto, Ontario."

Explorations:

Jack Layton, *Homelessness: The Making and Unmaking of a Crisis*
Marlene Webber, *Street Kids: The Tragedy of Canada's Runaways*
George Orwell, *Down and Out in Paris and London*
Rohinton Mistry, *A Fine Balance*
Susan Scott, *All Our Sisters: Stories of Homeless Women in Canada*
http://ryandale.org/ryanlinks.html
http://www.nationalhomeless.org
http://aspin.asu.edu/hpn
http://www.homelessness.gc.ca
http://www.parl.gc.ca/information/library/prbpubs/prb991-e.htm

Structure:

1. "Suitcase Lady" was a feature article in the Toronto *Globe and Mail.* As newspaper journalism, how does it differ from a typical ESSAY?
2. What does the opening *description* achieve?
3. How do the many quotations help the *description*?
4. Explain the IRONY of the closing.

Style:

1. Why is the vocabulary of "Suitcase Lady" so easy?
2. "With her words she spins herself a cocoon," states McLaren in paragraph 8. How appropriate is this METAPHOR?
3. Point out at least five concrete details that help you picture this homeless woman's life. Now think about your own writing: do you also give details, or do you hide behind GENERALIZATIONS?

Ideas for Discussion and Writing:

1. "It's not a life," says "the Vicomtesse" in paragraph 13. Is your province or city currently making life easier or harder for homeless people? Give *examples.*

2. How do you react to people who, like the suitcase lady, "bum on the street"? How often do you give? What makes you give to one person but not another?
3. In paragraph 6 the suitcase lady speaks of her son in Toronto: "We never got along well because I didn't bring him up. I was too poor. He never call me mama." In the area where you live, how much money does a family need to stay together? To avoid quarrels over money? To be hopeful about the future?
4. **PROCESS IN WRITING:** *Tape an interview with someone who in economic status, age, values or some other respect is very different from you. Then write a profile. Like McLaren, portray your subject through her or his best comments. Now add many* IMAGES *of physical appearance to build your* description. *Edit for conciseness and finally correctness. Then read your best version, with feeling, to the class.*

Note: See also the Topics for Writing on the Online Learning Centre at www.mcgrawhill.ca/olc/conrad.

CHARLES YALE HARRISON

In the Trenches

Charles Yale Harrison (1898–1954) was born in Philadelphia and grew up in Montreal. His independent spirit revealed itself early: in grade four he condemned Shakespeare's The Merchant of Venice *as anti-Semitic, and when his teacher beat him he quit school. At 16 he went to work for the* Montreal Star *and at 18 joined the Canadian army. As a machine gunner in France and Belgium during 1917 and 1918, Harrison witnessed the gruesome front-line scenes he was later to describe in fiction. He was wounded at Amiens and decorated for bravery in action. After the war Harrison returned to Montreal but soon left for New York, where he began a career in public relations for the labour movement and for numerous humanitarian causes. He also wrote several books, both nonfiction and fiction. By far the best is* Generals Die in Bed, *an account of trench warfare that shocked the public and became the best seller of 1930. Spare in style, biting and vivid, this autobiographical novel was described by the* New York Evening Post *as "the best of the war books." From it comes our selection.*

1 We leave the piles of rubble that was once a little Flemish peasant town and wind our way, in Indian file, up through the muddy communication trench. In the dark we stumble against the sides of the trench and tear our hands and clothing on the bits of embedded barbed wire that runs through the earth here as though it were a geological deposit.

2 Fry, who is suffering with his feet, keeps slipping into holes and crawling out, all the way up. I can hear him coughing and panting behind me.

I hear him slither into a water-filled hole. It has a green scum on 3
it. Brown and I fish him out.

"I can't go any farther," he wheezes. "Let me lie here, I'll come 4
on later."

We block the narrow trench and the oncoming men stumble on 5
us, banging their equipment and mess tins on the sides of the ditch. Some trip over us. They curse under their breaths.

Our captain, Clark, pushes his way through the mess. He is an 6
Imperial, an Englishman, and glories in his authority.

"So it's you again," he shouts. "Come on, get up. Cold feet, eh, 7
getting near the line?"

Fry mumbles something indistinctly. I, too, offer an explanation. 8
Clark ignores me.

"Get up, you're holding up the line," he says to Fry. 9

Fry does not move. 10

"No wonder we're losing the bloody war," Clark says loudly. The 11
men standing near-by laugh. Encouraged by his success, the captain continues:

"Here, sergeant, stick a bayonet up his behind—that'll make him 12
move." A few of us help Fry to his feet, and somehow we manage to keep him going.

We proceed cautiously, heeding the warnings of those ahead of us. 13
At last we reach our positions.

It is midnight when we arrive at our positions. The men we are reliev- 14
ing give us a few instructions and leave quickly, glad to get out.

It is September and the night is warm. Not a sound disturbs the 15
quiet. Somewhere away far to our right we hear the faint sound of continuous thunder. The exertion of the trip up the line has made us sweaty and tired. We slip most of our accouterments off and lean against the parados. We have been warned that the enemy is but a few hundred yards off, so we speak in whispers. It is perfectly still. I remember nights like this in the Laurentians. The harvest moon rides overhead.

Our sergeant, Johnson, appears around the corner of the bay, 16
stealthily like a ghost. He gives us instructions:

17 "One man up on sentry duty! Keep your gun covered with the rubber sheet! No smoking!"

18 He hurries on to the next bay. Fry mounts the step and peers into No Man's Land. He is rested now and says that if he can only get a good pair of boots he will be happy. He has taken his boots off and stands in his stockinged feet. He shows us where his heel is cut. His boots do not fit. The sock is wet with blood. He wants to take his turn at sentry duty first so that he can rest later on. We agree.

19 Cleary and I sit on the firing-step and talk quietly.

20 "So this is war."

21 "Quiet."

22 "Yes, just like the country back home, eh?"

23 We talk of the trench; how we can make it more comfortable.

24 We light cigarettes against orders and cup our hands around them to hide the glow. We sit thinking. Fry stands motionless with his steel helmet shoved down almost over his eyes. He leans against the parapet motionless. There is a quiet dignity about his posture. I remember what we were told at the base about falling asleep on sentry duty. I nudge his leg. He grunts.

25 "Asleep?" I whisper.

26 "No," he answers, "I'm all right."

27 "What do you see?"

28 "Nothing. Wire and posts."

29 "Tired?"

30 "I'm all right."

31 The sergeant reappears after a while. We squinch our cigarettes.

32 "Everything O.K. here?"

33 I nod.

34 "Look out over there. They got the range on us. Watch out."

35 We light another cigarette. We continue our aimless talk.

36 "I wonder what St. Catherine Street looks like—"

37 "Same old thing, I suppose—stores, whores, theaters—"

38 "Like to be there just the same—"

39 "Me too."

40 We sit and puff our fags for half a minute or so.

41 I try to imagine what Montreal looks like. The images are murky. All that is unreality. The trench, Cleary, Fry, the moon overhead—this is real.

42 In his corner of the bay Fry is beginning to move from one foot to another. It is time to relieve him. He steps down and I take his place. I look into the wilderness of posts and wire in front of me.

43 After a while my eyes begin to water. I see the whole army of wire posts begin to move like a silent host towards me.

44 I blink my eyes and they halt.

45 I doze a little and come to with a jerk.

46 So this is war, I say to myself again for the hundredth time. Down on the firing-step the boys are sitting like dead men. The thunder to the right has died down. There is absolutely no sound.

47 I try to imagine how an action would start. I try to fancy the preliminary bombardment. I remember all the precautions one has to take to protect one's life. Fall flat on your belly, we had been told time and time again. The shriek of the shell, the instructor in trench warfare said, was no warning because the shell traveled faster than its sound. First, he had said, came the explosion of the shell—then came the shriek and then you hear the firing of the gun....

48 From the stories I heard from veterans and from newspaper reports I conjure up a picture of an imaginary action. I see myself getting the Lewis gun in position. I see it spurting darts of flame into the night. I hear the roar of battle. I feel elated. Then I try to fancy the horrors of the battle. I see Cleary, Fry and Brown stretched out on the firing-step. They are stiff and their faces are white and set in the stillness of death. Only I remain alive.

49 An inaudible movement in front of me pulls me out of the dream. I look down and see Fry massaging his feet. All is still. The moon sets slowly and everything becomes dark.

50 The sergeant comes into the bay again and whispers to me:

51 "Keep your eyes open now—they might come over on a raid now that it's dark. The wire's cut over there—" He points a little to my right.

52 I stand staring into the darkness. Everything moves rapidly again as I stare. I look away for a moment and the illusion ceases.

53 Something leaps towards my face.

54 I jerk back, afraid.

55 Instinctively I feel for my rifle in the corner of the bay.

56 It is a rat.

57 It is as large as a tom-cat. It is three feet away from my face and it looks steadily at me with its two staring, beady eyes. It is fat. Its long tapering tail curves away from its padded hindquarters. There is still a little light from the stars and this light shines faintly on its sleek skin. With a darting movement it disappears. I remember with a cold feeling that it was fat, and why.

58 Cleary taps my shoulder. It is time to be relieved.

59 Over in the German lines I hear quick, sharp reports. Then the red-tailed comets of the *minenwerfer*° sail high in the air, making parabolas of red light as they come towards us. They look pretty, like the fireworks when we left Montreal. The sergeant rushes into the bay of the trench, breathless. "Minnies," he shouts, and dashes on.

60 In that instant there is a terrific roar directly behind us.

61 The night whistles and flashes red.

62 The trench rocks and sways.

63 Mud and earth leap into the air, come down upon us in heaps.

64 We throw ourselves upon our faces, clawing our nails into the soft earth in the bottom of the trench.

65 Another!

66 This one crashes to splinters about twenty feet in front of the bay.

67 Part of the parapet caves in.

68 We try to burrow into the ground like frightened rats.

69 The shattering explosions splinter the air in a million fragments. I taste salty liquid on my lips. My nose is bleeding from the force of the detonations.

70 SOS flares go up along our front calling for help from our artillery. The signals sail into the air and explode, giving forth showers of red, white and blue lights held aloft by a silken parachute.

71 The sky is lit by hundreds of fancy fireworks like a night carnival.

72 The air shrieks and cat-calls.

73 Still they come.

74 I am terrified. I hug the earth, digging my fingers into every crevice, every hole.

°*minenwerfer*: Mine-throwing trench mortars.

A blinding flash and an exploding howl a few feet in front of the 75
trench.

My bowels liquefy. 76

Acrid smoke bites the throat, parches the mouth. I am beyond 77
mere fright. I am frozen with an insane fear that keeps me cowering in the bottom of the trench. I lie flat on my belly, waiting....

Suddenly it stops. 78

The fire lifts and passes over us to the trenches in the rear. 79

We lie still, unable to move. Fear has robbed us of the power to 80
act. I hear Fry whimpering near me. I crawl over to him with great effort. He is half covered with earth and débris. We begin to dig him out.

To our right they have started to shell the front lines. It is about 81
half a mile away. We do not care. We are safe.

Without warning it starts again. 82

The air screams and howls like an insane woman. 83

We are getting it in earnest now. Again we throw ourselves face 84
downward on the bottom of the trench and grovel like savages before this demoniac frenzy.

The concussion of the explosions batters against us. 85

I am knocked breathless. 86

I recover and hear the roar of the bombardment. 87

It screams and rages and boils like an angry sea. I feel a prickly 88
sensation behind my eyeballs.

A shell lands with a monster shriek in the next bay. The concussion 89
rolls me over on my back. I see the stars shining serenely above us. Another lands in the same place. Suddenly the stars revolve. I land on my shoulder. I have been tossed into the air.

I begin to pray. 90

"God—God—please ..." 91

I remember that I do not believe in God. Insane thoughts race 92
through my brain. I want to catch hold of something, something that will explain this mad fury, this maniacal congealed hatred that pours down on our heads. I can find nothing to console me, nothing to appease my terror. I know that hundreds of men are standing a mile or two from me pulling gun-lanyards, blowing us to smithereens. I know that and nothing else.

93 I begin to cough. The smoke is thick. It rolls in heavy clouds over the trench, blurring the stabbing lights of the explosions.

94 A shell bursts near the parapet.

95 Fragments smack the sandbags like a merciless shower of steel hail.

96 A piece of mud flies into my mouth. It is cool and refreshing. It tastes earthy.

97 Suddenly it stops again.

98 I bury my face in the cool, damp earth. I want to weep. But I am too weak and shaken for tears.

99 We lie still, waiting....

EXPLORATIONS:

Charles Yale Harrison, *Generals Die in Bed*
Erich Maria Remarque, *All Quiet on the Western Front* (novel)
Ernest Hemingway, *A Farewell to Arms* (novel)
Timothy Findley, *The Wars* (novel)
Heather Robertson, ed., *A Terrible Beauty: The Art of Canada at War*
Tim Cook, *At the Sharp End: Canadians Fighting the Great War 1914–1916*
http://en.wikipedia.org/wiki/World_War_1
http://www.rootsweb.com/~ww1can/index.html
http://www.firstworldwar.com
http://www.worldwar1.com
http://gutenberg.net.au/ebooks05/0500061h.html
http://www.collectionscanada.gc.ca/firstworldwar/index-e.html

STRUCTURE:

1. In *narrating* his description of trench warfare, does Harrison ever deviate from straight chronological order? If so, where and how?
2. Harrison uses SENSE IMAGES so often that throughout this passage *description* carries the main weight of development. Find one example each of a strong appeal to our senses of sight, hearing, touch, taste and smell.

3. Many of the paragraphs are small, some only a word or two long. Examine paragraphs 25–30, 53–56, and 60–68, determining in each passage why the paragraphs are so short.
4. This account of an artillery attack ends with the words "We lie still, waiting…." Is the ending effective, and if so, how?

STYLE:

1. What degree of CONCISENESS has Harrison achieved in this selection?
2. Harrison tells of the rat: "I remember with a cold feeling that it was fat, and why" (par. 57). How does he convey so much horror in so few words?
3. Analyze the power of the deceptively simple events of paragraph 89: "A shell lands with a monster shriek in the next bay. The concussion rolls me over on my back. I see the stars shining serenely above us. Another lands in the same place. Suddenly the stars revolve. I land on my shoulder. I have been tossed into the air."
4. In describing, Harrison exploits FIGURES OF SPEECH. Point out at least one good SIMILE and one good METAPHOR.
5. Why is "In the Trenches" told in present tense, even though the book was published years after the war?

IDEAS FOR DISCUSSION AND WRITING:

1. Our narrator relates his first experience of war. What has it taught him?
2. Have you read books or seen films that show war in a positive light? Name them. In what ways does "In the Trenches" differ from those accounts?
3. "In the Trenches" is part of a book entitled *Generals Die in Bed.* Discuss the implications of this title.
4. If you have read "Coming of Age in Putnok," compare the conflict described by George Gabori with that described by Harrison. Does hostility between individuals contribute to hostility between nations?

5. **PROCESS IN WRITING:** *Have you lived through a violent or even life-threatening experience, as Harrison did? Close your eyes and remember it. Then in a rapid first draft,* describe *to your audience what it was really like. How did things look, sound, feel, smell or even taste? Use* SENSE IMAGES, *as Harrison does, to help your reader know too. The next day look your* description *over. Does it begin and end at the right spots, to emphasize the important things? If not, chop or add. Are there unimportant details? If so, chop. Are some parts "thin"? If so, add. Are paragraphs longer in the slower parts and shorter in the tenser parts, like Harrison's? If not, adjust them. Finally, edit for correctness and style before producing your final version.*

Note: See also the Topics for Writing on the Online Learning Centre at www.mcgrawhill.ca/olc/conrad.

Royalty-Free/CORBIS

"Once you see Earth from space, you can never again think of it in the same way."

—Marc Garneau, "Canada Must Put the Planet's Interests First"

4 CAUSE AND EFFECT

HERE'S WHY....

Have you heard the true story—and aren't they all supposed to be true?—of the philosophy prof who walked into class to give the final exam? He went to the blackboard and wrote one word: *Why?*

He knew that one of our most human traits is a desire to make sense of things by asking *Why?* If something good happens, we want to know *why* so we can repeat it. If something bad happens, we want to know *why* so in future we can avoid it. On news reports of earthquakes, hurricanes, fires, floods, accidents, crimes and terrorist attacks, victims are always shaking their heads and asking "*Why?*"

In the financial world investors bite their nails guessing what makes stocks go up or down. Will a growing economy push stocks up? Or will it cause inflation, which will cause us to stop buying things we can't afford, which in turn will lower company profits and cause stocks to fall? Will a controversial election send stocks crashing? Or will it just clear the air of uncertainty, making stocks soar?

Will a devastating earthquake harm the economy and the stock market? Or will the cleanup just create employment, sending stocks up? Using the same data, hundreds of experts reason that stocks will rise, while hundreds of others reason that they will fall. Do these experts, or do we, think cause and effect logic is easy?

Yet it is important. We use it in everyday life, and therefore many of our essays are based on it. So when you investigate causes and effects, think hard to get them right.

One of the most common sources of faulty cause-and-effect reasoning in everyday life is superstitions. Many students put a good-luck object on the desk in front of them while writing an exam, and may wear a good-luck item of clothing such as an old baseball hat or a certain pair of old shoes. Speaking of shoes, Canadian finance ministers customarily buy a new good-luck pair for every federal budget speech. Then there are the hockey players who observe lucky rituals such as letting their beards grow during playoffs. It is "bad luck" to wish an actor well before a theatre performance, so instead friends will say "break a leg," aiming for good luck through a reverse method. Many people, when realizing they have bragged or even expressed satisfaction, will knock on wood, to show their humility by touching an everyday object. Thus they will not be struck down by fate. Some superstitions are downright scary. It is said that the spouse who goes to sleep first on the wedding day will be the first to die. Even worse, it is said that "A green Christmas makes for full graveyards." In the vast majority of these and other superstitions, there is actually zero cause and effect, a deficiency that is called the *Post hoc, ergo propter hoc* fallacy ("After this, therefore because of this"). Only in the case of the graveyard may there be actual causality: if grass is green at Christmas, it means the weather has been milder than usual; and if the weather has been mild, then more microbes have survived to attack us. Of course, it could be equally argued that if the weather is warmer, we will suffer fewer chills and be healthier. As in the example of predicting stock market behaviour, does anyone think cause-and-effect logic is easy?

In summary, when you trace causes and effects, consider these principles:

JUST BECAUSE ONE EVENT FOLLOWS ANOTHER, DON'T ASSUME THE FIRST CAUSES THE SECOND. (As we have seen above, try to avoid the *Post hoc, ergo propter hoc* fallacy.) If a black cat crosses the road just before your car engine blows up, put the blame where it belongs: not on the cat but on the mechanic who forgot to replace your crankcase oil.

CONTROL YOUR PREJUDICES. If the bank manager refuses to give you a loan, is it because bankers are capitalist exploiters who like to keep the rest of us down? Or is it because this one had to call the collection agency the last time you took out a loan?

EXPLORE CAUSES BEHIND CAUSES. Your employer fired you because you didn't work hard enough. But *why* didn't you work hard enough? Because the job was a bore and the employer was a jerk? Or because you have two other jobs as well, and sleep only three hours a night? And if so, do you work these hours because the car you bought consumes every cent you earn? Finally, the real question may be *why did you buy the car?*

Many events have multiple causes and multiple effects:

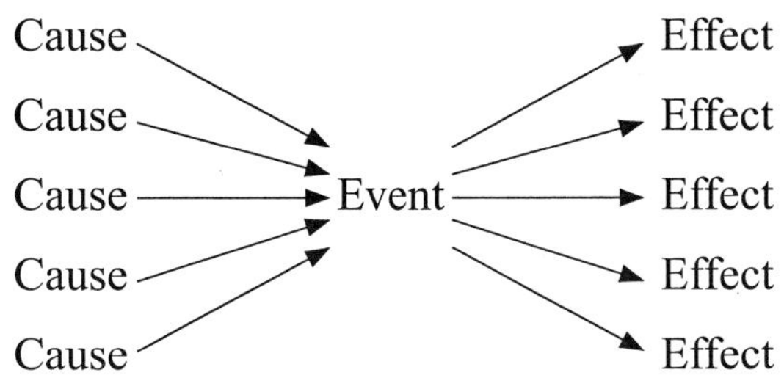

In addition, each cause may have one or more causes behind it, and each effect may produce further effects, leading to an infinite chain of causality receding into the past and reaching into the future.

Where, then, do you draw the boundaries as you plan an essay of cause and effect? The answer lies in your own common sense: include enough to make the point clearly and fairly, then stop. If your parents are workaholics, a description of their behaviour may help a reader understand your own. But do we need to hear about your grandparents as well? If we do, would a quick summary be enough, since we've already heard the details in your parents' case?

All the essays in this chapter show at least one clear-cut cause and at least one clear-cut effect. But while it is possible to give equal attention to both, constructing an essay may be easier if you concentrate *mostly* on cause or *mostly* on effect. Thus your attention can be focussed further, so you can delve deeper and end up with a more satisfying argument, saying more about less—rather than less about more.

Note also that while some essays in this chapter focus on one major cause or one major effect, others show several causes or several effects. For example, Patricia Pearson examines many possible causes of "the big C," while Linda McQuaig traces many effects of driving SUVs. As you choose your own approach to the organization of a cause-and-effect essay, remember above all your purpose: What kind of focus will most strongly explain and support your main point? Once you know, use it.

Note: Many essays in other chapters use cause and effect logic to help make their point. See especially these examples:

Karen Von Hahn, "Self-Serving Propaganda," p. 66
Stephanie Nolen, "Regine Mamba," p. 202
Catherine Pigott, "Chicken Hips," p. 196
Catharine Parr Traill, "Remarks of Security of Person and Property in Canada," p. 222
Lt.-Gen. Roméo Dallaire, with Major Brent Beardsley, "*Cri de coeur,*" p. 414

PATRICIA PEARSON

Avoiding the Big C: A Little Simple Advice

Patricia Pearson is the granddaughter of Lester B. Pearson, prime minister of Canada from 1963 to 1968, who won the Nobel Peace Prize for resolving the Suez Crisis of 1956 with his proposal to create a United Nations peacekeeping force. When Pierre Trudeau died in 2001, Patricia Pearson wrote a moving column in the National Post, *recalling how at age eight she was devastated by the death of her beloved grandfather, and how, like Trudeau's family, hers had to hear the events broadcast on the public media, and share the state funeral with the nation. Later she lived and wrote for several years in New York City. She has also lived in Mexico, and now resides with her husband and two children in the boreal forest north of Montreal. Pearson has written for the* National Post, USA Today, Maclean's, *the* New York Times, *the* Guardian, *and the* Times of London. *Her article on the notorious Canadian killer Karla Homolka, "Behind Every Successful Psychopath," won a National Magazine Award, and in 1997 appeared her widely read book* When She Was Bad: Violent Women and the Myth of Innocence, *which demolished the myth that women, unlike men, are incapable of violence. Then in 2003 was published her comic novel* Playing House, *in 2005 its sequel* Believe Me, *and also in 2005 a book of comic essays,* Area Woman Blows Gasket and Other Tales from the Domestic Frontier. *In 2008 she published* A Brief History of Anxiety (Yours and Mine). *Our own selection, a* National Post *column of August 28, 1999, showcases Pearson's witty and personal approach to journalism.*

1 The *New England Journal of Medicine* recently reported that "longer-legged people are significantly more prone to certain types of cancer." Indeed. Well, that's a huge relief for me. I can never see over anybody's head in a crowd. Guess I'll snicker at the supermodels and fry myself another burger.

2 What else, exactly, am I supposed to do with this information? Science, you may have noticed, pelts us daily with new studies on everything that causes cancer, everything that prevents it—and everything that they thought caused cancer before but they now realize actually prevents it.

3 At the moment, for example, I know that if I stay short, drink red wine, eat tomatoes and olive oil, avoid working in a coke foundry, avoid cigars, sleep more, take Aspirin, swallow Vitamin E, alter my estrogen levels, sip green tea, shun charcoal briquettes, dine on fish—but not from the Great Lakes—reduce my stress level and stay clear of Eastern Europe, my chances of dying from cancer will be reduced for the time being.

4 But it turns out that the sunblock that I've been slopping all over myself for five years may be carcinogenic, whereas sunburn is now thought to act as a cancer preventive. Meanwhile, the spinach and apples I've been eating all these years to bust cancer are laden with cancer-causing residues.

5 Likewise, Vitamin C, long touted as an antioxidant par excellence in megadoses, may actually change the structure of our DNA in such a way that ... guess what? It makes us more susceptible to cancer.

6 And those soft plastic dishes I've been using to microwave my anti-cancer vegetable recipes? They cause cancer.

7 You may recall that a cancer-fighting diet book came out a while back. After chumps like me went out and bought it, an army of doctors charged forth and repudiated its findings.

8 Well, isn't that just great. I wanted to phone my mom to tell her how I've had it up to here (writer's hand slicing sideways at chin level) with trying to keep track of every eensy-weensy obscure bit of research on health dangers. But I'd just read that cell phones were being implicated in brain tumours.

9 It seems to me, the more I think about it, that what this whole explosion in medical research is actually discovering is that sooner

or later people die. Of course, scientists are finding out other things that are useful to them, but they are not very useful to me. What all this research is generating in people is the expectation that somehow they don't have to die—that if they can only get *all the information* they can beat the odds.

If you talk to an insurance actuary, you'll be told what people actually die of, cancer-wise: smoking. Smoking is way, way up there with automobile accidents and heart attacks. And you don't need to read any more studies to know what to do about that one. Every other prevention strategy, in my opinion, is a crapshoot. 10

From now on, I follow the only recipe for longevity that's ever actually made sense to me: moderation in all things. A little wine, a nice walk, a good dish of pasta, a minimal amount of microwaving in Tupperware containers, a dash of olive oil, a soupçon of Vitamin C, a very brief visit to a foundry. Live life modestly—except during the holidays and when you've been dumped by your boyfriend—and hope for the best. It's all you can do. 11

EXPLORATIONS:

Patricia Pearson,

When She Was Bad: Violent Women and the Myth of Innocence

Area Woman Blows Gasket (humorous essays)

http://www.pearsonspost.com/bio2.html

http://www.randomhouse.ca/author/results.pperl?authorid=23494

http://www.pearsonspost.com

STRUCTURE:

1. Pearson starts right off with the odd idea that "longer-legged people are significantly more prone to certain types of cancer." What does this opening do for her readers?
2. Though Pearson informs us early as to her subject and point of view, her actual THESIS STATEMENT is kept in reserve till the first sentence of the last paragraph, where she advises "moderation in

all things." Name one advantage of placing it at the end. Name one potential disadvantage. Why in most essays does it come at or near the beginning?

3. Roughly what percentage of her essay space does Pearson devote to *examples*? Tell two or three of your favourites. Has she reached the recommended 50% level? Point out which paragraphs are built entirely or mostly of examples.
4. In this essay of *cause and effect*, Pearson first questions current medical views on what does or does not *cause* cancer, before going on to her own advice. Have you tried to follow any of the popularly believed techniques in paragraph 3? Do her exposés of once-accepted but now rejected beliefs in paragraphs 4–7 seem to question the validity of the beliefs in paragraph 3? Finally, does the fact that she has made fun of formerly accepted beliefs help us to accept her own points that (in par. 10) smoking is the most obvious *cause* of cancer, and (in her closing paragraph) that "moderation in all things" is the main *cause* of longevity?

STYLE:

1. Does Pearson's humorous TONE work with the very serious topic of cancer?
2. In paragraph 10 Pearson calls most cancer prevention strategies "a crapshoot." Where else does she use very informal, COLLOQUIAL language? Does it work in her argument, or does it make us doubt her seriousness?

IDEAS FOR DISCUSSION AND WRITING:

1. Do you try to follow all the latest techniques to achieve the *effect* of good health, or do you just enjoy life and hope for the best? Argue for one of these points of view, giving reasons.
2. If you have read Stephen Leacock's essay "How to Live to Be 200" (in Chapter 8), compare the attitude of Jiggins, who "dumb-belled himself to death," with that of modern health seekers who try to reach the ideal diet and lifestyle.

3. Who in your extended family has reached a very old age? Do you think this longevity was *caused* by the person's lifestyle, or was the cause genetic? Give *examples.*
4. **PROCESS IN WRITING:** *Patricia Pearson's basic message is "moderation," but in our time we are more likely to encounter the "extreme." Why do so many of us seek extreme lifestyles, in areas such as food and drink, drugs, financial life, career, relationships, or in risky outdoor adventures? Fill a page with notes on this question, then narrow your focus down to one item—such as an "extreme sport" that you practise yourself. Analyze all the* causes *you can think of, or all the* effects, *and explain them in a first draft filled with examples. Examine it the next day. Does the* THESIS STATEMENT *unify your argument? Have you reached at least 50%* example *content? Do your points rise up to the most important at the end? After editing for content, polish the style, then bring your argument to class to read aloud.*

Note: See also the Topics for Writing on the Online Learning Centre at www.mcgrawhill.ca/olc/conrad.

PAUL D'ANGELO

The Step Not Taken

Paul D'Angelo's usual idea of writing is to tell fish stories, and he admits that his, like most, will stretch the truth. But one day the writer and TV critic for Outdoor Canada *magazine stepped into a Toronto elevator, and lived the true and sobering story that follows. When it appeared in the* Globe and Mail *of April 3, 1995, it struck a deep chord: dozens of readers sent replies, one of them 5000 words long. Several recounted tragic experiences they had just had themselves, and told how D'Angelo's confession had helped them face their own trials. The author of this thought-provoking essay has an unusual background for a writer. Born in Toronto, D'Angelo never went to university but always read a lot, an activity that gave him a way with words. After high school he spent seven years in Europe and Africa travelling, working here and there, and just living life. In the meantime, on a visit home he launched a seasonal greeting card business, which still left him seven months a year to roam. For some years, now, he and his family have lived in Toronto, where he thinks of himself mostly as an entrepreneur, but goes north to fish pike and bass for fun, and then writes about it in several columns a year. "Write what you live!" he says. Though D'Angelo usually finds writing to be slow and tough, he felt our selection so strongly that he just wrote it right off, to "get it off his chest."* The *Globe *changed only one word. Though he "felt better," his hope that the young man in the elevator would see the article and respond never came true.*

1 A few weeks ago I was followed into an office-building elevator by a well-dressed young man carrying a briefcase. He looked very sharp. Very buttoned-down. Wearing gold wire-frame

glasses, he was of medium height and build with neatly trimmed brown hair and, I would guess, in his mid-20s. Typical junior executive material. There was nothing about him that seemed unusual. Nothing at all to indicate what was about to take place.

The elevator had only one control panel, and I excused myself as I 2
leaned over to his side of the car and pushed the button for the 10th floor. He pushed the button for the 15th. The doors of the elevator closed and we began to ascend. Employing typical Toronto elevator etiquette, I stood staring up at the row of floor numbers above the doors while purposely ignoring my fellow passenger. Then it happened. A sudden strained gasp. Turning toward the noise, I was astonished to see the young man drop his briefcase and burst into tears. Our eyes met for a split second and, as if slapped, he averted his face from me, leaned his head against the wood-panelled wall of the elevator and continued to weep.

And what I did next still shames me. 3

The elevator stopped at the 10th floor and, without looking back, 4
I stepped out. I stood in the hallway, a bundle of mixed emotions, wondering what to do. A combination of guilt and uncertainty washed over me. Should I go up to the 15th floor and make sure he's okay? Should I search him out from office to office? Should I risk the embarrassment it might cause him? Is he mentally disturbed? A manic depressive, perhaps? Is he a suicide just waiting to happen?

I didn't know what to do. So I did nothing. 5

And now he haunts me. Not with fear, of course, but with a sense of 6
regret. I see his face crumbling before he turns to the wall. I see his shoulders heave as he sobs in a combination of sorrow and shame. I wonder now what brought him to that moment in time. How long had he been holding his pain inside before he could no longer contain it? What could possibly have overwhelmed him to such an extent that he was unable to keep from crying out?

Had he just visited the doctor and been told that he had an incur- 7
able disease? Was he having marital problems? Was his wife ill? His child? Had someone dear recently died? Was he being laid off? Was he looking for a job and meeting with no success? Was he having financial woes? Was he without friends in the city and crushed by loneliness?

8 The sorrows of this world are endless.

9 The few people I have told about the incident all say I did the proper thing, the best thing, by leaving the young man alone.

10 But they are wrong.

11 Like so many things in life, I know now what I should have done then. I should have thrown caution to the winds and done the right thing. Not the big-city thing. The right thing. The human thing. The thing I would want someone to do if they ever found my son crying in an elevator. I should have given him the opportunity to unload his sadness onto my shoulders. I should have reached out a hand and patted him on the back. I should have said something like, "Why don't you let me buy you a cup of coffee and you can tell me all your problems. There's no reason to feel self-conscious. I'll listen for as long as you want to talk."

12 What would his reaction have been to that? Would he have turned even further to the wall? Or would he have turned on me? Cursing me? Telling me to mind my own damned business? Would he have lashed out at me? Sorrow and insecurity turning to rage? Would he have physically attacked me? Or would he have gone with me for that cup of coffee?

13 I don't know. I'll never know. All I can be certain of is that I left him in that elevator with tears streaming down his face. And that he was alone. All alone.

14 I hope that somehow he gets to read these words, because I want him to know that I'm pulling for him. That I hope things are looking up for him. That I hope his sorrow is in the past. That I hope he is never again burdened with such awful despair. That I am thinking of him. That I said a prayer for him. That I was wrong, dreadfully wrong, not to step forward in his time of need.

15 That I'm sorry.

EXPLORATIONS:

Joseph Hartog et al., eds., *The Anatomy of Loneliness*
John Glassco, trans., *Complete Poems of Saint Denys Garneau*
http://www.depressioncanada.com

http://www.nimh.nih.gov/healthinformation/depressionmenu.cfm
http://www.cfpc.ca/English/cfpc/programs/patient%20education/depression/default.asp?s=1

STRUCTURE:

1. D'Angelo begins with an ANECDOTE. Is this a good technique? Do you see it often? How well does this one work as an introduction?
2. In paragraph 1 D'Angelo refers to "what was about to take place"; in paragraph two he says "Then it happened"; and in paragraph 3 he says "And what I did next still shames me." Why does he keep building suspense? What does this do for his AUDIENCE?
3. Identify D'Angelo's THESIS STATEMENT.
4. Tell how paragraph 10 works as a TRANSITION between parts. Why is it only one sentence long?
5. Where does D'Angelo ask himself *why*? Where does he ask *what if*? What *causes* does he imagine? What *effects*? And how important are these to the essay?

STYLE:

1. How CONCISE is this selection? Can you find any wasted words at all?
2. Read paragraphs 14 and 15 aloud in class. Why has D'Angelo given us a series of partial sentences? Why do most begin with "That ..."? Is this repetition accidental or deliberate? What effect does it achieve?
3. Why does D'Angelo's last paragraph contain only three words?

IDEAS FOR DISCUSSION AND WRITING:

1. If you were Paul D'Angelo, what would you have done when the young man on the elevator began to cry? Why do you think he was crying? Do you, like our author, live in the big city? Describe a time when the actions of a stranger made you wonder how to react. Did you take the risk of involvement? Or did you do the

"big-city thing"? Why? And now what do you think you should have done?

2. Did this selection bring tears to your own eyes? If so, in which parts? Is it good for an essayist to seek emotion in the reader?
3. Describe the favourite techniques of subway, streetcar, bus and elevator riders to preserve their solitude in rush hour. Arrange chairs as in a public transit vehicle, and role-play the situation in class.
4. Our essay title, "The Step Not Taken," is probably a reference to "The Road Not Taken," a poem by Robert Frost, in which the poet wonders what his journey would have been like had he taken the other fork in the path. Is this a universal theme? Describe a fork in your own path. Imagine to what destination "the road not taken" might have led you.
5. **PROCESS IN WRITING:** *You were the young man—or, if you like, a young woman—who was in the elevator that day, and you have just read Paul D'Angelo's article. Now answer him in a letter telling the* causes *of your pain, and responding to his shame at not helping. Look over your first draft: Have you found all the main* causes*? Are there also important* causes behind causes*? Have you used* TRANSITION SIGNALS *to highlight the logic (words like "because," "therefore," "as a result of," "so," etc.)? Revise. Now check for punctuation and spelling before printing out your best version.*

Note: See also the Topics for Writing on the Online Learning Centre at www.mcgrawhill.ca/olc/conrad.

NAHEED MUSTAFA

My Body Is My Own Business

Born in England to parents from an Indo-Pakistani background, Naheed Mustafa moved as an infant to Canada. In 1992 she completed an honours degree in political science and philosophy at the University of Toronto, specializing in Third-World development. Then she studied journalism at Ryerson University. Mustafa currently lives in Toronto with her husband, and combines working as an editor and freelance writer with raising her three children. "Almost anybody who's willing to work hard enough can learn to write very well," Mustafa says. It was on July 29, 1993 that "My Body Is My Own Business" appeared in the Toronto Globe and Mail. *Since we first reprinted the essay it has become widely anthologized in print, has been widely circulated on the Internet and is still attracting commentary. Mustafa states, "I see myself as being on something of a journey around this issue...." Ironically, the author of "My Body Is My Own Business" recalls the first edition of a textbook that inspired her in high school: it had a photo of a lightning strike on its cover. Its title was* The Act of Writing.

I often wonder whether people see me as a radical, fundamental- 1
ist Muslim terrorist packing an AK-47 assault rifle inside my jean jacket. Or maybe they see me as the poster girl for oppressed womanhood everywhere. I'm not sure which it is.

I get the whole gamut of strange looks, stares and covert glances. 2
You see, I wear the *hijab*, a scarf that covers my head, neck and throat. I do this because I am a Muslim woman who believes her body is her own private concern.

3 Young Muslim women are reclaiming the *hijab*, reinterpreting it in light of its original purpose—to give back to women ultimate control of their own bodies.

4 The Koran teaches us that men and women are equal, that individuals should not be judged according to gender, beauty, wealth or privilege. The only thing that makes one person better than another is her or his character.

5 Nonetheless, people have a difficult time relating to me. After all, I'm young, Canadian born and raised, university-educated—why would I do this to myself, they ask.

6 Strangers speak to me in loud, slow English and often appear to be playing charades. They politely inquire how I like living in Canada and whether or not the cold bothers me. If I'm in the right mood, it can be very amusing.

7 But why would I, a woman with all the advantages of a North American upbringing, suddenly, at 21, want to cover myself so that with the *hijab* and the other clothes I choose to wear, only my face and hands show?

8 Because it gives me freedom.

9 Women are taught from early childhood that their worth is proportional to their attractiveness. We feel compelled to pursue abstract notions of beauty, half realizing that such a pursuit is futile.

10 When women reject this form of oppression, they face ridicule and contempt. Whether it's women who refuse to wear makeup or to shave their legs or to expose their bodies, society, both men and women, have trouble dealing with them.

11 In the Western world, the *hijab* has come to symbolize either forced silence or radical, unconscionable militancy. Actually, it's neither. It is simply a woman's assertion that judgment of her physical person is to play no role whatsoever in social interaction.

12 Wearing the *hijab* has given me freedom from constant attention to my physical self. Because my appearance is not subjected to public scrutiny, my beauty, or perhaps lack of it, has been removed from the realm of what can legitimately be discussed.

13 No one knows whether my hair looks as if I just stepped out of a salon, whether or not I can pinch an inch, or even if I have unsightly stretch marks. And because no one knows, no one cares.

Feeling that one has to meet the impossible male standards of beauty is tiring and often humiliating. I should know, I spent my entire teenage years trying to do it. I was a borderline bulimic and spent a lot of money I didn't have on potions and lotions in hopes of becoming the next Cindy Crawford. 14

The definition of beauty is ever-changing; waifish is good, waifish is bad, athletic is good—sorry, athletic is bad. Narrow hips? Great. Narrow hips? Too bad. 15

Women are not going to achieve equality with the right to bare their breasts in public, as some people would like to have you believe. That would only make us party to our own objectification. True equality will be had only when women don't need to display themselves to get attention and won't need to defend their decision to keep their bodies to themselves. 16

EXPLORATIONS:

Elizabeth Warnock Fernea, *In Search of Islamic Feminism: One Woman's Global Journey*
Richard Gordon, *Eating Disorders: Anatomy of a Social Epidemic*
Naomi Wolf, *The Beauty Myth: How Images of Beauty Are Used Against Women*
Bharati Mukherjee, *Jasmine* (novel)
Salman Rushdie, *Shame* (novel)
Under One Sky: Arab Women in North America Talk About the Hijab (NFB, 43 min., 1999)
http://en.wikipedia.org/wiki/Hijab
http://en.wikipedia.org/wiki/Burqa
http://www.usc.edu/dept/MSA/othersites

STRUCTURE:

1. Why does Mustafa open with two STEREOTYPES? Do they draw your attention? Do they go straight to her topic?
2. In her argument does Mustafa give more attention to *causes* or *effects*? Name the main causes. Name the main effects.

3. Why does Mustafa explore effects *first* and causes *after*, reversing the logical order of the two?
4. Identify the TRANSITION in which Mustafa actually asks "why" and answers with "because ... ," as she moves from *effects* to *causes*.

STYLE:

1. Ending on a key word is a powerful device of emphasis. Note the final word in each half of Mustafa's argument: What makes "freedom" and "themselves" good choices for these positions?
2. Language can speak through rhythm as much as through words. Read aloud the first sentence of paragraph 6, then analyze how its sound reinforces its meaning.

IDEAS FOR DISCUSSION AND WRITING:

1. Mustafa says male standards of beauty for women are "impossible" and that feeling the need to meet them is "humiliating" (par. 14). Is she right? Whatever your own gender, give examples to attack or defend her view.
2. Examine the PARADOX of paragraph 8: that the effect of covering oneself with the *hijab* is "freedom." Do non-Muslims have means of shielding themselves, as well, from the unreasonable scrutiny and expectations of others? Name any such techniques you have used.
3. In news coverage of the Canadian military presence in Afghanistan, we often see images of women wearing another garment that conceals the body, the *burqa.* Describe it. Tell any *effects* that you believe its use has on the wearer and on people observing the wearer. Can it offer "freedom," as Mustafa believes the *hijab* does?
4. Though part of her background is the culture of another country, Mustafa is Canadian. If you too have origins in another culture, to what extent do you see yourself retaining the clothes, the foods, the religion and the language of that culture, here in Canada. Predict the *effects* of your intended course of action.

5. Mustafa confesses that as a teen she was a "borderline bulimic" (par. 14). What do you see as the main *causes* of bulimia and anorexia nervosa? What *causes* women, not men, to be the main victims?
6. At the library look through an illustrated history of art, taking notes on how the ideal of beauty in women has changed through the centuries. Then report your findings to the class, showing illustrations as evidence for your conclusions.
7. Watch your favourite television channel for at least an hour, taking notes on how women are presented both in programs and commercials. Then report to the class on the attitudes, especially any STEREOTYPES, which you detected. What *effects,* in both male and female viewers, do you think these attitudes will *cause?*
8. **PROCESS IN WRITING:** *Do number 6 above, except as an essay. Look over your notes, then choose a THESIS STATEMENT that expresses the main* effect(s) *on viewers of the* examples *you observed. Now write a rapid first draft, supporting your thesis statement with large numbers of these* examples. *When the draft has cooled off, look it over. Do the* causes *and* effects *seem reasonable? Have you tried to be objective, rather than interpret according to your own prejudices? Are there* causes behind causes, *or* effects of effects, *that might enrich your analysis? Do TRANSITIONS such as "since," "because" and "therefore" help the audience follow your logic? If not, add. Finally, edit for things like punctuation and spelling before doing the final version. Read it to the class, and be ready to answer questions from other points of view.*

Note: See also the Topics for Writing on the Online Learning Centre at www.mcgrawhill.ca/olc/conrad.

LINDA McQUAIG

Killing Machines*

Linda McQuaig is one of our nation's most hard-hitting social and economic critics. In her newspaper columns and in her books, she tirelessly battles vested interests such as big oil and other polluters, powerful transnational corporations and governments that favour the wealthy over the poor. Bringing research, wit and a vivid writing style to bear upon her subjects, she excels at tracing webs of cause and effect, such as the corruption and greed for oil that she argues lay behind the American invasion of Iraq. These and other petroleum-related subjects are exposed in her bestselling 2004 book It's the Crude, Dude: War, Big Oil and the Fight for the Planet. *(Our own selection, attacking gas-guzzling SUVs, comes from the same book.) Among McQuaig's many other published volumes have been* Behind Closed Doors: How the Rich Won Control of Canada's Tax System *(1987);* The Quick and the Dead: Brian Mulroney, Big Business and the Seduction of Canada *(1991);* Shooting the Hippo: Death by Deficit and Other Canadian Myths *(1995); and* Holding the Bully's Coat: Canada and the U.S. Empire *(2007). McQuaig has also written regularly for the* Globe and Mail, *the* Toronto Star, Maclean's *magazine, the* National Post *and CBC Radio. She is also a popular speaker, bringing to her audiences the same sharp wit and vivid examples that fill her writings.*

1 Having paid insufficient attention to car advertisements in the 1990s, I somehow didn't get the concept of an SUV. I didn't realize, for instance, that it was a symbol

*Editor's title.

of a bold, adventurous, sporty kind of life, driven by people with a tendency to go off-road—just as, elsewhere in their lives, they have a tendency to break with the pack, to do things their way, to think outside the box. To show how far out of the loop I was, I didn't even know there was a difference between an SUV and a minivan. They both just seemed like awkward, bulky, oversized versions of a car—useful, no doubt, for those trips to Price Chopper when one comes home laden with several extra cases of Coke and a year's supply of toilet paper.

Of course, I was dead wrong. I've learned that there's a world of difference between a utilitarian minivan, which is designed for the Price Chopper trip as well as carting around children's soccer equipment, and an SUV, which is not only bold and adventurous but also glamorous, the car of choice these days among Hollywood stars and others with limitless resources. Still, one can appreciate the role advertising has played in making this sort of distinction clear to people, in establishing the SUV as the symbol of everything chic. The sheer brilliance of this advertising coup can perhaps best be measured by the extent of the image transformation the SUV has undergone since its first incarnation as a vehicle with few uses outside the funeral business. As Keith Bradsher has noted in his book *High and Mighty*, the forerunner of the SUV—the Chevy Suburban—dates back to the 1930s, and it managed to survive in the early decades largely because its body was the perfect height and width for the easy loading and unloading of coffins. This feature is retained today but omitted from SUV advertising. 2

So effective has the advertising campaign been that the public seems largely unaware that SUVs are generally difficult to handle, with poor agility and manoeuvrability—exactly the opposite of the sports car, which of course, used to be the sexy car of choice. While a sports car, with its low-slung body and road-gripping tires, can zip around corners at great speed, the rigid, high-set body of the SUV makes its way around corners with considerably more difficulty, which explains why ads typically show SUVs motionless at the top of a mountain or charging straight ahead (got to get straight home with all that toilet paper), rather than driving on the kind of winding, exotic cliffside roads typically seen in sports car ads. 3

4 Much of the appeal of today's SUV may have less to do with sportiness and glamour, and more to do with security in an age of fear. Huge and growing ever larger, the SUV offers its riders a massive, wraparound steel exterior with the feel of a tank—a mobile version of a gated community. Bradsher reports that this is deliberate, that the tough, even menacing-looking appearance of many SUVs is intentionally and consciously designed by automakers for an era when civility on the roads has been replaced with unabashed hostility, a kind of me-first aggressiveness. In the age of everything from road rage to anthrax to SARS, you can't have too much steel between you and the rest of what's driving around out there.

5 And it's true: SUVs *are* a threat to others on the road—a fact that was appreciated as early as thirty years ago by researchers trying to draw attention to the dangers of designing vehicles with the sort of stiff, high front ends that are the hallmark of the SUV. In an accident, an SUV is two and a half times more likely than a mid-size car to kill the occupants of the other vehicle, due to the fact that SUVs are heavier (by a thousand pounds on average), stiffer and taller. These characteristics effectively turn SUVs into "battering rams in collisions with other vehicles," notes a recent report by the Union of Concerned Scientists. When an SUV hits a car from behind, it is more likely to ride up over the car's bumper, leaving the car (and its occupants) essentially defenseless. When an SUV hits a car from the side, it can ride up over the car's door frame and right into the passenger compartment. (Well, hello there!) This mismatch of sizes has been dubbed "vehicle incompatibility," but another possible name would be "vehicle homicide." And one-on-one against an unarmed pedestrian, an SUV is more lethal still, hitting the pedestrian higher up on the body, closer to vital organs, than a regular car does. Yet this greater height, stiffness and body weight seems to be something of a selling point, rather than a signal that perhaps something is seriously wrong with these oversized killing machines.

6 Even if the thought of killing others isn't a deterrent, one would think the thought of killing oneself and one's loved ones would count for something. But apparently not. SUV sales have skyrocketed despite the fact that they are also a danger to their own passengers because, with their considerable height, they have a tendency to roll

over. More than 51,500 occupants of SUVs (and light trucks) died in rollovers from 1991 to 2001. The overall fatality rate for SUVs was 8 percent worse than for cars in 2000.

But the more far-reaching problem with SUVs—at least in terms of 7
the survival of the planet—is the devastating amount of greenhouse gases they spew out into the air. An SUV produces roughly 40 percent more greenhouse gas emissions than a regular car does, and with SUV sales soaring—sales have increased seventeen-fold in the past two decades—their emissions have become a significant part of the problem of global warming. At a time when the dangers of global warming are blatantly evident and of serious concern to people all over the world, the breezy marketing of SUVs in North America makes a mockery of any claim that we are addressing the problem. While common sense would call for a special effort to move away from these over-emitting vehicles, exactly the opposite has been happening. Both the U.S. and Canadian governments have contributed to the SUV problem by offering SUVs regulatory controls far looser than those applied to regular cars. (The regulations were established in the U.S., but Canada has effectively adopted matching standards, which the automakers have agreed to deliver on a voluntary basis.) The extraordinary growth in SUV sales over the last two decades, then, can be attributed as much to government favouritism as to the massive advertising campaign that has left prospective SUV buyers thinking of off-road adventure rather than the ease of moving coffins.

The story of the SUV is in many ways a microcosm of the human 8
folly that has led us to the brink of a climate change disaster. Perhaps it seems unfair to pick on the SUV. After all, it isn't, by any means, the only source of greenhouse gas emissions. It is, however, one of the fast-growing sources. SUVs now account for an astonishing 24 percent of all new cars sold, up from just 2 percent in 1980. (Overall, the transportation sector accounts for 26 percent of U.S. greenhouse gas emissions. Along with coal-fired power plants, transportation is one of the key sources of the global warming problem.)

I'm picking on the SUV partly because it somehow serves as a 9
metaphor for the absurdity of the situation we find ourselves in, if for no other reason than that these enormous, awkward vehicles seem so ... well ... unnecessary. There's another aspect to this story that

makes it emblematic of the saga of global warming: how easily the problem could be corrected if there were any serious political will. The technology exists to make enormous strides in cutting back the greenhouse gas emissions currently spewing out of SUVs (and other vehicles, but particularly SUVs) on highways across North America. I'm not talking about exotic space-age cars that run on hydrogen in some dream scenario (that's likely a couple of decades or so down the road), but about technology that already exists—and currently sits on shelves—in the offices of our big automakers. This, then, is the story of how Luddites° in the auto sector, fearful of risking their dominant market position, have declined to take us to where any sane person can see we must go, hiding behind claims of technological "can't do," hoping the public won't realize that what we have here is, in fact, a tale of technological "won't do."

°Luddites: In 1811 in Nottingham, England, textile workers led by Ned Ludd revolted against factory owners who were replacing craftsmen with new technology. They smashed the weaving machines, to protect their own jobs, until authorities put down the uprising. Since then, those who oppose new technology have often been called "Luddites."

EXPLORATIONS:

Linda McQuaig,

It's the Crude, Dude: War, Big Oil and the Fight for the Planet

The Cult of Impotence: Selling the Myth of Powerlessness in the Global Economy

Keith Bradsher, *High and Mighty: SUVs—The World's Most Dangerous Vehicles and How They Got that Way*

Al Gore, *An Inconvenient Truth* (feature-length documentary, and book)

Who Killed the Electric Car? (feature-length documentary, on DVD)

http://www.rabble.ca/about_us/bios.shtml?x=814

STRUCTURE:

1. Why does McQuaig begin by confessing her former ignorance about sports utility vehicles (SUVs)?

2. Identify McQuaig's THESIS STATEMENT.
3. Point out how in paragraph 3 McQuaig exploits the device of *contrast.*
4. McQuaig explores both *causes* and *effects* of the SUV phenomenon. First point out all the *causes* she gives, then all the *effects.*
5. What technique does McQuaig exploit in closing on the very words "'won't do'"?

Style:

1. In places Linda McQuaig uses academic words such as "emblematic," "microcosm" and "Luddites," but in other places more conversational language such as "got to get straight home with all that toilet paper" (par. 3) or, as the SUV is riding up over another car's door frame and into the passenger compartment, "Well, hello there!" (5). Is this mixture of TONE effective? Why or why not?
2. What FIGURES OF SPEECH does McQuaig apply when she likens an SUV to a "tank," a "gated community" (par. 4) and a "battering ram" (5)?

Ideas for Discussion and Writing:

1. In our era of consumerism, many people speak of "moving up" to a bigger car or house, rather than making a "lateral move." Do you aspire to drive an SUV? What do you think would be the *effects* on your status level? Your driving habits? Your bankbook?
2. McQuaig argues that SUVs are two and a half times more likely to kill occupants of another vehicle (par. 5), are more lethal to pedestrians (5), are 8% more likely to kill even their own passengers (6) and emit 40 percent more greenhouse gases (7), thus hastening planetary disaster. Why, then, do automakers promote these vehicles so heavily? And why do these "Luddites," as she calls them, refuse to take new technology off the shelf to improve the vehicles?
3. "I'm picking on the SUV," McQuaig openly states in paragraph 9. Has she gone too far in only criticizing and ridiculing? Should she have included positive points, in order to be fair? Or would that just diminish the whole idea of arguing a case?

4. In paragraph 7 McQuaig points out how Canada has followed the United States in adopting the same loose SUV emission standards. What are all the *causes* of this fact? What are the *effects*? Are we a nation of followers, or are there areas of public policy that are all our own?
5. What is the solution: Drive less? Car-pool? Drive a small car? (Are they safe?) Use public transit? Cycle or walk? Give your own conclusions.
6. **PROCESS IN WRITING:** *Write an essay on the* causes and/or effects *of owning one of the following: a bicycle, a motorcycle, a very small car, a sports car, a pickup truck, a Hummer or a luxury car. First rough out a page or two of notes. Then look to see if you have mentioned mostly* causes, *mostly* effects, *or both. Accordingly, plan your argument, arrive at a THESIS STATEMENT, and write a rapid first draft filled with* examples. *The next day look it over. Have you left out any obvious* causes and/ or effects*? If so, add. Do logic signals such as "because," "therefore," "so that" and "as a result" highlight your cause-and-effect argument? If not, add. Finally, look over the punctuation and sentence structure before printing out your best version.*

Note: See also the Topics for Writing on the Online Learning Centre at www.mcgrawhill.ca/olc/conrad.

JUNE CALLWOOD

Forgiveness

Founder or co-founder of some 50 humanitarian organizations, author of over a dozen books and of some 2000 articles and columns, for over six decades a fighter for the rights of women and children and the vulnerable everywhere, June Callwood became the nation's most effective social justice advocate. She was born in 1924 in Chatham, Ontario, grew up in the poverty of the Great Depression, dropped out of high school to help support her family, got her first journalism job at $7.50 a week in Brantford, then in 1942, at age 18, won a post at the Toronto Globe and Mail. *But her celebration of progressive values in journalism was not enough: she also took direct action, creating institutions in response to public need. In the sixties she founded Digger House, a shelter for homeless young people; then in 1974 Nellie's, a shelter for battered women; in 1982 Jessie's Centre for Teenagers; and in 1988 Casey House, a hospice for AIDS victims. Meanwhile she was a founding member of PEN Canada and of the Canadian Civil Liberties Association. Callwood hosted numerous television series, and ghost-wrote some ten autobiographies, as well as authoring her own books on humanitarian themes. Honoured with the Order of Canada and many other civic prizes, and granted 17 honorary degrees, Callwood never slowed down. Late in life she still drove her sports convertible around town, and maintained her pilot's licence. It was in April 2007, while Callwood was 82 and suffering from a long illness, that* The Walrus *published our selection, "Forgiveness." Later that month the nation lost one of its most exemplary citizens.*

1 A small boy in an industrial city in Ontario was beaten severely many times by his father, to the extent that the boy not infrequently required a doctor to stitch up the wounds. His father, a policeman, sincerely believed that if he beat his son with chains, belts, sticks, and his fists, the boy would not grow up to be gay. That boy, now in his thirties and indelibly a gay man, says he will never forgive his father.

2 "What he did is not forgivable," the man says with composure. "How can it ever be all right to abuse a child? But I have let it go."

3 And a woman, raised on the Prairies in a Finnish home, married a black man and had a son. She showed the infant proudly to her mother, whose reaction was a look of naked disgust. Her mother and that son, now a charming and successful adult, have since developed an affectionate relationship, but the daughter has not forgotten or forgiven the expression on her mother's face.

4 "The best I can do," she says, "is that I have stopped hating her."

5 The ability to forgive is a central tenet of every major religion in the world—Christian, Judaic, Hindu, Buddhist, and Islamic. Those faiths urge followers to forgive their enemies and, indeed, even to find a way to love those who wrong them. As the twenty-first century dawns, however, the world is making a spectacular mess of such pious admonitions. Instead of goodwill, this is the age of anger, the polar opposite of forgiveness. Merciless ethnic, tribal, and religious conflicts dominate every corner of the planet, and in North America individuals live with high levels of wrath that explode as domestic brutality, road rage, vile epithets, and acts of random slaughter.

6 Many people, like the gay man or the woman in a biracial marriage, find forgiveness an unreasonable dictate. Some assaults on the body or soul are unconscionable, they feel, and forgiveness is simply out of the question. It satisfies the requirements of their humanity that they gradually ease away from the primitive thoughts of revenge that once obsessed them.

7 When Simon Wiesenthal, the famed Nazi hunter, was in a German concentration camp, he found himself in a strange situation. He was taken to the bedside of a dying SS officer, a youth who had killed many

Jews, and the young man asked him, a Jew, for forgiveness. Wiesenthal was silent and left the room, but was haunted ever after. Thirty years later, he contacted some of the world's great thinkers and asked, what should I have done? Theologians such as Bishop Desmond Tutu and the Dalai Lama gently hinted that he should have been forgiving, for his own sake, but others, notably philosopher Herbert Marcuse, said that great evil should never be forgiven. In *The Sunflower*, a collection of fifty-three responses to Wiesenthal's question, Marcuse wrote sternly that forgiveness condones the crime.

The moral vacuum left by the pervasive disuse and misuse of religious tenets has allowed a secular forgiveness industry to spring into being. People who yearn desperately to rid themselves of an obsession for vengeance will seek help in curious places. Since 1985, the University of Wisconsin–Madison has offered forgiveness studies, and an International Forgiveness Institute was founded there. Four years ago, the world's first international conference on forgiveness drew hundreds of delegates to Madison. Stanford University has a forgiveness research project and people in California, a state on the cutting edge of self-absorption, are taking part in studies on the art and science of forgiveness. Self-help shelves in bookstores abound in titles such as *Forgive Your Parents: Heal Yourself.* 8

An odious US daytime television show, *Forgive or Forget,* features guests who say they owe someone an apology. They describe their offence, and then, *ta-dah,* the injured party appears on the appropriately tacky set and either grants or withholds forgiveness. Will the former foes embrace one another? The titillated audience can't wait. 9

Apologies are iffy because often they are contrived or coerced. Apologies extracted by judges, mediators, and parents are thin gruel for the wronged person. One familiar genre of apology, the one which commences, "I am sorry you are feeling badly," is particularly counterproductive because there is no admission of any responsibility; it is the other person's problem for being thin-skinned. A sincere and remorseful acceptance of blame, however, can close a wound. 10

Psychologists are engrossed by the topic and so are theologians, philosophers, psychiatrists, and—surprise—cardiologists. Unforgiving 11 people, some studies show, are three times more likely to have heart disease as people who don't carry grudges. These findings raise the suspicion that the researchers may have the cart before the horse. Heart attacks occur more often in blow-top people who have unfortified egos, the very ones most apt to be relentlessly unforgiving. On the other hand, people who hold tolerant views of human nature and don't seem to nurse grievances unduly tend to have blood pressures in the normal range.

12 Clergy, counsellors, and people who lecture and write books about forgiveness all preach reductionism as a strategy for overcoming hot resentment of someone's nasty behaviour. They say that people who have been harmed should see the hurtful as deeply flawed human beings working out nameless aggressions. Pitiable and inferior, they are examples of failure to thrive. Adults still distressed by abuse, neglect, or rejection in childhood are urged to consider what happened in their parents' childhoods—often, bad parenting comes from being badly parented. The theory is that understanding the reasons for their parents' limitations will enable the offspring to acquire a measure of compassion.

13 Maybe it works. Hillary Clinton apparently forgave her sleazy husband because she knows he had an unhappy childhood.

14 This technique can be applied to almost any injustice and falls within the rapists-were-beaten-as-children, *poor them* school of thought, which for some skeptics veers perilously close to non-accountability. The law and commonsense hold that adults are responsible for what they do. While empathy may help people appreciate why others behave badly, the exercise is somewhat patronizing. The offender is reduced to a contemptible hive of neuroses and ungovernable aberrations, which accordingly elevates the injured party to a morally superior person.

15 Demonizing the enemy is a common coping mechanism in times of adversity. In military terms, it captures the high ground.

16 Catastrophes such as divorce, job loss, rape, robbery, infidelity, and slander are all assaults on personal dignity and self-respect. A sense of being intact—*safe*—has been violated, and people are dismayed to find themselves for some time emotionally crippled by anger and grief. Betrayal and loss take big chunks out of people's confidence and leave them feeling excruciatingly vulnerable to random harm.

The starting place, some therapists say, is to accept that something appalling has happened, and it hurts. Denial, a recourse more favoured by men than by women, won't help. The next step, they say, is to develop an off switch. When fury threatens to make the brain reel, people should grasp for distractions. Brooding about revenge only serves to unhinge reason. If people don't rid themselves of wrath, personal growth stops cold. The hard part comes at the end of the process. The choices are to enter a state of forgiveness, which is a triumph of generosity, or just to put the matter in a box, cover it with a lid, place a brick on the lid, and move on. In healthy people, a perverse state of mind eventually wears itself out. 17

In yoga, they say that it takes six years of regularly practising meditation to gain spiritual insight. Forgiveness of a great wrong may take longer. The process can't even begin until the injured person stops crying. 18

Some people are marvellously unbroken by great injustices. Nelson Mandela smiled gently at his adversaries after twenty-seven years of brutal imprisonment. A worldwide figure of wonder, he even invited his white jailer to his inauguration as South Africa's president. In Cambodia, a pastor whose family had been wiped out by the Khmer Rouge baptized and forgave a notorious Khmer Rouge leader known as Duch. A university professor in Virginia had an urge to kill the intruder who beat his mother to death, but stopped himself with the thought, "Whose heart is darker?" And the father of a young girl casually murdered in a street encounter with a teenager she didn't know attended the trial and sat quietly throughout the appalling testimony. He said he would visit the youth in prison. "I do not think I can forgive him," he explained, "but perhaps if I know him I will not hate him." 19

Forgiveness is hard work. A woman, a devout Roman Catholic who forgave the man who tortured and killed her seven-year-old daughter, said, "Anyone who says forgiveness is for wimps hasn't tried it." The reward for giving up scalding thoughts of reprisal is peace of mind. It is worth the candle. 20

EXPLORATIONS:

June Callwood, *Twelve Weeks in Spring*
Anne Dublin, *June Callwood: A Life of Action*
Simon Wiesenthal, *The Sunflower*
http://www.cbc.ca/thehour/video.php?id=1513
http://en.wikipedia.org/wiki/June_Callwood
http://archives.cbc.ca/arts_entertainment/media/topics/1393
http://www.caseyhouse.com/en/june_callwood/biography/march_2007
http://www.mayoclinic.com/health/forgiveness/MH00131

STRUCTURE:

1. This argument of *cause and effect* makes strong use of *examples.* Roughly what percentage of the total argument is devoted to them? In which paragraph do they begin? Which speak most strongly to you?
2. After the two dramatic introductory *examples* in paragraphs 1–4, Callwood's THESIS STATEMENT is all of paragraph 5. Point out how it is built on a *contrast.*
3. In paragraphs 8–10 Callwood criticizes what she calls the "secular forgiveness industry." Why, in her view, are its attempts at forgiveness not very successful? What actually works better?
4. In a particularly concrete example of *cause and effect,* Callwood reports in paragraph 11 that "unforgiving people, some studies show, are three times more likely to have heart disease as people who don't carry grudges." To what extent do you believe good attitudes *cause* good health? Give examples from your own experience or observation.
5. In paragraph 14 Callwood describes what she calls the "rapists-were-beaten-as-children, *poor them* school of thought." Study the rest of this paragraph, then review the essay by Nathalie Petrowski in this chapter, "The Seven-Minute Life of Marc Lépine." In her search for the *causes* of the infamous Montreal Massacre, to what

extent does Petrowski conclude that Lépine was a victim of his own past?

6. Callwood packs paragraph 19 with a succession of dramatic acts of forgiveness. How do these lead to her closing?

STYLE:

1. Some of Callwood's paragraphs are quite long. Is this a flaw, or are there reasons?
2. How CONCISE is this essay? Do you see wasted words, or does everything contribute?

IDEAS FOR DISCUSSION AND WRITING:

1. The greatest hero of our time is widely thought to be Nelson Mandela, who emerged from decades as a political prisoner to lead his country of South Africa to democracy. Analyze his act of forgiveness in paragraph 19: inviting his own white jailer to his inauguration as South Africa's president. What may have *caused* Mandela's ability to forgive? What *effects* do you think the forgiveness may have achieved?
2. As in the opening examples of the gay man (paragraphs 1–2) and of the mother in a biracial marriage (3–4), forgiveness may not always be possible. But at least he has "let it go" and she has "stopped hating" her mother. Is this enough to help the offended persons? Is any step toward forgiveness a good step?
3. In paragraph 7 Callwood tells of the Nazi hunter Simon Wiesenthal, who pondered the question of whether "great evil" should ever be forgiven. What is your view? Could you have forgiven the dying SS officer? Or do you agree with philosopher Herbert Marcuse that "forgiveness condones the crime."
4. Put yourself in the place of June Callwood, whose own son Casey was killed by a drunk driver, while riding his motorcycle to university. Could you ever forgive? And if not, how do you imagine trying to contain your anger so it would not ruin your life? Reflect on the fact that in memory of her son (who did not have

AIDS), Callwood founded Casey House, a hospice for people living with AIDS.

5. **PROCESS IN WRITING:** *Think of the worst offence anyone has ever committed against you: perhaps an act of racism, or sexism, or betrayal, or violence, or even a crime. If the event is something you can share, make a page of notes on your own reactions: How have you responded, and what have been the* effects *of your response (for example, have you gone for anger, hate and revenge, or have you made attempts at closure, reconciliation or even forgiveness?)? Now develop a* THESIS STATEMENT *that tells your subject and your viewpoint toward it. Write a quick draft of your* cause and effect *essay. The next day look it over. Is there an opening and a closing? Have you given plentiful* examples, *like Callwood? Do* TRANSITION SIGNALS *move the argument forward? Now cut waste: surplus words, or even whole sections that do not support your main point. Last, check for spelling and punctuation. Now print out your best version. If it's something you cannot share with the class, then share it with a trusted friend.*

Note: See also the Topics for Writing on the Online Learning Centre at www.mcgrawhill.ca/olc/conrad.

NATHALIE PETROWSKI

The Seven-Minute Life of Marc Lépine*

Translated from the French by Ronald Conrad

Born 1954 in Paris and educated in Montreal, Nathalie Petrowski is a radio and TV personality, and one of Quebec's favourite print journalists—quirky, personal, satirical. In 1995 she also published Maman Last Call, *and wrote the script for the book's feature film version released in 2005. In her newspaper column for* Le Devoir *of December 16, 1989 Petrowski had a special challenge: ten days before, 25-year-old Marc Lépine had walked into an engineering class at the University of Montreal's École Polytechnique, shouted at the women students "You're all a bunch of feminists, and I hate feminists," ordered the men to leave—then lifted his rifle and shot the women. Six died. During the next minutes of terror he roamed the building, shooting. Altogether he gunned down 27 students, killing 14, all women. Then Lépine had turned the weapon on himself and died too. Canada felt a shock wave of anger and remorse, for this was the worst one-day mass murder in the nation's history, and its selectivity seemed to express a general sexism in society. In the next days, as the flag over Parliament flew at half-mast, citizens learned that Lépine's father had beat him and divorced the mother, and that the boy, though intelligent, had problems both academically and socially. He loved war movies, and from a paratrooper uncle had learned to handle firearms. His unemployment benefits were running out, the army would not take him, and the Polytechnique had refused him admission to its engineering program.*

*Editor's title.

Now on December 6 of every year, ceremonies across the nation honour the 14 young women, training for a profession still dominated by men, who were killed by a man whose suicide note blamed feminists for ruining his life. The essay that follows (originally entitled "Pitié pour les salauds"*) has a special poignancy, for Nathalie Petrowski wrote it in shock, as she and the nation first struggled to see meaning in the event.*

1 Pardon if I insist, pardon if I don't just mourn and forget, but it's stronger than I am, for a week I can't stop thinking about Marc Lépine. A psychoanalyst would say I'm identifying with the aggressor. But I'd say that inside every aggressor, every villain, there hides a victim.

2 I think of Marc Lépine to block out all the talk that just confuses things: Rambo, television, violence towards women, pornography, abortion, and firearms in display windows.

3 I think of Marc Lépine, still wondering what happened and exactly when the hellish countdown of his act was unleashed. Was it the morning of December 6, was it November 21 when he bought his rifle or September 4 when he applied for the firearm permit? Was it the day of his birth, the first time his father beat him, the day his parents divorced, the week when he suddenly quit all his courses, the night a girl didn't want to dance with him? What about all the hours, the days, the weeks, the years that passed before the bomb inside him went off?

4 Still, journalists have told us everything: where he lived, the schools he went to, the names of teachers and students he knew. We know how much he paid for his rifle and how he loved war movies. But once all this has been said, nothing has been said.

5 We know nothing of the ache that consumed him, of the torture inside him. We know nothing of the evil path he slipped into smiling the cruel smile of the angel of destruction, no longer himself, knowing only that he was put on earth to destroy.

6 I think of Marc Lépine but equally of Nadia,° his sister who was beaten, too, for singing out loud in the morning, Nadia who came

°Nadia: Lépine's sister Nadia Garbi later became a drug addict. In 1996 she died of cardiac arrest from an overdose.

from the same family but didn't fall prey to the same madness. Why Marc and not Nadia, why Marc and not another? That's what I ask myself when facts only deepen the mystery, when social criticism only confuses things.

No one remembers him from grade school, or from Sainte-Justine Hospital where he spent a year in therapy with his mother and sister. Until last week Marc Lépine did not exist. He was an unknown quantity, a number, an anonymous face in the crowd, a nobody who no one would even look at or give the least warmth, the slightest affection. In a few moments he went from a nothing to one of a kind, a pathological case who the experts claim in no way represents the society where he was born and grew up. 7

For a week I've been talking with these experts, hoping to understand. For a week all I've seen is that there is no one answer, there are a thousand. For a week I've dealt with the official and professional voices who keep their files under key, who keep repeating that there's no use wanting to know more, that Marc Lépine is dead, that he can no longer be healed or saved, that it's too late to do anything at all. Sometimes their excuses and justifications sound like lies. 8

But I refuse to hear the silence of death that falls like snow, the shameful silence that freezes my blood. Somewhere deep in the ruins of our private space we hide the truth, we try to protect ourselves saying that families—ours, his, the victims'—have been traumatized. 9

Forget about the past, say the authorities, let's move on and not let Marc Lépine's act dictate our choices. Yet the surest way to let this act dictate our choices is to hide it, to let it become a medical, psychological and criminal secret, to push it into the smallest hollow of our collective memory till it's erased and we can say it never existed at all. 10

In this province where memory is reduced to a slogan on a licence plate,° we want to forget Marc Lépine like we forget all events that can disturb us and make us think. Though I know nothing of Marc Lépine's story, I've met enough young people in the high schools and colleges to know that chance as well as reasons, randomness as well as all the wrong conditions in one person's life, caused this act. 11

°a slogan on a licence plate: Quebec licence plates bear the motto *"Je me souviens"* ("I remember"); Quebeckers consider this a reference to their history, and especially the Conquest.

His tragic destiny looks more and more like a tangle of shattered hopes, of frustrated dreams, of hopeless waits on a long and cold road without a single hand extended to help, and no guardrail.

12 Marc Lépine died the evening of December 6, but unlike his victims, he had died long before. In the end his life lasted just seven minutes. Before and after, he was forgotten.

13 So pardon my pessimism, but I cannot help believing that somewhere, at this moment, there are other Marc Lépines who won't ask for anything because they don't even know what to ask for—other children turned into monsters by abusive fathers and impersonal school systems, by a society so intent on excellence that every day it hammers the nail of Defeat further in, and plants seeds of frustration and violence in the fragile spirits of its children.

14 Though nothing can be done now for Marc Lépine, something can still be done for the others, whose inner clock has already begun the terrible countdown. It would be a mistake to forget them.

EXPLORATIONS:

Nathalie Petrowski, *Il Restera toujours le Nébraska* (novel; available only in French)
Louise Malette and Marie Chalouh, eds., *Polytechnique, 6 décembre* (writings on the Montreal Massacre; available only in French)
Elliott Leyton, *Hunting Humans* (book on multiple murders)
Neil Boyd, *The Beast Within: Why Men Are Violent*
Heidi Rathjen and Charles Montpetit, *December 6: From the Montreal Massacre to Gun Control*
After the Montreal Massacre (NFB/CBC video, 27 min.)
Camilo José Cela, *Pascal Duarte's family* (novel, Spain)
Gabriel García Márquez, *Chronicle of a Death Foretold* (novella, Colombia)
Anne Hébert, *The Torrent* (novella)
http://www.whiteribbon.ca
http://www.litterature.org/ile32000.asp?numero=373
http://www.infoculture.ca/?page=5&view=2&numero=5223

http://www.radio-canada.ca/radio/indicatifpresent/Chroniques/47790.shtml
http://en.wikipedia.org/wiki/Marc_L%C3%A9pine
http://archives.cbc.ca/IDD-1-70-398/disasters_tragedies/Montreal_massacre

STRUCTURE:

1. Identify Nathalie Petrowski's THESIS STATEMENT.
2. Tragic events leave people asking "Why?" Point out all the reasons that Petrowski examines to explain Marc Lépine's acts. How fully is her argument built on *cause-and-effect* reasoning?
3. How does paragraph 6 use *comparison and contrast*?
4. What popular technique of conclusion gives force to the closing?

STYLE:

1. In paragraph 1 and elsewhere, Petrowski groups sentences together with commas. Do you view this as faulty punctuation, or is it a way for Petrowski to express strong feeling? Are we ever justified in breaking rules of punctuation and sentence structure?
2. Identify all the FIGURES OF SPEECH in paragraph 9. What do they contribute?
3. What feeling does paragraph 3 convey in its flurry of questions?

IDEAS FOR DISCUSSION AND WRITING:

1. After murdering 14 engineering students because they were women, Marc Lépine used the last bullet on himself. But in what sense had he "died long before" (par. 12)? In what sense did his life last only "seven minutes" (par. 12)?
2. Petrowski opens her essay with the belief that "inside every aggressor, every villain, there hides a victim." Can we and should we view Marc Lépine, the killer, as himself a victim? If so, a victim of who or what? What might have been done, and by whom, to help Lépine before it was too late?

3. In its issue covering the Montreal Massacre, *Maclean's* reported that in Canada one of every four women is harassed sexually at some time in life, and that a million women are abused each year by their husbands or partners. It also quoted a study by Rosemary Gartner who found that "as women move into non-traditional roles, they run a significantly higher risk of being killed." Do you see a link between this information and the act of Marc Lépine? Explain.
4. By the tenth anniversary of that terrible day, the number of female students in Canadian engineering programs had doubled. Are the problems being solved? Or do you believe women and their goals are still at risk?
5. In a *Fifth Estate* documentary, *Legacy of Pain*, marking the massacre's tenth anniversary, correspondent Francine Pelletier spoke of one survivor, Nathalie Provost, now an engineer and a mother. "The first time her little boy went bang-bang to her, she said she went white," reported Pelletier. "She took him by the arm and said, 'Don't you ever do that to me. Because mommy's been there.'" Would you allow your own children to have toy weapons? To play cops and robbers, or other traditional games of violence? What could be the *effects*? Defend your response with evidence.
6. On that day, Lépine carried one of the most popular rifles in Canada, a .223-calibre Sturm, Ruger semiautomatic, with two 30-clip magazines holding shells with expanding slugs. Are firearms such as this a danger in your city or town? Attack or defend the sale of arms, including handguns, over the counter. Are our gun laws an attack on civil liberties, as many hunters maintain, or are they still too weak to stop the next Marc Lépine?
7. Go to reliable websites and read about other mass murders that have taken place in schools, such as Columbine High School (Colorado, 1999), or Virginia Tech University (2007). What seem to be the main *causes*?
8. **PROCESS IN WRITING:** *Lépine used a rifle, but handguns are the weapon of choice for shootings. At the library or at reliable websites, gather information on the role of handguns in crime in Canada. Research also our current regulations for their sale and use. Now decide on your* THESIS STATEMENT: *whether Canada should end, more severely limit or continue*

to permit the sale of handguns to civilians. List your reasons. From this short outline write a fast discovery draft of your essay, developed mainly through cause-and-effect *logic, not stopping now to fix things like spelling or punctuation. The next day look it over. Is every point backed by a reason or* example? *Does your* evidence *lead clearly to your* conclusion? *(Remember that many essayists will change a conclusion or even a thesis statement when the act of writing uncovers better ideas.) Finally, edit for correctness as you produce your final version.*

Note: See also the Topics for Writing on the Online Learning Centre at www.mcgrawhill.ca/olc/conrad.

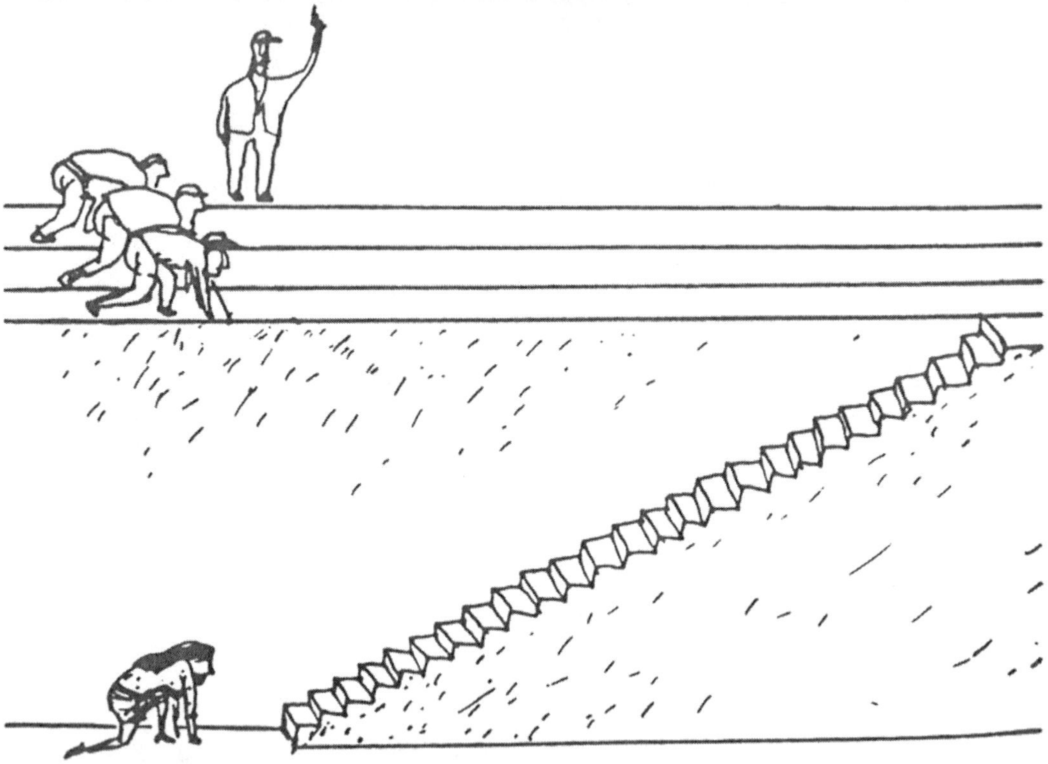

Mike Constable

"Women workers earn, on an average, only 70 cents for every $1 a man gets—even though on an average, women are better educated than men."

—Doris Anderson, "The 51-Per-Cent Minority"

5 Comparison and Contrast

IT'S JUST THE OPPOSITE OF....

You may have heard the old Chinese proverb "I felt sorry for myself because I had no shoes, until I met a man who had no feet." How much more we suddenly know about both the shoes and the feet, thinking of them together! This is the power of comparison and contrast.

See Mike Constable's cartoon on the opposite page. What is happening? All the runners are in starting position, awaiting the same shot from the same referee, and no doubt aiming for the same finish line. These are the *comparisons* (similarities). Yet at the same time there are *contrasts* (differences). Three of the runners are men, but only one is a woman. The referee holding his gun is also a man, unlike the woman contestant. She will run in skirt and high heels, while the men clearly will not. Worst of all, the men will run straight ahead, while she must race uphill to reach their level. Is there any way the woman can win this race?

Though the cartoon shows both comparisons and contrasts, clearly it is the contrasts that send the message—men have advantages in the race of life. In the essay that follows, Doris Anderson uses words to send the same message through the same logic. Though of course there are similarities between the lives of women and men, it is the differences, the *contrasts,* that build Anderson's point that women, though a "majority" in numbers, are a "minority" in power.

When using the logic of comparison and contrast in your own essays, you, too, may find both similarities and differences. Though it is possible to explore both, the need to focus means that using one is often better—and the choice is often the more dramatic one: *contrast.*

You have experienced contrast if you have ever known culture shock. As you enter a new country, the look of the buildings and streets, the smells in the air, the sounds, the language and customs, all seem strange—because you are contrasting them to what you just left. And if you stay a long time, the same happens in reverse when you return: home seems strange because you are contrasting it to the place where you've just been. The cars may seem too big, the food too bland, the pace of life too fast. Travel is one of the great educational experiences: through contrast, one place puts another in perspective.

In a comparison and contrast essay, it is essential to choose two subjects *of the same general type:* two countries, two sports, two poems, or two solutions to unemployment. For example, a person who knows both Vancouver and Montreal might choose to compare and/or contrast these two cities: their cuisine, their night life, cost of rent, traffic, air pollution, crime, level of unemployment, level of multiculturalism, etc. By the end of the essay—whether or not we agree with the author's point of view or preference of city—we would have the impression of reading a logical argument. After all, Vancouver and Montreal are in the same category: major Canadian cities.

But suppose that instead of comparing two cities, the author had compared a city and an anthill. After all, there are similarities: both are crowded, both are highly organized, both have housing with many rooms located off corridors, etc. But no matter how much fun she might have had or what insights she might have got across, she would prove nothing—for the simple reason that people are not insects. The essay would be an *analogy*, a more imaginative but less logical kind of argument, which we will explore in the next chapter.

Once you have chosen your two subjects of the same general type, you face another choice: how to arrange them. There are two basic ways:

DIVIDE THE ESSAY INTO HALVES, devoting the first half to Vancouver and the second to Montreal. This system is natural in a short essay, because your reader remembers everything from the first half while reading the second half. It is also natural when for some reason the items are more clearly discussed as a whole than in parts.

DIVIDE THE SUBJECTS INTO SEPARATE POINTS. First compare the cuisine in both cities, then the night life, then the cost of rent, and so on through your whole list of points. This system is most natural in long essays: putting related material together helps the reader to grasp comparisons or contrasts without the strain of recalling every detail from ten pages back.

Although "halves" are often best for short papers and "separate points" are often best for long papers, be open to the needs of your particular subject, treatment and purpose. Choose the approach that will most strongly deliver your message.

For example, Catherine Pigott, in her essay "Chicken-Hips" in this chapter, uses halves. This fits the chronology of her subject, since she spends time first in Africa, then in Canada. More importantly, it fits her subject, which is cultural. We appreciate more easily the many cultural aspects of life in Gambia that lead to Pigott's new idea of body image, since they are all presented together. Later we have the same experience with aspects of Canada's culture, which drag her back to her old ideas of body image. Finally, Pigott's essay is fairly short, so the halves are not too long to master.

By contrast, "Apocalypse Soon," by Jon Evans, is a much longer essay, which might already suggest a point-by-point approach, to make things easier for the reader. Indeed, Evans places his contrasts of the paper book and its electronic competitors throughout the essay, as the many different subpoints come up, ranging from the economics of publishing, to physical comfort in reading, to the decline of the newspaper, to environmental implications of paper books, to commercial and moral implications of downloading. It is difficult to imagine readers mastering all this material if it were not presented in pieces small enough to digest.

Finally, the very act of comparing or contrasting means you need *examples*—either a large number of short ones or a small number of long ones. If these do not make up at least half the content of your essay (as they do in both Pigott and Evans), you are probably losing power. Add more.

To generate your examples and points, why not draw a line down the middle of a blank page and put the name of your subjects at the top of each column? Now brainstorm a list of points under each heading. Connect related items from left to right with lines, and, seeing relationships, decide on your thesis statement. Is cash better than credit? Is income tax fairer than sales tax? Are motorcycles more dangerous than cars? Whatever you believe is the truth, now write your essay, letting the many examples show your reader why.

Note: Many essays in other chapters use comparison and contrast to help make their point. See especially these:

Crisanta Sampang, "Trading Motherhood for Dollars," p. 176
Samantha Bennett, "It's Not Just the Weather That's Cooler in Canada," p. 264
Martin Hocking, "Capping the Great Cup Debate," p. 354
Kildare Dobbs, "The Scar," p. 361
Joy Kogawa, "Grinning and Happy," p. 373
Margaret Atwood, "Letter to America," p. 392

CATHERINE PIGOTT

Chicken-Hips*

How does a piece of writing begin? Here is an example. Seeing a documentary film about eating disorders, The Famine Within, *and interviewing its director Katherine Gilday for a magazine article, Catherine Pigott recalled her own time in Africa. It was several years earlier, while teaching English at a teachers' college, that she had shared the home and culture of a Gambian family. Then returning to Canada, she suffered culture shock: through African eyes she now saw North American ideas of eating and bodily appearance as cruel and misguided. In response to this mix of new experience and earlier memories, she wrote the essay that follows (*Globe and Mail, *March 20, 1991), a celebration of the natural life she knew in Africa. Not only is its message cross-cultural but also its form: Pigott says "I was aware of speaking as I wrote," as in the oral tradition of African narrative. Now she applies this philosophy daily in her profession. After her return she worked for a time in print journalism, then entered the world of radio: first the* CBC Radio News, *then the CBC'S celebrated* Morningside, *where she found guests for host Peter Gzowski, and researched and developed a broadcast a day. From there she moved on to* Sunday Morning, *then to CBC Radio's national program* This Morning. *At present she is a producer for the CBC in Yellowknife. Pigott thinks of her writing for radio as "not for the eye but the ear." It is direct, simple, natural. She offers similar advice to students writing essays: "Write for the ear as well as the eye."*

*Editor's title.

The women of the household clucked disapprovingly when they saw me. It was the first time I had worn African clothes since my arrival in tiny, dusty Gambia, and evidently they were not impressed. They adjusted my head-tie and pulled my *lappa*, the ankle-length fabric I had wrapped around myself, even tighter. "You're too thin," one of them pronounced. "It's no good." They nicknamed me "Chicken-hips." 1

I marvelled at this accolade, for I had never been called thin in my life. It was something I longed for. I would have been flattered if those ample-bosomed women hadn't looked so distressed. It was obvious I fell far short of their ideal of beauty. 2

I had dressed up for a very special occasion—the baptism of a son. The women heaped rice into tin basins the size of laundry tubs, shaping it into mounds with their hands. Five of us sat around one basin, thrusting our fingers into the scalding food. These women ate with such relish, such joy. They pressed the rice into balls in their fists, squeezing until the bright-red palm oil ran down their forearms and dripped off their elbows. 3

I tried desperately, but I could not eat enough to please them. It was hard for me to explain that I come from a culture in which it is almost unseemly for a woman to eat too heartily. It's considered unattractive. It was even harder to explain that to me thin is beautiful, and in my country we deny ourselves food in our pursuit of perfect slenderness. 4

That night, everyone danced to welcome the baby. Women swivelled their broad hips and used their hands to emphasize the roundness of their bodies. One needed to be round and wide to make the dance beautiful. There was no place for thinness here. It made people sad. It reminded them of things they wanted to forget, such as poverty, drought and starvation. You never knew when the rice was going to run out. 5

I began to believe that Africa's image of the perfect female body was far more realistic than the long-legged leanness I had been conditioned to admire. There, it is beautiful—not shameful—to carry weight on the hips and thighs, to have a round stomach and heavy, swinging breasts. Women do not battle the bulge, they celebrate it. A body is not something to be tamed and moulded. 6

7 The friends who had christened me Chicken-hips made it their mission to fatten me up. It wasn't long before a diet of rice and rich, oily stew twice a day began to change me. Every month, the women would take a stick and measure my backside, noting with pleasure its gradual expansion. "Oh Catherine, your buttocks are getting nice now!" they would say.

8 What was extraordinary was that I, too, believed I was becoming more beautiful. There was no sense of panic, no shame, no guilt-ridden resolves to go on the miracle grape-and-water diet. One day, I tied my *lappa* tight across my hips and went to the market to buy beer for a wedding. I carried the crate of bottles home on my head, swinging my hips slowly as I walked. I felt transformed.

9 In Gambia, people don't use words such as "cheating," "naughty," or "guilty" when they talk about eating. The language of sin is not applied to food. Fat is desirable. It holds beneficial meanings of abundance, fertility and health.

10 My perception of beauty altered as my body did. The European tourists on the beach began to look strange and skeletal rather than "slim." They had no hips. They seemed devoid of shape and substance. Women I once would have envied appeared fragile and even ugly. The ideal they represented no longer made sense.

11 After a year, I came home. I preached my new way of seeing to anyone who would listen. I wanted to cling to the liberating belief that losing weight had nothing to do with self-love.

12 Family members kindly suggested that I might look and feel better if I slimmed down a little. They encouraged me to join an exercise club. I wandered around the malls in a dislocated daze. I felt uncomfortable trying on clothes that hung so elegantly on the mannequins. I began hearing old voices inside my head: "Plaid makes you look fat.... You're too short for that style.... Vertical stripes are more slimming.... Wear black."

13 I joined the club. Just a few weeks after I had worn a *lappa* and scooped up rice with my hands, I was climbing into pink leotards and

aerobics shoes. The instructor told me that I had to set fitness goals and "weigh in" after my workouts. There were mirrors on the walls and I could see women watching themselves. I sensed that even the loveliest among them felt they were somehow flawed. As the aerobics instructor barked out commands for arm lifts and leg lifts, I pictured Gambian women pounding millet and dancing in a circle with their arms raised high. I do not mean to romanticize their rock-hard lives, but we were hardly to be envied as we ran like fools between two walls to the tiresome beat of synthesized music.

We were a roomful of women striving to reshape ourselves into some kind of pubertal ideal. I reverted to my natural state: one of yearning to be slimmer and more fit than I was. My freedom had been temporary. I was home, where fat is feared and despised. It was time to exert control over my body and my life. I dreaded the thought of people saying, "She's let herself go." 14

If I return to Africa, I am sure the women will shake their heads in bewildered dismay. Even now, I sometimes catch my reflection in a window and their voices come back to me. "Yo! Chicken-hips!" 15

EXPLORATIONS:

Joan J. Brumberg, *Fasting Girls: The History of Anorexia Nervosa*
Richard Gordon, *Anorexia and Bulimia: Anatomy of a Social Epidemic*
Jean Kilbourne, *Slim Hopes: Advertising and the Obsession with Thinness* (video, 1995, 30 min.)
Naomi Wolf, *The Beauty Myth: How Images of Beauty Are Used Against Women*
Joetta Schlabach, *Extending the Table: A World Community Cookbook*
http://home3.inet.tele.dk/mcamara/gam.html
http://www.phac-aspc.gc.ca/publicat/miic-mmac/chap_6_e.html
http://ca.dir.yahoo.com/Health/Diseases_and_Conditions/Anorexia_Nervosa
http://www.pbs.org/wgbh/nova/thin/program.html# (several short online videos about eating disorders)

STRUCTURE:

1. "Chicken-Hips" is mainly a *contrast* of ideals of beauty in Gambia and Canada. Point out at least two other things that the essay *compares.*
2. Does Pigott organize her *contrast* mainly "point by point" or by "halves"?
3. How selectively does the author choose details from her year in Africa? In paragraph 1, for example, has she told anything at all that is not vital to her theme?
4. What classic techniques of organization does Pigott exploit in her opening and closing?

STYLE:

1. The Gambian women nicknamed our author "Chicken-hips" because of her relative thinness. Create five other METAPHORS they could have used to say the same thing.
2. Where do SENSE IMAGES most strongly help us "see" the author's point?
3. Judging by Pigott's vocabulary, what sort of *audience* is she aiming at in her essay?

IDEAS FOR DISCUSSION AND WRITING:

1. Review "My Body Is My Own Business" (p. 149), then *compare* and/or *contrast* the struggles of Naheed Mustafa and of Catherine Pigott with body image. Has either writer found a solution to the problem?
2. How important to you is the appearance of your body? Are you trying for an ideal size or shape? Describe it to the class. And what sources gave you this ideal?
3. Why, in Canada, is it mostly women who go on diets, and mostly women who suffer and die from anorexia nervosa?
4. In paragraph 5 thinness reminds Gambians of "things they wanted to forget, such as poverty, drought and starvation." On the other hand, the Duchess of Windsor once remarked, "Never too rich

and never too thin." How do *you* see thinness? *Compare* or *contrast* your view to one of the above, and give reasons.

5. Have you, like Pigott, lived in another country? Tell the class one major thing the other culture taught you about life. Now that you are here, are you remembering or forgetting the lesson?
6. Many Canadians go abroad, as Pigott did, to teach in developing countries. But imagine her Gambian friends coming to your school to teach you. What might some of their "lessons" be?
7. In paragraph 10, watching the "skeletal" Europeans at the beach, Pigott states "My perception of beauty altered." Examine the illustrations in a book of art history, taking notes on how our current view of human beauty differs from those of past periods. Report these differences to the class, showing illustrations as examples.
8. **PROCESS IN WRITING:** *Remember a time when you set out to change your body through a diet, athletics, aerobics, bodybuilding or other means. On a blank piece of paper draw a vertical line. Entitle the left column "BEFORE" and the right column "AFTER," then brainstorm to develop the* contrast. *Now looking at these notes, decide on your thesis: In which version of yourself did you actually feel happier, the before or after? Now write a rapid first draft, proceeding either by "halves" or "point by point." The next day look it over: Do images help your audience "see" you? If not, add. Is your draft at least 50% examples? If not, add. Are any words wasted? If so, cut. Finally, edit for things like grammar and spelling, then produce your good version.*

Note: See also the Topics for Writing on the Online Learning Centre at www.mcgrawhill.ca/olc/conrad.

STEPHANIE NOLEN

Regine Mamba

As Africa correspondent for the Toronto Globe and Mail, *Stephanie Nolen has a special mission to inform the world about the HIV/AIDS pandemic in Africa. Having lived now for several years in Johannesburg, South Africa, and having reported from some 40 countries around the world, including two dozen in Africa, and being able to speak seven languages, Nolen has built a formidable background of knowledge and of contacts to pursue her goal. She has long garnered journalism awards, such as the 2003 National Newspaper Award for International Reporting, then the same award in 2004 for her writings about the genocide in Rwanda. Nolen has won the Amnesty International Award for Human Rights Reporting three times. It was in 2007, though, that she stunned readers around the world with her book* 28: Stories of AIDS in Africa. *(The title refers to her profiles of 28 Africans, one for each million people living with HIV/AIDS in Africa.) While the book conveys statistics that amply define the challenge, it is Nolen's anecdotal portraits of AIDS victims that opens the eyes of her readers. She took substantial risks gathering her information, for example travelling with a long-distance trucker to see first-hand the lifestyle, and all the prostitution, that have so quickly spread the pandemic. Our selection comes from this volume, which Stephen Lewis, former Canadian ambassador to the U.N., has called "the best book ever written about AIDS."*

1 In the natural order of things, these would be quiet days for Regine Mamba. She would sit in the shade of the large neem tree in her swept dirt yard in Malala in southern Zambia. She

might sift through a basket of beans in her lap, picking out the stones and twigs, and she might keep an eye on a pudgy baby just learning to totter. They should be peaceful, these days at the end of her life.

2 Instead, Regine works. She is up before the sun to start a fire for the maize porridge the children eat, and still up well after the sun has set, trying to comfort them with a story or a hymn when they sit by the embers of that fire. And although she is exhausted, she often lies awake long after the children have fallen asleep all crammed together in two round mud houses—there is much to occupy her mind. Instead of the quiet twilight of old age that should be hers, Regine has work and worries and children.

3 A huge number of children: so many that when I arrived at her house, on a walk through Malala, I thought at first that it was a primary school. There were children peeping around the doors of the houses and children sitting in the shade of the thatch-roof overhang, children tussling by the kindling pile and children beneath the tree.

4 "These children, their mothers and fathers died," Regine said by way of introduction.

5 We sat beneath that tree and Regine told me about the past few years, how it came to be that they are all her children now. As a young woman, she had given birth to seven who survived, most of whom went off to the capital, Lusaka, to work as teachers and clerks and maids. There they got married and had children of their own. In the usual way of things in a place like Malala, those children would have come home every few months, bringing their own families—they might time their visit to help with the planting, and bring a sweater or a fluffy new Chinese-made blanket as a gift. Regine would have sat on a rough wood chair and listened to the stories from the city. Her children would have stayed for a couple of days, and then they would have gone home again, taking their own children with them.

6 It didn't work out that way. In 1998, one of her daughters died in Lusaka, and she took a rickety shared taxi into the city. "I went and assessed the situation. Their father did not have much life left in him. According to our tradition, as the grandmother you are responsible. You cannot just disregard your grandchildren." So she brought those children home to Malala. Then a second daughter and son-

in-law died, and their children were sent to Regine. Then her third daughter, Lovegirl, lost her husband and came home, bringing her one surviving child and two orphans from another daughter. Before long there were more than a dozen children, in city clothes rapidly starting to fray, and at the age of seventy-four, Regine's days of sitting in the shade were over.

7 In Zambia today, basic demographics are horribly skewed. One in three children is an orphan. One in five people has HIV/AIDS. In a country of eleven million, at least 600,000 people have already died, almost all of them young adults. They have left behind a good part of a generation of children without parents. And in so many cases those children have wound up, after a few detours to aunts or neighbours, with their grandmothers.

8 Nearly two-thirds of orphans in southern and eastern Africa are in the care of grandparents. One in three heads of household in Zambia is over fifty years of age; two-thirds of them are female. In other words, grandmothers. It is the grannies, more than any other group, who carry this burden. Regine was already widowed and long past the days of sexual activity when the virus took hold in Zambia—women her age have largely escaped it. They remain healthy as their children waste away by the age of thirty. When I met her in 2003, Regine had lived to twice a Zambian woman's life expectancy, by then reduced to just thirty-seven years because of AIDS.

9 Regine and her family live at the end of a winding dirt track on a low hill. There is one big rondavel, about two metres across with smooth mud-plastered walls, where she sleeps with the little ones; one rough rondavel where they cook and keep their small store of maize; a third, small rondavel where the older children sleep; and one last round hut. Regine led me inside this one and introduced her youngest daughter, Jacqueline, who was then exactly my age, thirty-two. She was lying on the floor on a fresh grass mat, and dying. Every hour or two her toddler daughter crept up to the door and peered around it to where her mother lay. Sometimes Jacqueline gave her a little wave.

10 Regine has a constant struggle to care for this brood, ranging from one lanky fifteen-year-old boy to several grubby babies. Lovegirl, the

only other adult in the family, is fifty-one, has grandchildren of her own and could also reasonably expect to be retiring. Instead she had moved back home to help her mother.

"It's trying, it's difficult—the only way I manage is that what little I get, I give them," Regine said. "Even if it's not very nice food—as long as it helps them to live. The biggest problem is that I have to till the land, and I have no animals to help me plant a big maize field." Her back aches, and it pains her to hoe and plow, but she has no cash to hire labourers from the village and must rely on the work of the older children. Her worries have given her high blood pressure; after she slowly lowered herself to the ground, to sit and rest for a minute or two, she rubbed her swollen calves with gnarled hands. 11

The children were dust-smeared and grimy, wearing short trousers made out of feed sacks. It is a source of some shame for Regine, who knows that her grandchildren are less well off than her own children were. The newest child in the house that day was an infant a few weeks old, born to a fourteen-year-old granddaughter. Regine said, looking pained and embarrassed, that she was surprised by the pregnancy, but then, it isn't uncommon for orphaned village girls to have sex with older men for cash or food. 12

She wants the children to go to school, but in Zambia it costs 8,850 kwacha per year per child, or about $2.50—a huge burden. On the holidays and between terms, the oldest children go out to hoe the fields of better-off farmers near town to earn a few kwacha; thus far, it had been enough to keep them all enrolled for another term. Sometimes there is a bit left over for a new shirt or a pair of shoes, shoes that are worn only to school and church and otherwise kept stored away. 13

Regine's situation, the sheer quantity of children she has inherited, should be extraordinary. And yet in Malala, this story—of the young people dying and their wide-eyed children turning up back in the village—has become the norm. In 1999, the old women decided to organize, to pool their resources. They made a registry, and came up with 376 orphans, out of a total population of four thousand in Malala and two villages nearby. In other words, nearly one of every ten people in these villages is a child whose parents have died of AIDS. The grandmothers made a plan: committee members set out 14 to visit each family with orphans, to see how they were coping. That chance to talk is important, Regine said—it gives the guardians an opportunity to share their worries, and the children time to air their grievances. The local branch of the Salvation Army said it would help, with blankets, food parcels and pens and notebooks. But there wasn't enough money for the one thing every grandmother wanted: money to pay the fees and keep all the children in school.

15 As I sat with Regine that day, several of her neighbours, elderly ladies dressed, as she was, in a print wrap and blouse, scarves knotted round their heads, walked slowly up over the hill. They joined us in the shade of the neem tree, stretching out callused bare feet. The grannies said they could cope with the young orphans, but the pain of their parents' deaths makes the older ones a handful. "There's a problem with teenagers," one neighbour confided, while Regine slowly nodded in agreement. "With younger children you can manage, but teenagers say, 'You are not my mother or father.' Like any teenager, they go out and we are afraid they will be infected themselves, by the older men in the drinking places." Regine glanced toward her teenage granddaughters, one with the new baby on her back.

16 Regine was keeping the children fed and clothed—in itself something of a miracle—but she worried a great deal about their spirits. "I try by all means to make the children happy; because if I look sad they will worry and wonder what is happening, so I must tell them jokes. In the evenings when we sit around the cooking fire, I tell them stories, I sing them songs. I wish them happiness."

17 She and the other grandmothers listed off the people who were sick in Malala; they could name almost two dozen children who would lose their parents in the coming year. What, I asked, would happen to those children? Someone will take them in, the women said. We will continue to take care of them until all of us are dead.

18 But that, of course, was Regine's predominant worry. She was acutely conscious of her age. What will happen if she dies? If Lovegirl gets sick or can't manage? She told me that her great fear is that if the children are orphaned again, they will be separated, each one parcelled out to a different family; no one, she knows, could be expected to take all thirteen. "I worry. I think the children will suffer ... I am old now, but we thank God that I can still manage."

She was sitting with her back against the tree trunk, and one by one the smaller children had crept forward to listen to the visitors. First one, then a second, jostled for space in her lap; she moved her legs so that a couple more could cuddle up beside her. An impish girl of about four wanted to drape around her granny's neck, and Regine made room for her too. 19

"I never imagined it this way," she said. 20

EXPLORATIONS:

Stephanie Nolen, *28: Stories of AIDS in Africa*
Stephen Lewis, *Race Against Time* (2nd ed.)
Albert Camus, *The Plague*
http://www.theglobeandmail.com/special/aidsinafrica
http://www.cbc.ca/thehour/video.php?id=1549
http://www.stephenlewisfoundation.org
http://en.wikipedia.org/wiki/AIDS

STRUCTURE:

1. Stephanie Nolen starts her essay off with a vivid *contrast.* Point it out. And point out the THESIS STATEMENT to which it leads.
2. In developing her essay of *contrast,* why does Nolen devote more space to the way life has turned out for Regine Mamba than to the way it would have turned out if the pandemic of HIV/AIDS had not hit?
3. What widely used device of closing does Nolan place in her final sentence?
4. To what extent does Nolen also exploit patterns of *cause and effect*? Point out several examples.

STYLE:

1. Why does Nolen put a section break between paragraphs 9 and 10? Does it serve an organizational purpose?

2. Read paragraph 3 aloud. Why does the word "children" appear four times in these two lines—not to mention more times in the paragraphs before and after? Is this *repetition* accidental or deliberate?
3. How well has Stephanie Nolen given us a picture in words of Regine Mamba's family and surroundings? Can you picture yourself there? Where are her best passages of *description*?

IDEAS FOR DISCUSSION AND WRITING:

1. In her book from which our selection comes, Stephanie Nolen portrays a stunning change in the demographics of Sub-Saharan Africa: vast numbers of parents have died of AIDS because they are at a sexually active age, while most of the children have survived because they are young, and the grandparents because they are old. According to Nolen, what are the main *effects* on society of this disappearance of a generation?
2. Would you mostly *compare* or *contrast* the lifestyle of your own grandparents to that of 74-year-old Regine Mamba in Zambia? Do your grandparents still work hard taking care of their descendants, or are they now at ease, experiencing travel and leisure? To what extent is their lifestyle determined by economics, and to what extent by culture?
3. Why do some employees wish to retire earlier, and others later? What *effects* does choice of retirement age have on the individual? On society? And what do you see as the ideal age to retire? Defend your answer with reasons.
4. Nolen says the average woman in Zambia can expect to live 37 years (half the age of Regine Mamba), and tells how almost all Regine Mamba's children have died. Yet in the developed world HIV/AIDS has become more of a chronic than a fatal disease. People are now "living with AIDS" for decades. How have these improvements taken place here? And why have they mostly not taken place in Zambia?
5. In paragraph 13 Nolen tells how the $2.50 a year it costs for a child to go to school is "a huge burden" barely affordable to Regine Mamba's family. What does your own tuition cost in Canada? Look over the web sites of some nonprofit agencies that work in

Africa. Find one you like. Describe it to the class. If there is interest, mount a fundraising project to help the agency do its work in education or health.

6. **PROCESS IN WRITING:** *Which kind of home is better to grow up in, the "nuclear" family of parents and children, or the "extended" family that may also include grandparents, uncles, aunts and cousins? Close your eyes as you think of this topic. Then write an essay of* contrast. *First draw a line down the middle of a page, and write "nuclear" at the top left and "extended" at the top right. Now jot down many notes on both sides. Next develop a clear* THESIS STATEMENT *that tells your viewpoint on the question. Decide whether to develop your topic by* "halves" *or by* "separate points," *then write a quick draft, using many* EXAMPLES *on both sides. Later look it all over. Does every example contribute to your point? Do* TRANSITION *words speed your argument? Is the language* CONCISE*? Finally check the punctuation and spelling, and print your best version. Bring it to class to read aloud, and be ready to defend your point of view.*

Note: See also the Topics for Writing on the Online Learning Centre at www.mcgrawhill.ca/olc/conrad.

LAWRENCE HILL

Black + White = Black

In 2001 Maclean's *published an excerpt from Lawrence Hill's book of the same year,* Black Berry, Sweet Juice: On Being Black and White in Canada. *In the* Maclean's *version reprinted here, Hill tells much of his life story. But there is more. Not only did his African-American father become Director of the Ontario Human Rights Commission, and later the province's ombudsman, but his brother Dan Hill became a noted singer/songwriter of the 70s and 80s. Lawrence himself moved from his upper-middle-class white suburb of Toronto to Quebec City, where in 1980 in French he completed a B.A. in economics from Université Laval. In 1992 he went on to an M.A. in writing from Johns Hopkins University in Baltimore. Having lived and worked abroad, Hill is fluent in French and Spanish. In 1982 he began reporting for the* Toronto Globe and Mail, *then moved to* The Winnipeg Free Press. *Eventually he went on to write for ministries of the Ontario government. Meanwhile his own writing career took shape. In 1992 appeared Hill's first novel,* Some Great Thing, *then two nonfiction books about being black in Canada. His second novel,* Any Known Blood, *was published in 1997, and his third,* The Book of Negroes, *in 2007. It spent 13 weeks in the top-ten fiction list, won the best book award for the Commonwealth Writers' Prize (for Overall Best Book) and won the Rogers Writers' Trust Fiction Prize. Also in 2007 Hill collaborated with Joshua Key, a young American seeking refugee status in Canada, in writing* The Deserter's Tale: The Story of an Ordinary Soldier Who Walked Away from the War in Iraq. *To learn more about Lawrence Hill, read* Black Berry, Sweet Juice, *and see Hill's excellent website at http://www.lawrencehill.com.*

My childhood was punctuated with sayings about black people. My father's relatives sometimes said, "The blacker the berry, the sweeter the juice." On one level, the meaning is obvious: a raspberry or strawberry that is full and dark and pregnant with its own ripeness is sweeter than its pink, prematurely plucked counterpart. But there is also a sexual undertone to the saying, a suggestion of the myth of the overcharged, overheated, high-performing black body. Presumably, the blacker berry tastes richer, more full and is juicier. The trouble with this expression is that it has always struck me as a limp-wristed effort to help black people believe that it was OK to be black. It seemed to me sad and pathetic that we even felt a need to pass around a saying like that. 1

But I wasn't the only one who found that the words itched more than they tickled. My father bombed the pious saying to smithereens with his own sarcastic version: "The blacker the berry/The sweeter the juice/But if you get too black/It ain't no use." I absolutely loved that variation. Why? Because it turned self-affirmation on its head with a mere 10 additional words, offering a bittersweet reminder of the hopelessness of being black in a society that doesn't love—or even like—black people. There were many other sayings, such as "If you're white/You're all right/If you're brown/Stick around/If you're black/Stay back." Black people said these words and laughed. All the sayings underscored the utter futility of being black. 2

I discovered, very early, that some people had strange ideas about the children of interracial unions, and seemed inclined to believe that life for us would be miserable. When I was 12, my best friend was a white girl, Marilyn (as I shall name her), whose mother would embarrass the dickens out of me by singing my praises to her own children. "Look how well Larry does in school. Why can't you be like that, Marilyn?" Astoundingly, this same mother who thought I was doing so well once took me aside and said, "Frankly, Larry, don't you think it is terrible, mixing races like that? It ruins the children! How are they to make their way in life?" 3

As a child, my own experience of race, including my concept of my own racial identity, was shaded quite differently from that of my parents. They were both born and raised in the United States, and their 4 racial identities were clearly delineated all their lives. The America of their youth and early adulthood was replete with laws that banned interracial marriages and upheld segregation in every domain of public life. One of the most telling details came to me from my mother, who was working as a secretary for a Democratic senator when she met my father in Washington in 1953: "When I started dating your father, even the federal government cafeterias were segregated." In the United States, there was never any doubt that my father was first and foremost a black man. Or that my mother was a white woman. And there is no question that, had my siblings and I been raised in the United States, we would have been identified—in school, on the street, in community centres, among friends—as black.

5 But my parents threw their unborn children a curveball. They came to Toronto right after they married, had us and we all stayed here. They had had enough of racial divisions in their country of birth. And although they spent their lives at the forefront of the Canadian human-rights movement, they were also happy and relieved to set up in suburban, white, middleclass Toronto, where race faded (most of the time) into the background.

6 When I was growing up, I didn't spend much time thinking about who I was or where I fit in. I was too busy tying my shoelaces, brushing my teeth, learning to spell, swinging baseball bats and shooting hockey pucks. But once in a while, just as my guard was down, questions of my own identity would leap like a cougar from the woods and take a bite out of my backside.

7 I found that race became an issue as a result of environmental factors. The average white kid growing up in a white suburb didn't have to think of himself as white. Gradually, my environment started talking to me and making me aware that I could never truly be white. There's nothing like being called "nigger" to let you know that you're not white.

8 Learning that I wasn't white, however, wasn't the same as learning that I was black. Indeed, for the longest time I didn't learn what I was—only what I wasn't. In the strange and unique society that was Canada, I was allowed to grow up in a sort of racial limbo. People knew what I wasn't—white or black—but they sure couldn't say what I was. I have black American cousins, of both lighter and darker com-

plexions, who attended segregated schools and grew up in entirely black communities. They had no reason to doubt their racial identity. That identity was wrapped around them, like a snug towel, at the moment of birth.

In 1977, when I decided to take a year off university, I went to visit my cousins in Brooklyn before flying to Europe, which must have appeared to them a quintessentially white thing to do. My cousin Richard Flateau took me under his wing, and was patient until I asked if he liked to play squash. An indignant retort exploded from his lips: "Larry! That's a white folks' game!" Today, looking back, I find irony in that memory. There I was, son of a black American Second World War veteran and a white American civil-rights activist, playing squash, a sport virtually unknown to inner-city blacks in the United States. 9

These days, I think of the factors that contributed to my sense of identity, and of how malleable that sense of identity was and still is. There were days when I went straight from my exclusive, private boys' high school to family events populated by black relatives or friends who idolized the icons and heroes of my childhood—Angela Davis, with her intelligence and her kick-ass Afro; sprinters Tommie Smith and John Carlos, with their black-gloved fists raised on the Olympic podium in Mexico City; Muhammad Ali, who stood up to the white man and spoke the words that moved the world: "I ain't got no quarrel with the Viet Cong." I bounced back and forth between studying Latin, playing squash and revering black American cultural icons, but who exactly was I? 10

Lately, I have been looking at some family photos and mulling over what they mean to me. In my home office, I have some 30 framed shots of relatives. There are my three children, running, cavorting, picking apples. The eldest, Geneviève, is 11, and I wonder how she will come to see herself, racially, as she moves into adolescence. She has been a ballerina for six years, and you don't find a world much whiter than that, not even in Oakville, where we live. She knows who she is, and has had much contact with the black side of her family—but the girl has blue eyes and skin even lighter than mine, and I can see that if she is going to assert her own blackness one day, she may have to work hard at it. Nine-year-old Caroline, the middle child, is 11 the darkest of my three, and has that uncanny middle-child ability to relate to anybody of any age. I have noticed that she already bonds vigorously with black women. Andrew, who is 7, is about as interested in race as he would be in nuclear physics. Interestingly, though, he has already called out a few times, "I'm not black, I'm white," and shot a look my way to test for a reaction. He looks white, too.

12 Would you like to know how my children would once have been categorized, racially? Quadroons. They have a father who is supposedly half-black and a mother who is white, and that parentage, according to the traditional racial definition blender, would have made them quadroons. Quadroons, of course, were most definitely black, and enslaved like the rest of us in Canada and the United States. Quadroon women were favoured by slave owners for features deemed exotic and sexy but not too black, thank you very much. I shudder to imagine children who looked just like mine dancing in the infamous Quadroon Balls in New Orleans, where hot-looking young women were bought and consumed until they were no longer young or beautiful.

13 Today in Canada, black people still contend with racism at every level of society. And yet, the way my children will define themselves, and be defined by others, remains up for grabs. Racial identity is about how you see yourself, about how you construct a sense of belonging, community, awareness and allegiance.

14 To this date, I have mostly seen myself as black. My black American relatives, who lived in Brooklyn, Washington, Baltimore and North Carolina, were much closer to us and much easier to visit than my mother's family. Apart from her twin, Dottie, whom we all adore, we never really got to know my mother's relatives. My mother spoke negatively of her brothers when we were young, describing how they gave her a hard time—one even questioned her sanity—when she announced that she would be marrying a black man. As a result, as a child I came to nourish a minor grudge against some of these relatives. On my father's side, however, family was like an extension of my own body and psyche.

15 My first sense of blackness, sprang from warm places. Our house boomed with jazz and blues on weekends. Dan, Karen and I watched—entranced, intrigued—as our parents danced in the living room to

Ella Fitzgerald, Billie Holiday and Duke Ellington. Dad has an amazing voice. When he sang, he waltzed up and down the tunes with a playfulness and irreverence that we found absolutely infectious.

I remember being laid up with the flu when I was 5. My father asked: "Any musical requests, sir?" And I said, "Put on Joe Williams." *Every Day I Have the Blues* began to jump off the record player. I listened to my dad and Williams nailing the notes as Basie hammered the piano, and trumpets, trombones and saxophones erupted with glee. It's one of the happiest songs I've heard—even if it is about the blues. *Nobody loves me/nobody seems to care/between bad luck and trouble/well you know I've had my share.* Just about any words could have flown from Joe Williams's lips and soared, ecstatically, as if to prove that nothing could keep this man from living and loving. Jazz and blues were already showing me the sweet alchemy of trouble and joy that defined black musical expression, and black people themselves. 16

I don't recall early moments with family members that gave me a negative sense of race, but my siblings do. Perhaps because he was the firstborn, Dan had a rockier time with our father. Dan has no doubt that our father gave us mixed racial messages. When my brother was 11 or so, Dad gave him a stocking to wear on his head at night. The idea was to straighten out Dan's hair while he slept, or at the very least to keep it from getting too curly on the pillow. I asked Dan if Dad had told him why he had to wear it. 17

"It wasn't good to have curly hair. He'd pull a hair out of my head and put it on the table and say, 'See? This is curly. It's not good to have curly hair.' And I remember feeling extremely hurt and ashamed, and I started wearing the stocking cap. I remember feeling very concerned that my hair was curly, and I remember being frantic about straightening it." 18

Dan now attributes the incident to the strange paradoxes of human nature. "I think that kind of behaviour is common among people like our father, who have worked in the field of human rights. Very often, people go into these fields as compensation for their own feelings of inadequacy. That way, they can still bring those feelings of inadequacy and self-hatred—self-racial-hatred—into the house." 19

Dan, Karen and I learned early that you can have a white parent and still be considered black, but you can never have a black parent 20 and be considered white. It ain't allowed. You'll be reminded of your "otherness" more times than you can shake a stick at it. This is one of the reasons why I self-identify as black. Attempts at pleasant symmetry, as in "half-white, half-black," trivialize to my eye the meaning of being black. This doesn't mean I don't love my mother. I love her as profoundly as I love any person on earth. But I just don't see myself as being the same race as she is. I raised this issue with my mother recently. "Listen," she told me, "when I married your father, I knew that our children would be black. I would have been an idiot to fail to see that. Look where we came from."

21 However, the suburb of Don Mills in which they eventually settled became as suffocating for their children as D.C. had been for them. There were no blacks in my school, on my street. Because I looked so different from everyone else, I feared that I was ugly. I worried about having frizzy hair, big ears, a big nose and plump lips. When I looked in the mirror, I felt disgust. None of the people I admired looked the least bit like me. Listening to stories of my father's working world instilled in us a measure of black pride. We also derived a sense of connection from family moments around the television, which is odd because we weren't that interested in TV. But the late 1960s and the early 1970s featured big stand-up comedy numbers by Bill Cosby and Flip Wilson. When I watched these shows, I felt alive. I felt that there were people in the world who were speaking to me.

22 I had to find other ways to connect with them. So I ate up every bit of black writing that I could find. Langston Hughes, Ralph Ellison, Richard Wright—whom I approached gingerly because my mother confessed that *Native Son* had upset her so much, it had made her vomit. James Baldwin. Eldridge Cleaver—now that cat fascinated me, especially when, in *Soul on Ice,* he speculated as to why black men and white women end up together. I read Alex Haley's *Autobiography of Malcolm X,* and had to struggle through the section of Malcolm X's life when he ardently believed that white people were the devil incarnate. I knew this to be false. My mother was white, and she was no devil.

23 Without knowing exactly what I was doing, I was forming my own sense of blackness and my own connection to the black diaspora. Soon, this exploration blossomed into creative writing. Every time I wrote, my mind wandered into the lives of black characters. Slowly, I

was developing a sense of myself. These days, when I'm invited into schools with black students, I feel a tinge of nostalgia for a past not lived. I can't help wondering what it would have been like to have black people around me when I was young. I can't help wondering what it would have been like to go out with black girls, or to drift into a friend's home and find myself surrounded by black people. What a different life that would have been.

EXPLORATIONS:

Lawrence Hill,
Black Berry, Sweet Juice: On Being Black and White in Canada
Any Known Blood (novel)
George Elliott Clarke, ed., *Eyeing the North Star: Directions in African-Canadian Literature* (anthology)
Frances Henry, *The Caribbean Diaspora in Toronto: Learning to Live with Racism*
Henry Gates and Nellie McKay, eds., *The Norton Anthology of African American Literature*
Arnold Rampersad, ed., *The Oxford Anthology of African-American Poetry*
Richard Wright, *Native Son* (novel)
Toni Morrison, *Beloved* (novel)
http://www.lawrencehill.com
http://www.wier.ca/lhill.html
http://www.quillandquire.com/authors/profile.cfm?article_id=7654
http://www.cbc.ca/arts/books/book_of_negroes.html

STRUCTURE:

1. How do you interpret the equation in Hill's title, "Black + White = Black"? Is it a good start to the essay? What does it do? Compare another mathematical title in this book, Doris Anderson's "The 51-Per-Cent Minority."

2. Like many essayists, Hill opens with a quotation. Point out all the ways it moves us into his topic. Do you ever use this technique? If you don't have the right quotation to start your essay, where do you look for it?
3. Is Hill's argument all *contrast* between his black roots and white roots, or is there also *comparison*? If so, where?
4. In this argument of *contrast*, Hill organizes not by "halves" but "point by point." As a class, split into ten groups, each choosing a passage listed below. Examine your section in your small group, then report to the class what aspect of the total subject it analyzes through *contrast*: paragraphs 1–2, 3, 4–8, 9, 10, 11–12, 14–19, 20, 21–22, and 23.

STYLE:

1. Why do you think Hill's paragraphs are longer than those of many other writers in this book? Are they too long? Are your own ever too short? What is a good typical length, and why?
2. In paragraph 8 Hill describes his American cousins growing up in black communities where "that identity was wrapped around them, like a snug towel, at the moment of birth." Where else does Hill use strong METAPHORS?

IDEAS FOR DISCUSSION AND WRITING:

1. Do you, too, have roots in two or more races or cultures? Do you, like Hill, identify more with one than with the others(s)? Try to explain why, giving examples.
2. With a father who was Director of the Ontario Human Rights Commission and later the province's ombudsman, Lawrence Hill had a privileged upper-middle-class childhood. Do working-class people have a different experience of racial issues? Give examples.
3. Canada—especially in its big cities—is said to be the most cosmopolitan, multicultural country in the world. Do you agree? Is your own neighbourhood multicultural? If so, name all the places where its different population groups have their roots.

4. *Contrast* the American and Canadian examples of racism that Hill gives. Was Canada the more open society when Hill's parents were young? Is it now? Give examples.
5. Do interracial couples, like Hill's parents, still face extra challenges in society, or by now has fairness been achieved?
6. *Compare* or *contrast* Lawrence Hill's portrayal of racism in society with those of George Gabori (p. 26), Carol Geddes (p. 45), Goran Simic (p. 84), Naheed Mustafa (p. 149) or Joy Kogawa (p. 373).
7. **PROCESS IN WRITING:** *If, like most Canadians, you have roots in more than one geographical area, language, culture or race, draw a line down the middle of a page. At the top left and right, name the two most important components of your own roots (such as "Iran" and "Germany," or "Mandarin" and "English"). Make sure that both items, as in these pairs, are from the same category: two countries, two languages, etc. Below them, on each side, make many notes on their characteristics. Now look over what you have produced: What* contrasts *do you see? Draw lines across the page to link the contrasting items. Next put your overall point in a* THESIS STATEMENT, *then write a discovery draft using your* examples. *(Choose to organize your contrast either by "*halves*" or "*point by point.*") When this version has cooled off, look it over. Is it filled with* examples, *like Hill's essay? If not, add. Does it use transition signals like "but," "on the other hand," "however" and "by contrast" to heighten your* contrast*? If not, add. Finally, edit for correctness and conciseness before printing out your best version. Share it with the class.*

Note: See also the Topics for Writing on the Online Learning Centre at www.mcgrawhill.ca/olc/conrad.

CP (Chuck Stoody)

"Yet as fast as the woodsmen cut, as much as they cut, it was never fast enough. The quantity always fell short of the expectations of the weendigoes, their masters."

—Basil Johnston, "Modern Cannibals of the Wilds"

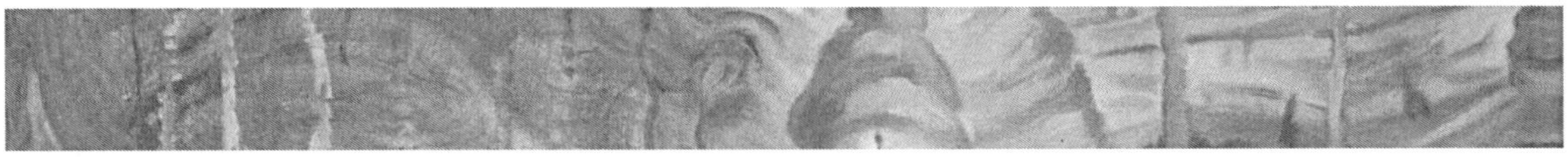

6 Analogy and Related Devices

IN A WAY, IT'S LIKE….

One student wrote this childhood memory:

> I heard and felt a rumbling from the ground, looked up and saw a huge red metallic monster with a tail on the end approach us. "Run, run," I said, "before it eats us." My mother reassured me that no fear was necessary. The monster slowly rolled up beside us, opened its mouth, and we went in.

As adults, we know monsters have not roamed Canada for millions of years, and we know they were not red but probably green! We also know that monsters and streetcars have little in common. Yet who would say this *analogy* does not clearly express the child's first encounter with a streetcar? It may even help us, as adults, to view with new eyes something we had taken for granted. *(A caution, though: as explained below, what an analogy will* not *do for us is prove anything at all logically. An essay based on this device is more in the realm of creative writing than of factual argumentation.)*

In this chapter Basil Johnston describes another monster—the weendigo of Native American legend that eats humans who wander outside at night. In its new version the weendigo consumes not humans but pine, spruce, cedar and the wildlife that lives there. Though we know the forest industry is not staffed by monsters but by decent men and women trying to make a living, we cannot help but see, through Johnston's eyes, the "monstrous" destruction of clearcutting.

In the last chapter we discussed how two items from the same category—say, two cities—can be explained logically through comparison and contrast. By seeing how Vancouver and Montreal are alike or unlike, we gain a clearer understanding of both. An *analogy*, though, brings together two apparently *unlike* items from *different* categories (such as a monster and a modern industry). Instead of using the two to explain each other, it more often uses one as a device to explain the other. It is not the monsters we investigate, but the monstrous aspects of the streetcar or the forest industry.

In the last chapter we speculated whether, instead of comparing two cities, we could compare a city and an anthill. To those of us who live in chambers along the corridors of apartment buildings or who each day crowd into holes in the ground to take the subway, the similarities may be all too clear. We do see right away that such an argument is hardly logical, for the very good reason that people are not insects. And we would certainly not want to base a factual paper, such as a research essay, on this device. Yet in a very informal or humorous paper, an analogy may be a fresh, thought-provoking way to express aspects of city life.

Topics that are unfamiliar or abstract almost cry out for analogies to explain them. Thus, a generation ago the term "computer virus" swept the world. These electronic "diseases" "infect" computer programs, "spreading" an "epidemic" of "contagion." The "outbreaks" of various "strains" feature names such as AIDS.II, Amoeba A, Anthrax, BW.Hepatitis, Cancer.2528, Cholera.A, Ebola 3000, Encephalitis, Leprosy, Measles.212 and Plague.2647.

These plagues "contaminate" programs, erase memory and even attack hardware. Of course "antiviral" software to "vaccinate" the patient was soon developed, with brand names like "Flu Shot +," "Data Physician," "Antidote," "AntiVirus," "Virus RX," "ViruSafe" and "Vaccine 1.0." In addition, "safe computing practices" have been recommended to avoid infection by viruses such as AIDS.II.

Have we already seen the first big analogy of the new millennium? In a 2005 *Globe and Mail* article, business reporter Andrew Willis wrote, "Spurned suitors, unrequited passion. A final, joyful union. The latest round of takeovers is the stuff of romance novels.

"Just look at the flirting going on before Gillette finally fell into Procter & Gamble's waiting arms, and before SBC Communications got a ring on the finger of AT&T.... for years, chief executives at these companies met in secret spots or whispered into their phones late into the night. We've also learned they contemplated walking down the aisle with any number of other partners."

Apparently an optimist, Willis says nothing of divorce. But he has already exploited the power of the analogy. It comes not so much from its originality as its breadth, especially the heavy borrowing of vocabulary from the one item (romance) to the other (corporations). The further you develop such links between your two items, the stronger the analogy.

Yet even a brief statement, such as "A corporate merger is like a wedding," can have value. As a *simile* it is not much of an argument in itself, but is a concrete statement that can be used in support of another argument. While a *simile* states that one thing is *like* another, a *metaphor* states that one thing *is* another ("A corporate merger is a wedding"). Both devices occur often in poetry and fiction, and also occur in essays. Review Nathalie Petrowski's selection "The Seven-Minute Life of Marc Lépine," in Chapter 4. It offers a wealth of these devices, especially from paragraph 9 through the end. These carry a strong load of emotion, as the author struggles to make sense of a recent event, the worst mass murder in Canadian history. The images may not prove anything logically, but they convey a strong sense of the author's consternation, and they vividly express the violence not only of Lépine's story, but all too likely the stories of many others feeling the same pressures from our society.

In closing, again a caution*: Do not confuse the pleasures of the analogy with the logic of argumentative devices such as comparison and contrast, or cause and effect. Of course a brief figure of speech or a small analogy can help explain a point in other kinds of arguments; but the full analogy, a device on which a whole paper is based, is best saved for personal essays, humorous pieces, and satires, where its freewheeling poetic nature is most appropriate.*

Note: For more examples of analogy and related devices, see these essays in other chapters:

Analogy:
Nathalie Petrowski, "The Seven-Minute Life of Marc Lépine," p. 169
Kildare Dobbs, "The Scar," p. 361
Lt.-Gen. Roméo Dallaire, "*Cri de coeur,*" p. 414

Simile, metaphor and other figures of speech:
Emily Carr, "D'Sonoqua," p. 117
Nathalie Petrowski, "The Seven-Minute Life of Marc Lépine," p. 169
Dr. Mark Bernstein, "Yes, It Is Brain Surgery," p. 311
Joy Kogawa, "Grinning and Happy," p. 373

BASIL JOHNSTON

Modern Cannibals of the Wilds

Basil Johnston is well known as a writer, storyteller and teacher of Ojibway (Anishinabe) language, mythology and history for 25 years in the Department of Ethnology of Toronto's Royal Ontario Museum. Born in 1929 on the Parry Island Reserve in Ontario, he attended Cape Croker public school, then at the Spanish Residential School lived the cultural dislocations of the residential school system which he later described in his book Indian School Days *(1988). He completed his education at Loyola College in Montreal and the Ontario College of Education. Fluent in his original language and culture, Johnston has long been a strong voice of First Nations People in Canada. Though he lectures widely on Ojibwa history, culture and language, it is his books that reach the largest audience:* Ojibway Heritage *(1976),* How the Birds Got Their Colours *(1978),* Moose Meat and Wild Rice *(1978),* Tales the Elders Told *(1981),* Ojibway Ceremonies *(1982),* By Canoe and Moccasin *(1986),* Tales of the Anishinaubaek *(1993),* The Manitous: The Spiritual World of the Ojibway *(1995),* The Bear-Walker and Other Stories *(1995),* The Star Man and Other Tales *(1997),* Mermaids and Medicine Women *(1998),* Crazy Dave *(1999) and* Honour Mother Earth *(2003). Our selection is from the August 1, 1991 Toronto* Globe and Mail. *In it Johnston goes beyond his usual role of imparting Ojibway culture; his portrait of the new "weendigo" cuts right to the heart of modern Canadian values.*

1 Woods and forest once mantled most of this land, this continent. It was the home of the Anishinabek (Ojibway, Ottawa, Potowatomi, Algonquin), their kin and their neighbours. It

was also the home of the moose, the deer, the caribou, the bear, their kindred and their neighbours. It was as well the home of the thrushes, the sparrows, the hawks, the tanagers, the ravens, the owls, their cousins and their neighbours. Mosquitoes, butterflies, caterpillars, ants, moths, their kin and their neighbours had a place therein.

Not only was it home, but a wellspring from which all drew their sustenance, medicine and knowledge. 2

Also dwelling in the woods and forests were weendigoes, giant cannibals who fed upon human flesh to allay their perpetual hunger. They stalked villages and camps, waiting for, and only for, the improvident, the slothful, the gluttonous, the promiscuous, the injudicious, the insatiable, the selfish, the avaricious and the wasteful, to be foolish enough to venture alone beyond the environs of their homes in winter. 3

But no matter how many victims a single weendigo devoured raw, he could never satisfy his hunger. The more he ate, the larger he grew, and the larger he grew, the greater his hunger. The weendigo's hunger always remained in proportion to his size. 4

Even though a weendigo is a mythical figure, he represents real human cupidity. What the old-time storyteller meant to project in the image of the weendigo was a universal and unchanging human disposition. But more learned people declared that no such monster ever existed, that he was a product of superstitious minds and imaginations. 5

As a result, the weendigo was driven from his place in Anishinabe traditions and culture, ostracized through disbelief and skepticism. It was assumed, and indeed it appeared as if, the weendigo and his brothers and sisters had passed into the Great Beyond, like many North American Indian beliefs and practices and traditions. 6

Actually, the weendigoes did not die out; they have only been assimilated and reincarnated as corporations, conglomerates and multinationals. They have taken on new names, acquired polished manners and renounced their craving for human flesh for more refined viands. But their cupidity is no less insatiable than their ancestors'. 7

One breed subsists entirely on forests. When this breed beheld forests, its collective cupidity was stirred as it looked upon an endless, boundless sea of green—as in greenbacks. They saw beyond, 8 even into the future. Money. Cash. Deposits. Bank accounts. Interest. Reserves. Investments, securities, bonds, shares, dividends, capital gains, assets, funds, deals, revenue, income, prosperity, opulence, profits, riches, wealth, comfort.

9 They recruited woodsmen with axes, crosscut saws and Swede saws, sputters, shovels, cant hooks, grapples, chains, ropes, files and pikes, and sent them into the woods to fell, hew, saw, cut, chop, slash and level. The forests resounded with the clash of axes and the whine of saws as blades bit into the flesh of spruce, pine, cedar, tamarack and poplar to fill the demands of the weendigoes in Toronto, Montreal, Vancouver, New York, Chicago, Boston, wherever they now dwelt. Cries of "Timber!" echoed across the treetops, followed by the rip and tear of splintering trees, and thundering crashes.

10 And as fast as woodsmen felled the trees, teamsters delivered sleighload after sleighload to railway sidings and to the rivers. Train after train, shipload after shipload of logs were delivered to the mills.

11 Yet as fast as the woodsmen cut, as much as they cut, it was never fast enough. The quantity always fell short of the expectations of the weendigoes, their masters.

12 "Is that all? Should there not be more? We demand a bigger return for our risks and our investments. Only more will satisfy us. Any amount will do, so long as it's more, and the more the better."

13 The demands were met for more speed and more pulp, more logs and more timber. Axes, saws, woodsmen, horses and teamsters were replaced, and their blows and calls no longer rang in the forest. In their place, chainsaws whined, Caterpillar tractors with huge blades bulled and battered their way through the forest, uprooting trees to clear the way for automatic shearers that topped, limbed and sheared the trunks. These mechanical weendigoes gutted and desolated the forests, leaving death, destruction and ugliness where once there was life, abundance and beauty.

14 Trucks and transports operated day and night delivering cargo with a speed and quantity that the horses and sleighs could never have matched.

15 Yet the weendigoes wanted still more, and it didn't matter if their policies and practices of clear-cutting their harvest of timber and

pulp resulted in violations of North American Indian rights or in the further impairment of their lives.

16 Nor does it matter to them that their modus operandi permanently defiles hillside and mountainside by erosion. They are indifferent to the carnage inflicted upon bears, wolves, rabbits, thrushes, sparrows, warblers. Who cares if they are displaced? What possible harm has been done? Nor does it seem as if these modern weendigoes have any regard for the rights of future generations to the yield of Mother Earth.

17 The new, reincarnated weendigoes are little different from their forebears. They are more omnivorous than their ancestors, however, and the modern breed wears elegant clothes and comports itself with an air of cultured and dignified respectability.

18 Profit, wealth, comfort, power are the ends of business. Anything that detracts from or diminishes the anticipated return, be it taking pains not to violate the rights of others, or taking measures to ensure that the land remains fertile and productive for future generations, must, it seems, be circumvented.

19 And what has been the result of this self-serving, self-glutting disposition? In 10 short decades, these modern weendigoes have accomplished what at one time seemed impossible; they have laid waste immense tracts of forest that were seen as beyond limit as well as self-propagating, and ample enough to serve this generation and many more to come.

20 Now, as the forests are in decline, the weendigoes are looking at a future that offers scarcity. Many others are assessing the weendigoes' accomplishments not in terms of dollars but in terms of damage—the damage they have inflicted on the environment and the climate and on botanical and zoological life.

EXPLORATIONS:

Basil Johnston,
How the Birds Got Their Colours
Indian School Days

Agnes Grant, ed., *Our Bit of Truth: An Anthology of Canadian Native Literature*

Linda Jaine and Drew Hayden, eds., *Voices: Being Native in Canada*
Elizabeth May, *At the Cutting Edge: The Crisis in Canada's Forests*
M. T. Kelly, *A Dream Like Mine* (novel)
Margaret Atwood, *Strange Things: The Malevolent North in Canadian Literature*
http://www.nativewiki.org/Basil_Johnston
http://www.turtle-island.com/rolemodels.html
http://www.whetung.com/basil.html
http://www.ipl.org/div/natam/bin/browse.pl/A41
http://archives.cbc.ca/IDD-1-75-679/science_technology/clearcutting

STRUCTURE:

1. "Modern Cannibals of the Wilds" is a FABLE. (See this book's glossary.) How do fables work? How does this one?
2. Why does Johnston open by listing so many animals, birds and insects whose "home" was once most of this continent?
3. Point out the paragraph of TRANSITION where we move from the old weendigo to the new one. Point out the THESIS STATEMENT.
4. Analyze how paragraphs 15 and 16 employ *cause and effect.*
5. Point out all the ways Johnston portrays the forestry industry as a monster and cannibal. How fully has he developed the *analogy*? Now invent an *analogy* for those who support the forestry industry, and tell it to the class.

STYLE:

1. In what kind of writing do we more often see words like "mantled," "kindred," "improvident" and "slothful"? Describe Johnston's TONE. Why do you think he chose it for this subject?
2. Read paragraph 9 aloud to the class, with feeling, so all can experience its ONOMATOPOETIC language. Which words sound like what they mean? What is the overall effect?

3. How CONCISE is Johnston's analogy? What techniques make it so?
4. Why is the METAPHOR "flesh" of paragraph 9 appropriate to Johnston's portrayal of the weendigoes?

IDEAS FOR DISCUSSION AND WRITING:

1. If our human forestry industry is a "cannibal," then in what sense is it "eating" us as well as trees?
2. "The more he ate, the larger he grew, and the larger he grew, the greater his hunger" (para. 4). What if one day the monster's "food" runs out? When our forestry industry can no longer "eat" and "grow," will it "starve"? What can we do now to either reduce its appetite or extend its food supply?
3. Defend or attack the clearcutting of forests that continues in British Columbia and most other provinces. Defend or attack the actions of environmentalists in convincing many European companies not to buy Canadian paper made through clearcutting.
4. Conservationists often say that in Canada we do not "harvest" but "mine" the forests. Extend these images into *analogies*, by giving parallels. *Contrast* the philosophies behind both.
5. What particularly qualifies Basil Johnston, a First Nations person, to write on this subject?
6. **PROCESS IN WRITING:** *In paragraph 16 Johnston refers to our "Mother Earth." Expand this widespread* metaphor *into an essay of* analogy. *First write the term "Mother Earth" in the centre of a page, then fill the surrounding space with other words it brings to mind. Connect related items with lines. Determine your main point. Now draw upon this cluster outline as you do a rapid first draft. When it has "cooled off," look it over. Do* examples *always help the reader "see" your point? If not, add. Does your* TONE *fit this important subject? If not, adjust. Is everything on topic? If not, cut. Finally, revise for spelling and punctuation as you produce your best version.*

Note: See also the Topics for Writing on the Online Learning Centre at www.mcgrawhill.ca/olc/conrad.

JupiterImages

"The scurry of feet grew louder as more sailors began to pour out through the hatches onto the deck."

—Hugh MacLennan, "A Sound Beyond Hearing"

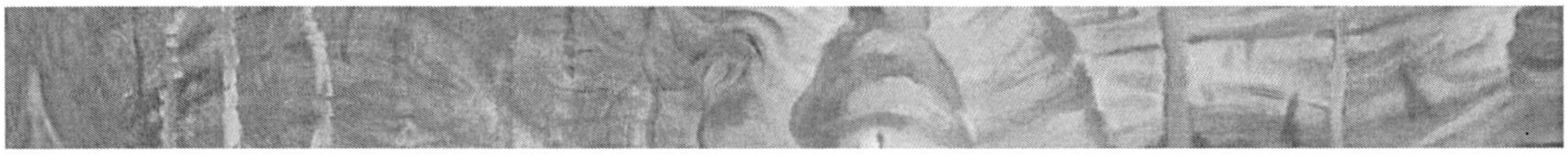

7 CLASSIFICATION

THERE ARE THREE KINDS OF THEM....

Our world is so complex that without classification we are lost. To make a phone call we use an alphabetized phone book. To find oranges in the supermarket we head for the fruit section. To buy a used canoe we go to the *classified* section of the newspaper. Putting things into categories is one of our most common methods of thought. Who would search the whole dictionary when the word in question begins with "T"? What student, *classified* into grade five, would look for the grade six *class*room?

For the essayist, classifying can be a powerful way of organizing. Tackling a large or detailed subject, for example, is a real challenge. One way to start making sense of it is to see it as several parts, so that, instead of thinking about everything at once, the writer can focus on one section, then focus on the next section, and so on. Of course this is also true of a comparison and contrast essay, whether developed by halves or point by point. Do remember, though, that a comparison and contrast involves only two items of the same general type, while a classification involves at least three, with a maximum of perhaps 5 or 6.

Read Ian and Will Ferguson's essay in this chapter, "Theatre." See how it presents six categories to explain its subject of theatre in Canada. This is no doubt close to the upper limit of sections we might want in a short essay, but the argument seems of reasonable size because the sections are compressed and short. Notice, by the way, how the Fergusons actually number their points, to be super-clear in their organization.

Read also "Pulling Together" by former British Columbia Governor General David Lam. In examining the ways for the province's citizens to "pull together," Lam presents three categories: "acceptance," "belonging" and "contribution" (abbreviated as A, B and C). This minimum number of categories for a classification works well here, because the sections are somewhat longer than those of the Fergusons. Thus Lam is able to give many examples to support his points.

A classification, which has more parts than a comparison and contrast, requires a somewhat larger system of logic. Observe the following guidelines:

CLASSIFY ALL ITEMS BY THE SAME PRINCIPLE. An essay on kinds of cars might be organized by any one of several different principles: size, quality, safety level, cost, fuel economy, performance, body type, engine type, etc. The important thing, though, is to work with only one of these major criteria at a time, not diluting your focus across categories. For example a focus on *size* might include the large (or "full-size") car, the midsize car, the compact car and the small car. But it certainly would not include the diesel, which concerns a fuel type and engine technology found in cars of all sizes. Neither would it include the sports car, which comes in many sizes, or the pickup truck, which is not a car at all.

DO NOT LEAVE OUT AN OBVIOUS CATEGORY. Suppose you had reasons to classify cars by the *number of cylinders* in the engine. You would probably want to have as your categories the 4, the 6 and the 8. It is true that other configurations exist: there have been cars with 1 cylinder, and others with 2, or 3, or 5, or even 12 or 16. How many of those are on the road, though? If they are rarities, they would only clutter up an argument about the engine types that do power almost all cars driven today. Just as illogical would be an argument that left out the 8-cylinder engine. It may be falling out of favour because of high fuel prices and environmental concerns, but there are millions of them still on the road. Ignoring these would leave the argument incomplete.

DO NOT LET CATEGORIES OVERLAP. A classification of cars by *quality level* might reasonably feature the categories of high quality, medium quality and low quality. After all, do these choices not cover the whole spectrum of quality? But you would not want to add the hatchback, the station wagon or the crossover utility vehicle—because each of these represents a kind of body type, rather than any aspect of quality.

Classifying is not easy; it's a real exercise in logic. Keep applying the guidelines.

Also observe the main principle of any essay: *Know your purpose.* Exactly *why* are you comparing, say, the three kinds of parents or the four kinds of teachers or the five kinds of friends? Is it because you have a vision of what a good parent or teacher or friend is, and want to share it with others? Is it because bad experiences have led you to warn against certain kinds of parents or teachers or friends? Like any argument, an essay of classification makes a point; otherwise it is "pointless." Try freewriting or brainstorming for five or ten minutes to get thoughts flowing and ideas out in the open. Then look these over. Let them help you decide not only what the content of your classification will be, but also its overall point, its thesis statement. Since thinking is not easy, you need all the help you can get—and some of the best help comes from your own pen or computer: while it is writing, you are thinking.

THE HONOURABLE DAVID LAM

Pulling Together

The Honourable David See-Chai Lam, born in Hong Kong in 1923, has had a long career in business and public life, culminating in his term from 1988 to 1995 as Lieutenant-Governor of British Columbia. With a B.A. from Lingnam University and an M.B.A. from Temple University, he became in 1960 the CEO of Ka Wah Bank Ltd. of Hong Kong. Then, immigrating to the "golden mountain" which he celebrates in his essay, he became in 1968 the president of Canadian International Properties Limited. When Dr. Lam was invited ten years later to be the Lieutenant-Governor of his new home, British Columbia, he underwent the uncertainties described in his essay below, at first declining because he was "living in a province with a history of discrimination against Chinese," because he was "getting old," and because English was not his first language. Reconsidering, though, he did accept the post, and, with the aid of his much-loved wife Dorothy Lam, found great fulfillment in the job through "building bridges" among the many population groups of British Columbia. Our selection, published in Maclean's *of January 30, 1995, reflects this experience in acceptance, belonging and contribution. Now retired from government, Dr. Lam lives in Vancouver, where he directs a charitable foundation that gives grants to universities, hospitals and other public institutions.*

1 Once, Asians came to North America for jobs, albeit somewhat menial ones. Particularly in the West, there was ready work on the railway, in laundries and in chop suey houses.

With the gold rush and its opportunity to strike it rich, this continent became known in China as the "golden mountain."

Today, Canada continues to attract Asians, although the lure is no longer gold. Instead, they come for things that a lot of us in Canada take for granted: stability, a peaceful life, law and order, education, generally friendly and understanding people. 2

As one of those who chose to settle in Canada over 28 years ago, I would like to offer a brief ABC for others hoping to make a new home here. 3

The A is for acceptance. And that goes two ways. Prospective immigrants must be accepted by the federal immigration department. But even if the government accepts you, your peace of mind and happiness will depend very much upon how you are accepted in your community. 4

Of course, newcomers could reject the broader Canadian community and choose to live only among their own people. But that choice is self-defeating: one becomes inward-looking, cut away from the mainstream of society. There is really no way to enjoy what Canada has to offer if one lives in either a physical or psychological ghetto. So, it is a duty of sorts to strive for acceptance. 5

There are always difficulties arising from different value systems, a different cultural style. Speaking loudly, getting things done in the quickest manner, bragging about accomplishments and wealth—all might be commonplace in Hong Kong and totally acceptable in many other parts of the world. But they are not so in Canada. 6

Here, we try to minimize friction between people. We downplay displays of wealth. We respect good manners. Such simple courtesies as saying good morning and thank you are daily expressions of respect for others. 7

The B represents belonging. This is a very important feeling. People who do not belong always feel impermanent. As with people who reside in a hotel, no matter how beautiful it may be, they are constantly reminded that they are transients. 8

People who divide their time between Canada and another country become "astronauts"—flying too high and fast to put down real roots or to feel a sense of belonging. They are not found just among Chinese immigrants. Some Canadians who spend half of their time 9 in California or in Florida might also be considered astronauts. When they are asked to become involved in community services, many say: “Ah, but in a couple of months I will return to Canada ...,” or, “... I’ll be leaving for the States.”

10 If you want to feel that you belong, ask yourself: how much do I care about what happens in my community and related issues such as crime, a clean neighborhood, volunteering to pitch in.

11 The C stands for contribution. And this is the easiest thing of all to achieve. In this new country, in this new community, in this new neighborhood in which we have started to take root, commitment makes a strong statement that you belong. You can give without loving; but you cannot love without giving.

12 When I was initially approached to consider being nominated as lieutenant-governor of British Columbia, I turned it down. My negative side told me: “You are living in a province with a history of discrimination against Chinese. You are getting old. You speak English as a second language. Don’t do it.”

13 Fortunately, however, my positive side saw an opportunity to build bridges among people of different cultures, different ethnic backgrounds and different races. After 6½ years, I have experienced tremendous love and respect from the people of Canada as a whole, and particularly from those in British Columbia. I feel proud to be a Canadian, because I truly appreciate the quality of its people.

14 I was brought up in Hong Kong to be so conscious of racial differences that we had derogatory nicknames for everyone. That is no way to go through life. It is like carrying a little bit of poison in the mind. And the world is changing. The day is quickly coming when people with only one culture will find it difficult to compete, let alone to prosper.

15 Don’t talk to me about “tolerance.” Tolerating someone is like holding your breath: you are telling the world that you can hold your breath longer than anyone else. I say, let us celebrate differences—not tolerate them.

16 I believe in multiculturalism because it adds to our strength. The Asia-Pacific region is the fastest-growing region in the world. And it is

just across the ocean from British Columbia. Let us turn the people of all the races living in Canada into partners. Let us build a "golden mountain" for all of us.

EXPLORATIONS:

Reginald H. Roy, *David Lam: A Biography*
Bennett Lee and Jim Wong-Chu, eds., *Many-Mouthed Birds: Contemporary Writings by Chinese-Canadians*
Wayson Choy, *Paper Shadows: A Chinatown Childhood* (memoir)
Sky Lee, *Disappearing Moon Cafe* (novel)
Amy Tan, *The Joy Luck Club* (novel; also made into a feature film and DVD)
Peter S. Li, *The Chinese in Canada* (2nd ed.)
http://www.fccbc.ca/NewsletterArticles/DavidLam.htm
http://archives.cbc.ca/IDD-1-69-1433/life_society/chinese_immigration
http://en.wikipedia.org/wiki/Chinese_Canadian
http://www.asian.ca/community
http://www.ccnc.ca/toronto/history/timeline.html

STRUCTURE:

1. Why does David Lam both open and close his essay with the same expression, "golden mountain"? What effect does this repetition achieve?
2. How do you rate Lam's "brief ABC" as a *classification*? Are its three categories enough? Is any obvious category left out? Are all *classified* by the same principle? Do you think the organizational device of the "ABC" is a good fit for Lam's categories?
3. How does the device of *comparison and contrast* heighten the power of paragraph 9?
4. Why does Lam wait almost till the end to describe his own decision to become Lieutenant-Governor of British Columbia?

STYLE:

1. How easy or hard is the vocabulary of "Pulling Together"? How short or long are its sentences? Its paragraphs? Who do you see as its intended AUDIENCE?

IDEAS FOR DISCUSSION AND WRITING:

1. While stating "I believe in multiculturalism because it adds to our strength" (par. 16), Lam also advises New Canadians not to live "in either a physical or psychological ghetto" (par. 5). What is your view? Do you prefer the traditional American "melting pot" which is supposed to assimilate immigrants, or the Canadian "mosaic," in which New Canadians are encouraged, even funded, to retain their first language and culture? Which path is better for the individual? For the nation?
2. David Lam's adopted home of British Columbia is part of the Asia Pacific rim, and is itself one of the most multicultural spots on earth. If you live there, describe how the cosmopolitan mix of its population has influenced your own life. Or if you live in Toronto, Montreal or another cosmopolitan place, apply this topic to your own city.
3. Lam says "The day is quickly coming when people with only one culture will find it difficult to compete, let alone to prosper" (par. 14). Do you think this is true for your own intended profession? Why or why not? If so, what have you done to prepare? If your family has immigrated, what are you doing to keep your first language and culture? If your family has earlier roots in Canada, what other languages, if any, have you learned to speak? And what experiences have you had to make yourself feel at home with other cultures?
4. **PROCESS IN WRITING:** *Whether you have immigrated, yourself, or only know others who have, think about the main challenges that face immigrants to Canada. Fill a page with brainstorming on this topic, then look it over. Circle or highlight the main points, choose your THESIS STATEMENT, then rearrange these thoughts into a short conventional outline that* classifies *the challenges. Are there at least three categories in your* classification *? Are any main ones missing? Are all* classified *by the same principle? Do*

any seem to overlap? Now write a rapid version of your essay of classification. *The next day look it over. Does it have enough* examples? *If not, add. Do* TRANSITIONS *move the argument from one point to the next? If not, add. Finally, check the punctuation and spelling before printing out your best version.*

Note: See also the Topics for Writing on the Online Learning Centre at www.mcgrawhill.ca/olc/conrad.

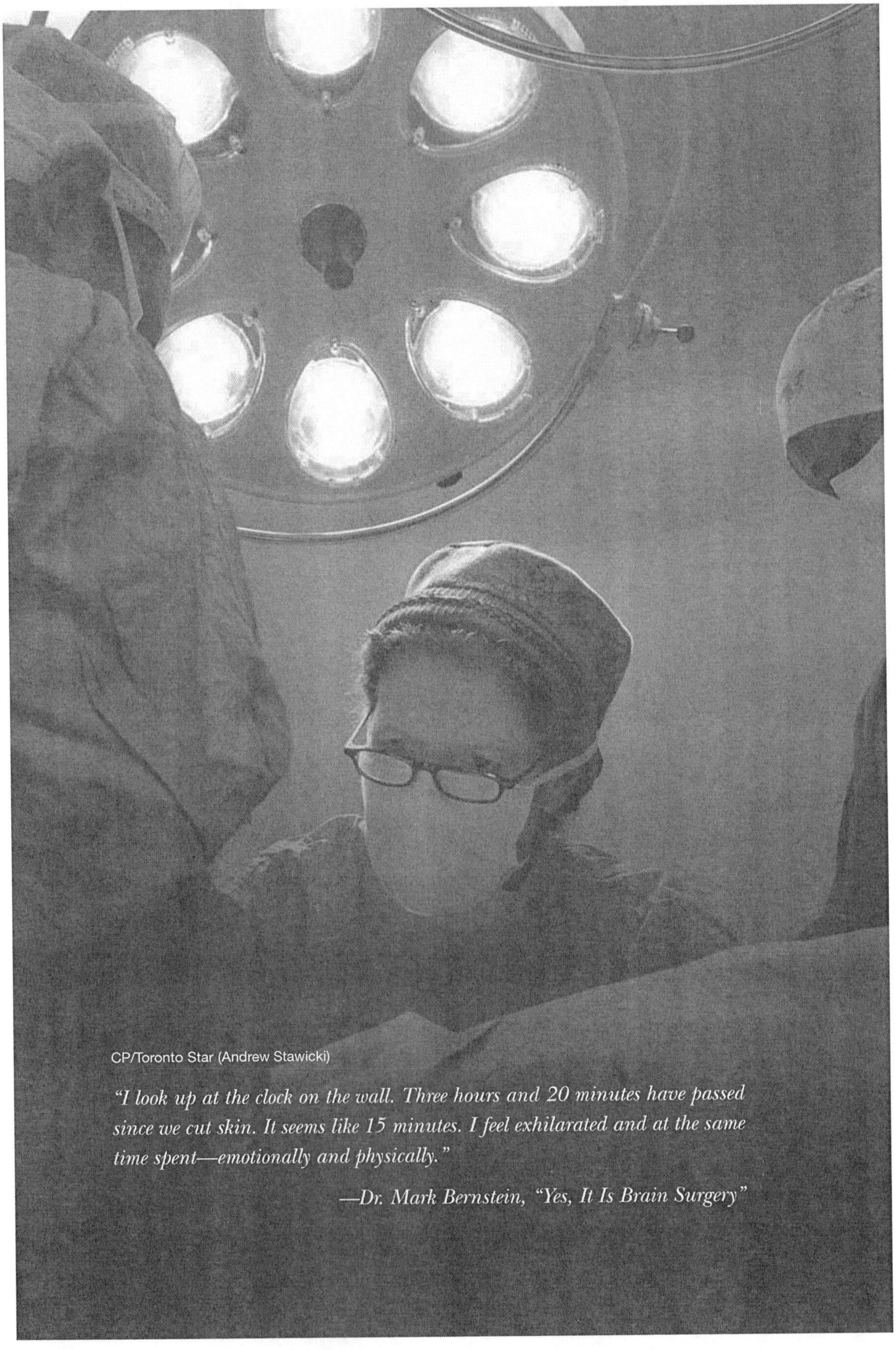

CP/Toronto Star (Andrew Stawicki)

"I look up at the clock on the wall. Three hours and 20 minutes have passed since we cut skin. It seems like 15 minutes. I feel exhilarated and at the same time spent—emotionally and physically."

—Dr. Mark Bernstein, "Yes, It Is Brain Surgery"

8
Process Analysis

HERE'S HOW IT'S DONE....

Whenever you enter a large bookstore, it won't be long before you notice titles like these: *Success Without College, How to Make People Like You in 90 Seconds or Less, Think and Grow Rich, Massage Made Easy*, and *The Complete Snowboarder.* Look a little further and you might see *Awaken the Giant Within*, or *Secrets of Power Persuasion*, or *Parenting Your Out-of-Control Teenager.* Then there are the "Idiot" and "Dummy" books: *The Complete Idiot's Guide to Plumbing, The Complete Idiot's Guide to Grandparenting*, and *Italian Cooking for Dummies*—not to mention *Norton for Dummies* and all the other computer titles for still more dummies. Clearly many people want to do things, and there is a great need to learn how. But the writer who tells how has some serious thinking and organizing to do.

Consider the last time you bought something in kit form and tried to assemble it. Maybe you were lucky and everything fit together. But more likely, you were sweating to make out tiny diagrams, to understand terminology you had never heard of and to follow vague directions with spelling errors that left out steps or got them in the wrong order. With your new exercise machine or computer desk or amplifier lying in parts on the floor, you wondered if you would *ever* get it together. And when you finally did, mysterious parts were left over.

It doesn't have to be this way. We are not "dummies," but we do need explanations that are clear and easy to follow. And so does your own reader. Writing that tells *how* to do things is often called *process analysis.* Sometimes we write an essay that gives what could be called a **directional** process analysis. It is a sort of *narrative,* taking readers from the beginning to the end of a task, usually in the time order required to grow tomatoes, write a résumé, tune up a car, or do whatever else readers set out to do. It includes every step, for each is vital to the success of the project. And unless it is written for the specialist, it includes all the details right down to the spacing and depth of seeds in the soil, the order of items in your résumé, or the size of the paintbrush.

Did you ever eat something so good that you just had to have the recipe? An experienced cook has a hard time explaining. Instead of giving quantities, temperatures and measurements of time that we can actually apply, the old pro will say things like "add some yeast" or "now put in a little salt" or "take it out of the oven when it's done." The writer of recipes in a book, though, puts his or her own experience in the background and thinks instead about what the *audience* needs to know. The result is a set of directions so exact that, even if we have never cooked before, the product is likely to turn out.

If you are an "old pro" at other tasks, the challenge will be the same. Suppose you have a digital camera and regularly order prints online. The process may seem easy and transparent to you, but what about your parents or even grandparents? Imagine all the details you would have to explain about matters such as choice of website, access to it and uploading digital photos first to the computer, and from there to the website. Then there are photographic improvements to make such as editing out the "red-eye" factor, turning images to different orientations, cropping to get the best picture, etc. Then there are still more steps: recording your choice of prints (how many, what sizes, what texture, etc.), not to mention the matter of paying online. Imagine in your mind's eye the less technically sophisticated person you might be instructing, and the ways you will need to put things so they are clear.

When you are writing directions, on whatever topic, this is the main challenge: keeping your *audience* in mind. You may try to take shortcuts, skipping details you assume anyone would know. But respect the person you are writing for; remember your own encounters with procedures you have not yet learned yourself. If you estimate your reader's level of knowledge and explain accordingly, your directions—whether verbal or written—will very likely succeed.

Another kind of process analysis could be called **informational**, for it satisfies not our practical needs but our curiosity. We may wish to know how airliners are hijacked, how stockholders are swindled, how the greenhouse effect causes tornadoes and tsunamis or how the Second World War was won—knowing we will never do these things ourselves. Not every detail is given in this kind of armchair reading: only as many as it takes to inform and interest the reader. In this chapter Dr. Mark Bernstein tells how he saved a patient's life with a brain operation. His account is not a how-to-do-it set of directions, with the dose of every medication spelled out to the milligram—because he knows we're not going to operate on someone ourselves. But he does relate all the main points, and describes what happens with an almost scary vividness of imagery. He knows his *informational* process analysis will succeed if it keeps us on the edges of our seat.

Another writer in this chapter, Christie Blatchford, depicts the long process through which her mother became an alcoholic. Obviously Blatchford is not explaining to us how to do the same; she is generating an *informational* process analysis of how people fall into one of life's worst traps. The implied lesson is clear: Avoid alcoholism. At the same time, she also offers directions: in portraying her loving and heroic father, who never stops trying to help his wife, Blatchford shows readers how they, too, might help others in this dilemma.

Occasionally a writer will use the format of process analysis not really to instruct or inform, but as a means to other ends. When Stephen Leacock tells us "How to Live to Be 200," he advises us to eat cement—which seems a strange way to reach the goal, until we realize that his goal is not really longevity but laughs.

Whether you aim to help the reader accomplish a task, to satisfy the reader's curiosity, or even just to entertain, your process analysis will work only if you realize *why* you are writing it: Are you giving directions? Then follow all the advice above, so your reader's efforts will be successful. Are you explaining a task that only specialists perform? Then interest the reader with a multitude of examples. Are you even just writing humour, like Leacock? Then do anything that is fun. But even then, you will probably be making a serious point—like Leacock who advises us to enjoy life.

Note: For more examples of ***informational*** *process analysis, see these essays in other chapters:*

Patrick Lane, "There Is a Season," p. 37
Crisanta Sampang, "Trading Motherhood for Dollars," p. 176
Martin Hocking, "Capping the Great Cup Debate," p. 354

For more examples of ***directional*** *process analysis, see these essays in other chapters:*

Dr. Vincent Lam and Dr. Colin Lee, "Dr. Lam's Perspective: Go on a Canoe Trip," p. 253
Hon. David Lam, "Pulling Together," p. 284

ALBERT KOEHL

Hockey Etiquette for the Beginner

Albert Koehl is many things: a Maple Leafs fan, a fluent speaker of several languages, a wilderness canoeist and hiker, a lover of the arts, and a lawyer who hunts down and prosecutes corporate polluters. After graduating from Queen's Law School in 1987, Koehl spent six years as a prosecutor for the Ontario Ministry of the Environment, served in Guatemala as a volunteer human rights observer and United Nations investigator and worked in Toronto community legal clinics. Then in 2001 he joined Sierra Legal Defence (now called Ecojustice), a powerful Canadian environmental group that studies existing legislation to find new ways of bringing polluters to justice. As if this were not enough, Koehl has found time to join the boards of civic organizations for the poor; has run for political office; has travelled across Africa by box car, bush taxi and barge; has studied Mandarin in China; is fluent in French, German, Spanish and English; and also writes. (The essay that follows appeared in the Globe and Mail *of April 21, 2004.) Asked what changes he would like to see in his lifetime, Koehl replied, "We need to change our focus from a right to pollute, to a right to clean air, water, and land. I believe a clean environment is as crucial to a child as a good education and good health care."*

1 It is a common mistake, especially for theatre, opera, and symphony lovers, to conclude from the casual attire, beverage choice, and boisterous conduct of hockey fans that watching a game is a cultural event of a lower social order. In reality, the etiquette expected of ice hockey aficionados is quite refined. Ignorance of this etiquette risks turning an invitation to watch an NHL playoff game at the home of a friend, colleague or business associate, into a

social disaster. Fortunately, even the novice can avoid embarrassing blunders by learning a few simple rules:

Arrive on time for the start of a game. Hockey fans may not make you wait on the porch for the intermission, but if a goal is scored while you are being greeted your punctuality faux pas may prejudice a future invitation. 2

Cheer for the host's team unless you have announced a contrary affiliation in advance, much like a vegan properly reveals a dietary preference before attending a pig-roast fundraiser for the opera. And cheering for the other team simply because you like the colour of their jerseys is considered uncouth. 3

Remember, each hockey fan considers his or her role as important to the team's success as that of the players on the ice. Some fans contribute to their team by a complex set of superstitions. While guests may not believe in the power of the hockey gods, they are nonetheless expected to participate. For instance, if the opposing team takes a lead you may be asked to change seats. If you refuse, you can be blamed for the team's loss. In a recent game, our team was winning until my brother sent his toddlers to bed. Soon we were down by two goals. It turned out that the children's presence had been key to the team's lead and perhaps the reason they had so vigorously resisted bedtime. "I'll go wake up the kids," I volunteered. 4

Other fans contribute to the team by intensely concentrating on the game. It would be rude to mock this intensity, much like telling a mesmerized opera lover, "Relax, it's just singin' and yellin'." Hockey fans are willing to suffer tremendous anxiety for their team, even to pay the ultimate price. A recent study found that the anxiety suffered by fans during games sometimes brings on fatal heart attacks. At least the players have the chance to work off their nervous energy—a luxury the fan does not enjoy, except for the odd sprint to greet late arrivals at the door. 5

If the opposing team scores, quietly gauge the host's reaction. At the very least, allow the host to move uninterrupted through feelings of guilt, denial, anger, and acceptance. Later, it is always helpful to blame the referee, the seating arrangement or bad luck for the team's misfortune. On the other hand, remarking on the skill of the opposing team's scorer can be dangerous and is in any case considered déclassé, like hooting at a sexy stagehand at the theatre. 6

7 However, when the home team scores there are few rules to the proper conduct of the celebration, although damaging walls, smashing light fixtures (unless your host is a tenant) or interfering with the electrical cord to the TV are frowned upon. The euphoric mood of the host is also a perfect opportunity for a business associate or friend to bring up a delicate subject, such as the loss of a major contract or running over the family dog on the rush into the driveway to avoid being late.

8 Conversation during a game is properly limited to superficial topics. Generally, matters that can be answered with "yes" or "no" are acceptable, except during commercial breaks. Attempting to engage the host in a discussion about the war in Iraq, for example, would be like phoning your stockbroker during a symphony. It is worthwhile noting, however, that hockey fans are eager to share their extensive repertoire of trivial statistics. A fan may not remember his wife's birthday but would be happy to field a question such as, "Hey, do you know how much [Maple Leafs Captain] Mats Sundin weighs?" or "How tall is [Calgary star] Jerome Iginla?"

9 Similarly, telephone calls to a hockey fan during the playoffs are best kept to a minimum and, of course, restricted to the intermission. Never phone a hockey fan after 9:30 p.m. during the playoffs, since an overtime period may be in progress. If in doubt, do not call during evening hours until late June, when the playoffs end.

10 If the host's team is eliminated from the playoffs, behaviour that is appropriate at a funeral home is expected. For instance, you would never say "Look on the bright side, you still have other relatives." By the same token, clichés like "There's always next season" are not appreciated. Instead they expect the passing of their team from competition to be marked with profound solemnity. In fact, intimacy that might otherwise raise eyebrows is perfectly acceptable. A tender hug, even for a business associate, is remembered with fondness.

11 It is even acceptable for men to weep on the demise of their team. As one caller to a hockey talk show recently admitted, "I have cried only twice in my life, each time when the Maple Leafs were eliminated from the playoffs." To belittle a man at such a time is like mocking a person moved to tears by fair Juliet's plight.

12 By mastering these simple rules, a playoff game can become an enjoyable, even rewarding, cultural experience.

EXPLORATIONS:

Ken Dryden, *The Game*
Dave Bidini, *Tropic of Hockey*
Brian McFarlane, *Brian McFarlane's World of Hockey*
Hockey: A People's History (a six-disk DVD set of the CBC television series)
http://www.hhof.com/index.htm
http://en.wikipedia.org/wiki/Ice_hockey

STRUCTURE:

1. If Albert Koehl's essay is a process analysis, why does he begin paragraph 1 with a *comparison and contrast*?
2. Point out where else, throughout this selection, Koehl uses comparison and contrast.
3. Where is Koehl's thesis statement?
4. Is Koehl's essay a *directional* or an *informational* process analysis?
5. Does Koehl give his process analysis in the usual chronological order?
6. What common technique of closing does Koehl employ?

STYLE:

1. Parts of this piece are formal (big words, big sentences, big paragraphs), while other parts are informal ("'Relax, it's just singin' and yellin'"). What is Koehl doing through this contrast of styles?

IDEAS FOR DISCUSSION AND WRITING:

1. One fan in paragraph 11 admits, "I have cried only twice in my life, each time when the Maple Leafs were eliminated from the playoffs." Why do spectator sports move us? Tell of the time when you were most deeply affected by watching a sport.

2. Which does more for us, watching a sport or playing it ourselves? Give reasons.
3. Ken Dryden, one of the greatest goalies of all time, played for the Montreal Canadiens from 1971 to 1979, when they won six Stanley Cups. He also did a law degree (like Albert Koehl), wrote four bestselling books, became president of the Toronto Maple Leafs, then went on to be a federal MP and cabinet minister. Is his a rare story, or do sports build a character and ability that help athletes later in life?
4. Do high salaries, high ticket prices and labour-management conflicts mean NHL hockey is in trouble? Suggest long-term solutions to strengthen this favourite Canadian sport. And do you think hockey will remain our favourite?
5. Paragraph 4 describes typical superstitions of sports fans. Why, in an age of science, do we still believe things like these? Tell your own strongest superstition, and give evidence whether it works or not.
6. Do you prefer watching sports, or going to the symphony, theatre or opera? Or, like Albert Koehl, do you like them all? Argue why or why not.
7. **PROCESS IN WRITING:** *Write a humorous* process analysis, *like Koehl's, entitled "Concert Etiquette for the Beginner." (The concert may be of any kind, from classical to heavy metal.) Start with a page of notes, then put them in time order and select the best. Are there plenty of actual techniques? How do concertgoers do each thing? (Include such acts as obtaining tickets, entering the hall, finding one's place, enjoying the event, dealing with annoying neighbours, showing appreciation for the performance, etc.). Now do a quick draft. The next day look it over. Are words wasted? Then cut. Do examples fill at least half the essay? If not, add. Is word choice exact? If not, see your thesaurus. Do you move the reader on with* transitions *such as "first," "then," "next," "at last" and "finally"? Is the punctuation accurate? If not, edit. Finally, read your* process analysis, *with feeling, to the class.*

Note: See also the Topics for Writing on the Online Learning Centre at www.mcgrawhill.ca/olc/conrad.

STEPHEN LEACOCK

How to Live to Be 200

During his lifetime Stephen Leacock became the world's best-known humorist writing in English, a Canadian successor to the American writer Mark Twain. Reading in person, Leacock was so funny that once a member of his audience literally died laughing. Though he was for decades Canada's favourite author, Leacock has slipped into neglect. Born in England in 1869, at age six he came with his family to Ontario. He studied at Upper Canada College, the University of Toronto and the University of Chicago, where in 1903 he received a Ph.D. That year McGill hired him to teach economics and political science, and from 1908 till his retirement in 1936, he served as head of his department. He died in 1944. Leacock wrote over 60 books, many on academic subjects, but of course it is for his books of humour that he is remembered. The best-loved have been Literary Lapses *(1910),* Nonsense Novels *(1911),* Sunshine Sketches of a Little Town *(1912),* Arcadian Adventures with the Idle Rich *(1914) and* My Remarkable Uncle and Other Sketches *(1942). Our selection, from a later version of* Literary Lapses, *is vintage Leacock: through exaggeration and incongruities, it reduces to absurdity a topic that many people, today as in Leacock's time, take seriously. It may be worth noting that Leacock himself shunned the "health mania" to spend large amounts of time enjoying his favourite brandies in the McGill Faculty Club.*

1 Twenty years ago I knew a man called Jiggins, who had the Health Habit.

2 He used to take a cold plunge every morning. He said it opened his pores. After it he took a hot sponge. He said it closed the pores. He got so that he could open and shut his pores at will.

3 Jiggins used to stand and breathe at an open window for half an hour before dressing. He said it expanded his lungs. He might, of course, have had it done in a shoe-store with a boot stretcher, but after all it cost him nothing this way, and what is half an hour?

4 After he had got his undershirt on, Jiggins used to hitch himself

up like a dog in harness and do Sandow exercises. He did them forwards, backwards, and hind-side up.

He could have got a job as a dog anywhere. He spent all his time 5
at this kind of thing. In his spare time at the office, he used to lie on his stomach on the floor and see if he could lift himself up with his knuckles. If he could, then he tried some other way until he found one that he couldn't do. Then he would spend the rest of his lunch hour on his stomach, perfectly happy.

In the evenings in his room he used to lift iron bars, cannon-balls, 6
heave dumb-bells, and haul himself up to the ceiling with his teeth. You could hear the thumps half a mile.

He liked it. 7

He spent half the night slinging himself around the room. He said 8
it made his brain clear. When he got his brain perfectly clear, he went to bed and slept. As soon as he woke, he began clearing it again.

Jiggins is dead. He was, of course, a pioneer, but the fact that he 9
dumb-belled himself to death at an early age does not prevent a whole generation of young men from following in his path.

They are ridden by the Health Mania. 10

They make themselves a nuisance. 11

They get up at impossible hours. They go out in silly little suits 12
and run Marathon heats before breakfast. They chase around barefoot to get the dew on their feet. They hunt for ozone. They bother about pepsin. They won't eat meat because it has too much nitrogen. They won't eat fruit because it hasn't any. They prefer albumen and starch and nitrogen to huckleberry pie and doughnuts. They won't drink water out of a tap. They won't eat sardines out of a can. They won't use oysters out of a pail. They won't drink milk out of a glass. They are afraid of alcohol in any shape. Yes sir, afraid. "Cowards."

And after all their fuss they presently incur some simple old-fash- 13
ioned illness and die like anybody else.

Now people of this sort have no chance to attain any great age. 14
They are on the wrong track.

Listen. Do you want to live to be really old, to enjoy a grand, green, 15
exuberant, boastful old age and to make yourself a nuisance to your whole neighbourhood with your reminiscences?

Then cut out all this nonsense. Cut it out. Get up in the morning at 16
a sensible hour. The time to get up is when you have to, not before. If your office opens at eleven, get up at ten-thirty. Take your chance on ozone. There isn't any such thing anyway. Or, if there is, you can

buy a Thermos bottle full for five cents, and put it on a shelf in your cupboard. If your work begins at seven in the morning, get up at ten minutes to, but don't be liar enough to say that you like it. It isn't exhilarating, and you know it.

17 Also, drop all that cold-bath business. You never did it when you were a boy. Don't be a fool now. If you must take a bath (you don't really need to), take it warm. The pleasure of getting out of a cold bed and creeping into a hot bath beats a cold plunge to death. In any case, stop gassing about your tub and your "shower," as if you were the only man who ever washed.

18 So much for that point.

19 Next, take the question of germs and bacilli. Don't be scared of them. That's all. That's the whole thing, and if you once get on to that you never need to worry again.

20 If you see a bacilli, walk right up to it, and look it in the eye. If one flies into your room, strike at it with your hat or with a towel. Hit it as hard as you can between the neck and the thorax. It will soon get sick of that.

21 But as a matter of fact, a bacilli is perfectly quiet and harmless if you are not afraid of it. Speak to it. Call out to it to "lie down." It will understand. I had a bacilli once, called Fido, that would come and lie at my feet while I was working. I never knew a more affectionate companion, and when it was run over by an automobile, I buried it in the garden with genuine sorrow.

22 (I admit this is an exaggeration. I don't really remember its name; it may have been Robert.)

23 Understand that it is only a fad of modern medicine to say that cholera and typhoid and diphtheria are caused by bacilli and germs; nonsense. Cholera is caused by a frightful pain in the stomach, and diphtheria is caused by trying to cure a sore throat.

24 Now take the question of food.

25 Eat what you want. Eat lots of it. Yes, eat too much of it. Eat till you can just stagger across the room with it and prop it up against a sofa cushion. Eat everything that you like until you can't eat any more. The only test is, can you pay for it? If you can't pay for it, don't eat it. And listen—don't worry as to whether your food contains starch, or albumen, or gluten, or nitrogen. If you are a damn fool enough to want these things, go and buy them and eat all you want of them. Go to a laundry and get a bag of starch, and eat your fill of it. Eat it, and take a good long drink of glue after it, and a spoonful of Portland cement. That will gluten you, good and solid.

26 If you like nitrogen, go and get a druggist to give you a canful of it at the soda counter, and let you sip it with a straw. Only don't think that you can mix all these things up with your food. There isn't any nitrogen or phosphorus or albumen in ordinary things to eat. In any decent household all that sort of stuff is washed out in the kitchen sink before the food is put on the table.

27 And just one word about fresh air and exercise. Don't bother with either of them. Get your room full of good air, then shut up the windows and keep it. It will keep for years. Anyway, don't keep using your lungs all the time. Let them rest. As for exercise, if you have to take it, take it and put up with it. But as long as you have the price of a hack° and can hire other people to play baseball for you and run races and do gymnastics when you sit in the shade and smoke and watch them—great heavens, what more do you want?

°hack: A kind of horse-drawn carriage.

EXPLORATIONS:

Stephen Leacock,
    Sunshine Sketches of a Little Town
    Literary Lapses
    My Remarkable Uncle and Other Sketches
Robertson Davies, *Stephen Leacock*
D. Staines, *Stephen Leacock: A Reappraisal*
http://www.athabascau.ca/writers/leacock.html
http://archives.cbc.ca/IDD-1-41-615/sports/fitness
http://archives.cbc.ca/IDC-1-74-645-3540-20/that_was_then/people/stephen_leacock_obit

STRUCTURE:

1. This essay has two main parts. Where do they join? How do they differ?
2. We begin with Jiggins. How is his story organized? Were you surprised at his death in paragraph 9? Why? What literary device lies behind this effect? How does the death of Jiggins lead into Leacock's main argument?

3. Are Leacock's health tips given in order of application?
4. What is our first clue that Leacock's *process analysis* is meant more to entertain than to instruct?

STYLE:

1. Leacock writes "eat" ten times in paragraph 25. Read the passage aloud in class, with feeling. Is this repetition accidental? What effect does it have? In which other paragraph does Leacock exploit repetition?
2. Paragraph 25 states, "That will gluten you, good and solid." What effect does Leacock's unusual use of "gluten" have here?
3. Reduction to absurdity is a comic device Leacock often uses, as in the "bacilli" as insects to swat, or as a favourite dog run over by a car. Where else in this essay has he reduced something to total absurdity?

IDEAS FOR DISCUSSION AND WRITING:

1. Do you have the "Health Habit," like Jiggins, or do you prefer comfort and luxury, like our narrator? Give reasons.
2. Update Leacock's argument for our times. Which kinds of "Health Mania" would you drop? Which would you keep? Which might you add?
3. To women in the class: Why does Leacock refer only to men pursuing the "Health Mania"? Give a *process analysis* of your own actions to keep healthy and fit.
4. **PROCESS IN WRITING:** *Write a* process analysis *of how to reach old age in good health. First brainstorm or freewrite, then do a fast discovery draft. When it has cooled off, analyze it: Are the steps of your process in order? Are the instructions clear for your intended* AUDIENCE*? Have you supplied* examples*? Revise accordingly. Now sharpen word choice as well. Heighten* TRANSITIONS*. Cut deadwood. Finally, test the prose aloud before printing out your best version.*

Note: See also the Topics for Writing on the Online Learning Centre at www.mcgrawhill.ca/olc/conrad.

CP

"It is time that I tell the story from where I stood—literally in the middle of the slaughter for weeks on end."

—Lt.-Gen. Roméo Dallaire, with Major Brent Beardsley, "Cri de coeur"

9 ARGUMENTATION AND PERSUASION

THEREFORE....

So far the essays in this book have taken many paths in developing their subject. They have narrated events, they have described, they have explained, and some have entertained. But you have surely realized that in one way or another, whatever else they do, almost all the selections have tried to make a point. After all, an essay without a point is "pointless." The very use of a thesis statement implies a main idea or opinion. In this final chapter, we now focus more closely on how the writer makes that point. The process takes two complementary forms: *argumentation* and *persuasion.*

ARGUMENTATION

This word has a broad set of meanings, but here we will consider it the writer's attempt to convince the reader mostly *through logic.* This stance implies respect: it considers the reader a mature individual capable of independent thought. It assumes the reader will also respect the thoughts of the writer, if those thoughts are presented in a logical way. In summary, the writer and reader are *partners*: since the writer does not play on the reader's emotions, the reader considers the argument with a more open mind. If the logic makes sense, the reader may be convinced. Argumentation through logic takes two opposite forms, *deduction* and *induction*. Let's look at each.

DEDUCTION

Deduction accepts a general principle as true, then applies it to specific cases. For over two thousand years logicians have expressed this process in a formula called the *syllogism*. Here's a well-known example:

Major premise: All men are mortal.
Minor premise: Socrates is a man.
Conclusion: Socrates is mortal.

This chain of reasoning is about as foolproof as any: since no human in the history of the world has yet lived much longer than a century, we feel safe in assuming that no one ever will; therefore "all men are mortal." And since all historical records about Socrates portray him as a man—not, say, as a rock or horse or tree—we accept the minor premise as well. Logic tells us that if both the major and minor premises are true, then the conclusion will inevitably be true as well.

But now let's look at a syllogism whose logic is not as clear:

Major premise: Progress is good.
Minor premise: The automobile represents progress.
Conclusion: The automobile is good.

At first glance the argument may seem all right: it certainly reflects values common in our society. But let's examine the major premise, the foundation on which all the rest is built: is it true that "progress is good"? Well, how do we know until we define "progress"? Is it more jobs? More production? More cars? Higher sales? More consumption? A rising stock market? Or are all these the opposite of true "progress" because our natural resources are dwindling, our highways are choked with traffic, our lakes and forests are dying of acid rain, the greenhouse effect is disrupting our climate and around the world several species of life per hour are becoming extinct? Our values will determine our response.

If we cannot agree on what "progress" is, how can we say it is "good"? And how could we go on to our minor premise, saying that "the automobile represents progress"? How could we build even further on this shaky foundation, claiming in our conclusion that "the automobile is good"? Within its own framework the argument may be "valid" (or logical), but only those who accept the original premise will view the conclusion as true. Those who do not will reject it as false.

And that is the problem with deduction: not always can we agree on premises. A thousand years ago society ran almost entirely on deduction: the King or the Church or our parents told us what to believe, and we simply applied those principles to any case that came up. But in our millennium many of us do not accept being told what to think. Not only do many people now question systems of belief such as Marxism or codes of religion, but scientists even question the previously accepted "laws" of nature. How is a person to know what is true? It is therefore no coincidence that most contemporary essays argue not through deduction but through induction.

INDUCTION

We have discussed how deduction applies a general rule to explain particular cases. Induction is the opposite: it first observes particular cases, then from them formulates a general rule. This is the basis of the scientific way, the procedure that enables humans to conquer disease, multiply food production and travel to the moon. It can produce faulty results, just like deduction, but the open mind required to use it appeals to our modern sensibilities. Let's take an example:

> After a summer in the factory Joan thought she could afford a car, so the week before school began she bought a sporty red three-year-old Japanese model. Speeding around town with the stereo turned up was

> so much fun that she didn't mind the $350-a-month payments. But when the insurance company hit her for $2800 as a new driver, her savings took a dive. Each month she found herself paying $150 for gas and $200 for parking. A fall tuneup set her back $180, and new tires $500. Then came the repairs: $250 for brakes, $325 for a clutch, $225 for an exhaust system, and $380 for a timing belt. In desperation Joan took a part-time job selling shoes. That helped her bank book but took her study time. Two weeks after exams, holding a feeble grade report in her hand, Joan decided to sell the car. Nobody could have told her to, since, like most people, she likes to make up her own mind. But the long string of evidence did the teaching: now Joan knows, through *induction*, that as a student she cannot afford a car.

Induction is not infallible. Conceivably Joan's next car might never need a repair. Next year insurance might somehow drop from $2800 to, say, $75. Gas stations might sell premium for 10 cents a litre, and on Boxing Day a good tire might cost $1.99. Anything is possible. But Joan feels that the consistency of her results—the steady high cost of her car ownership—will *probably* not change. Likewise, the scientist believes that her or his years of research have yielded results that will not be disproved by the very next experiment. But in all humility both Joan and the scientist must consider the new principle not a fact, not an unchangeable law, but simply an idea with a very high probability of being true.

Finally, suppose that Joan analyzes her experience in an essay. If she sets up her paper as most essayists do, we will read her thesis statement near the beginning—even though the principle it states is the *result* of the evidence still to come. This positioning is not a flaw of logic: Joan simply *introduces* the main idea so we can see where we are going, then tells us how she arrived at it, letting her evidence lead inductively toward the main point which will be restated at the end. You will find this pattern at work in several of this chapter's inductive essays, for example the one by Martin Hocking.

You will also find that, although deduction and induction represent opposite methods of logic, sometimes both are used in the same argument (when the writer's original opinion is confirmed by the evidence). This does not necessarily mean weakness in logic either. Another link between these opposites is that most principles which we accept as true, and upon which we base our own deductions, originated in someone else's induction. (Newton arrived inductively at his theory of gravity, through evidence such as the famous apple that fell on his head; almost all of us now believe Newton and his theory without waiting for an apple, or anything else, to fall on our own heads.) Similarly, a conclusion we derive from our own induction might become the premise of someone else's deduction—a link in an ongoing chain of logic. To keep this chain from breaking, the individual has a double task: to evaluate any links provided by others, then to make her or his own link as strong as possible.

PERSUASION

We have just seen how *argumentation* seeks to convince through logic. But, whether deductive or inductive, is logic enough? Now let's look at the complementary approach of *persuasion*, which attempts to convince through emotion. A century of inductive research into psychology has shown that we humans are seldom rational. Even when we think we are "reasoning," we are often building arguments merely to justify what we thought or felt already. It is possible to write an argumentative essay with enough restraint to be almost purely logical. But to most people the effort is difficult and unnatural, requiring a great deal of revision, and the result may seem cold and uninviting to those who have not spent years reading the almost pure argumentation of scholarly journals. Most professional writers would say that a little feeling and a little colour can help an essay. But how do we take this approach without slipping into dishonesty? Let's look now at the major techniques of *persuasion*—both their uses and abuses.

Word choice: Is a person "slim," "thin" or "skinny"? Is a governmental expenditure an "investment," a "cost," a "waste" or a "boondoggle"? Is an oil spill an "incident," an "accident," a "mistake," a "crime" or an "environmental tragedy"? Essayists tend to choose the term that reflects their feeling and the feeling they hope to encourage in the readers. While deliberate choice of words is one of the central tasks of all writers, including essayists, let's not abuse the process. Bertrand Russell once quipped, "I am firm; you are stubborn; he is pig-headed." If too many of your word choices follow the model of "pig-headed," you will alarm an alert reader and unfairly overwhelm a careless one.

Example: Although examples form the basis of logical induction, they can also add colour and feeling to a persuasive essay. Choose vivid ones. An attempt to show old people as active may be helped by the example of your grandmother who skis. But avoid dubious cases like that of the man in Azerbaijan who is rumoured to have ridden a horse at age 155.

Repetition: Although we try to cut accidental repetition from our writing (as in the case of one student who used the word "tire" 55 times in an essay about, you guessed it, tires), intentional repetition can build feeling. Stephen Leacock builds emphasis by using the word "eat" over and over in paragraph 25 of his essay (see p. 340), and in paragraphs 14–17 of her selection (see pp. 375–376) Joy Kogawa builds feeling by starting a whole string of sentences with the contraction "it's."

Hyperbole (exaggeration): A humorist can exaggerate and get away with it, as Stephen Leacock does when he tells us "How to Live to Be 200." By contrast, an essay with a serious subject should stay strictly with the truth.

Analogy and figures of speech: You have seen in Chapter 6 how we can suggest a point by comparing one thing with another from a different category, such as a monster with the forestry industry, or a flower with a new baby. Analogies, and their shorter cousins similes and metaphors, are powerful tools of persuasion; avoid abusing them through name-calling. Think twice before casting a politician as a dinosaur, entrepreneurs as piranhas or police officers as gorillas. Remember, above all, that neither analogies nor figures of speech are logical proof of anything.

Irony: When in Chapter 2 the poet Goran Simic tells of his job moving clothes in a warehouse; when in Chapter 4 Naheed Mustafa covers herself with the traditional *hijab* in order to be free; when in Chapter 5 Stephanie Nolen shows us an African grandmother who now has to raise a second generation of children; and when in this chapter Rita Schindler "thanks" her son's assailants for not killing him—we feel the power of irony. A writer can use this device for a lifetime without exhausting its emotional power; yet irony lends itself less easily to abuses than do many tools of persuasion, for both its use and its appreciation demand a certain exercise of intelligence.

Appeal to authority or prestige: Opponents of nuclear weapons love to quote Albert Einstein on their dangers; after all, since his discoveries made this hardware possible, he should know. We also invite our reader to believe what a famous economist says about money, what a judge says about law, or what an educator says about education. This approach appeals to our reader's ethical sense: he or she believes these people know the facts and tell the truth. But avoid the common abuse of quoting people on matters outside their competence—a terrorist on peace, a disgraced politician on honesty or a convicted murderer on religion.

Fright: You can be sure that a frightened reader is an interested reader, for fright is personal: what you say in your essay could be important! Avoid cheap effects, though. Frighten a reader only with facts that really are scary (such as the number of times computer error nearly launched a third World War).

Climax: Whatever your argument, don't trail off from strong to weak. After a good introduction, drop to your least important or least dramatic point, then progress upward to your strongest. This very rise produces an emotion in the reader, like that of the concertgoer who thrills to the final dramatic chords of "The Hallelujah Chorus."

Cause and Effect: Review the introduction to Chapter 4. Note how answers to the question "why?" can themselves cause emotion in the reader: the sudden resolution of our doubts can be a deep and satisfying experience.

Comparison and Contrast: Review the introduction to Chapter 5, which discusses how a strong contrast—such as culture shock—can create feeling.

PLAYING FAIR IN ARGUMENTATION AND PERSUASION

We have looked at some abuses both of argumentation and of persuasion. Now read the following communication, an actual chain letter that arrived one day in the mail. (Versions of it also circulate on the Internet; you may have seen one.) What attempts does it make at *deduction* or *induction*? Are they logical? What attempts does it make at *persuasion*? Are they fair? (For your information, the person who received this letter did not send it on. So far he has not died or been fired—but then, neither has he won a lottery!)

> **KISS SOMEONE YOU LOVE WHEN YOU GET THIS LETTER AND MAKE SOME MAGIC**
> This paper has been sent to you for good luck. The original copy is in New England. It has been around the world nine times. The luck has sent it to you. You will receive good luck within four days of receiving this letter, provided you send it back out. THIS IS NO JOKE. You will receive it in the mail. Send copies to people that you think need good luck. Don't send money as fate has no price. Do not keep this letter. It must leave your hands within 96 hours. An R.A.F. officer became a hero. Joe Elliot received $40,000, and lost it because he broke the chain. While in the Philippines, Gene Welch lost his wife six days after receiving this letter. He failed to circulate the letter. However, before her death she had won $50,000.00 in a lottery. The money was transferred to him four days after he decided to mail out this letter. Please send twenty copies of this letter and see what happens in four days. The chain came from Venezuela and was written in South America. Since the copy must make a tour of the world you must make copies and send them to your friends and associates. After a few days you will get a surprise. This is true even if you are not superstitious. Do note the following: Constantine Dias received the chain in 1953. He asked his

secretary to type twenty copies and send them out. A few days later he won a lottery of $2,000,000. Aria Daddit, an office employee, received the letter and forgot that it had to leave his hands within 96 hours. He lost his job. Later, finding the letter again, he mailed out twenty copies. A few days later he got a better job. Dalen Fairchild received the letter and not believing, threw it away. Nine days later he died. PLEASE SEND NO MONEY. PLEASE DON'T IGNORE THIS. IT WORKS!

Note: No essay in this chapter adopts a stance of pure logic to the exclusion of emotion, or of pure emotion to the exclusion of logic. The nine essays represent different proportions of both elements, and are arranged in approximate order from most argumentative to most persuasive.

For more examples of argumentation, see these essays in other chapters:

Karen Von Hahn, "Self-Serving Propaganda," p. 66
Jeffrey Rosenthal, "Poker Power," p. 71
Doris Anderson, "The 51-Per-Cent Minority," p. 191
Catharine Parr Traill, "Remarks of Security of Person and Property in Canada," p. 222
Lawrence Hill, "Black + White = Black," p. 228

For more examples of persuasion, see these essays in other chapters:

Nathalie Petrowski, "The Seven-Minute Life of Marc Lépine," p. 169
Drew Hayden Taylor, "This Boat Is My Boat," p. 216
Samantha Bennett, "It's Not Just the Weather That's Cooler in Canada," p. 264

KILDARE DOBBS

The Scar*

Kildare Dobbs was born in Meerut, Uttar Pradesh, India in 1923, was educated in Ireland, then during the Second World War spent five years in the Royal Navy. After the war he joined the British Colonial Service in Tanganyika, then, after earning an M.A. at Cambridge, came in 1952 to Canada. Here Dobbs has been a teacher, editor for Macmillan, managing editor of Saturday Night, *and book editor of the* Toronto Star. *He was one of the founders, in 1956, of the* Tamarack Review. *He is also the author of many books, among them* Running to Paradise *(essays, 1962, winner of the Governor General's Award);* Canada *(an illustrated travel book, 1964);* Reading the Time *(essays, 1968);* Pride and Fall *(short fiction, 1981);* Anatolian Suite *(travel, 1989);* Ribbon of Highway *(travel, 1992);* The Eleventh Hour: Poems for the Third Millennium *(1997);* Casablanca, the Poem *(1997);* Historic Canada *(1998); and* Running the Rapids: A Writer's Life *(2005). Many of Dobbs' books are about faraway places, whether travel writing, serious analysis or both mixed. In a millennium project he visited 24 countries, logging over 27,000 miles, filing regular reports by satellite with the CBC. Our own selection, from* Reading the Time, *tells of an event Dobbs was not there to see, yet the vivid details that support his argument show all too clearly what that tragedy must have been like.*

*Editor's title.

1 This is the story I was told in 1963 by Emiko Okamoto, a young Japanese woman who had come to live in Toronto. She spoke through an interpreter, since at that time she knew no English. It is Emiko's story, although I have had to complete it from other sources.

2 But why am I telling it? Everyone knows how terrible this story is. Everyone knows the truth of what von Clausewitz said: "Force to meet force arms itself with the inventions of art and science." First the bow-and-arrow, then Greek fire, gunpowder, poison-gas—and so on up the lethal scale. These things, we're told, should be considered calmly. No sweat—we should think about the unthinkable, or so Herman Kahn suggests, dispassionately. And he writes: "We do not expect illustrations in a book of surgery to be captioned 'Good health is preferable to this kind of cancer.' Excessive comments such as 'And now there is a lot of blood' or 'This particular cut really hurts' are out of place.... To dwell on such things is morbid." Perhaps the answer to Herman Kahn is that if surgeons hadn't dwelt on those things we wouldn't now have anaesthetics, or artery forceps either, for that matter.

3 To think about thermonuclear war in the abstract is obscene. To think about any kind of warfare with less than the whole of our mind and imagination is obscene. This is the worst treason.

4 Before that morning in 1945 only a few conventional bombs, none of which did any great damage, had fallen on the city. Fleets of U.S. bombers had, however, devastated many cities round about, and Hiroshima had begun a program of evacuation which had reduced its population from 380,000 to some 245,000. Among the evacuees were Emiko and her family.

5 "We were moved out to Otake, a town about an hour's train-ride out of the city," Emiko told me. She had been a fifteen-year-old student in 1945. Fragile and vivacious, versed in the gentle traditions of the tea ceremony and flower arrangement, Emiko still had an air of the frail school-child when I talked with her. Every day, she and her sister Hideko used to commute into Hiroshima to school. Hideko was thirteen. Their father was an antique-dealer and he owned a house in the city, although it was empty now. Tetsuro, Emiko's thirteen-year-old brother, was at the Manchurian front with the Imperial

Army. Her mother was kept busy looking after the children, for her youngest daughter Eiko was sick with heart trouble, and rations were scarce. All of them were undernourished.

The night of August 5, 1945, little Eiko was dangerously ill. She was not expected to live. Everybody took turns watching by her bed, soothing her by massaging her arms and legs. Emiko retired at 8:30 (most Japanese people go to bed early) and at midnight was roused to take her turn with the sick girl. At 2 a.m. she went back to sleep. 6

While Emiko slept, the *Enola Gay*, a U.S. B-29 carrying the world's first operational atom bomb, was already in the air. She had taken off from the Pacific island of Iwo Jima at 1:45 a.m., and now Captain William Parsons, U.S.N. ordnance expert, was busy in her bomb-hold with the final assembly of Little Boy. Little Boy looked much like an outsize T.N.T. block-buster but the crew knew there was something different about him. Only Parsons and the pilot, Colonel Paul Tibbets, knew exactly in what manner Little Boy was different. Course was set for Hiroshima. 7

Emiko slept. 8

On board the *Enola Gay* co-pilot Captain Robert Lewis was writing up his personal log. "After leaving Iwo," he recorded, "we began to pick up some low stratus and before very long we were flying on top of an under-cast. Outside of a thin, high cirrus and the low stuff, it's a very beautiful day." 9

Emiko and Hideko were up at six in the morning. They dressed in the uniform of their women's college—white blouse, quilted hat, and black skirt—breakfasted and packed their aluminum lunch-boxes with white rice and eggs. These they stuffed into their shoulder bags as they hurried for the seven-o'clock train to Hiroshima. Today there would be no classes. Along with many women's groups, high school students, and others, the sisters were going to work on demolition. The city had begun a project of clearance to make fire-breaks in its downtown huddle of wood and paper buildings. 10

It was a lovely morning. 11

While the two young girls were at breakfast, Captain Lewis, over the Pacific, had made an entry in his log. "We are loaded. The bomb is now alive, and it's a funny feeling knowing it's right in back of you. Knock wood!" 12

13 In the train Hideko suddenly said she was hungry. She wanted to eat her lunch. Emiko dissuaded her: she'd be much hungrier later on. The two sisters argued, but Hideko at last agreed to keep her lunch till later. They decided to meet at the main station that afternoon and catch the five-o'clock train home. By now they had arrived at the first of Hiroshima's three stations. This was where Hideko got off, for she was to work in a different area from her sister. "Sayonara!" she called. "Goodbye." Emiko never saw her again.

14 There had been an air-raid at 7 a.m., but before Emiko arrived at Hiroshima's main station, two stops farther on, the sirens had sounded the all-clear. Just after eight, Emiko stepped off the train, walked through the station, and waited in the morning sunshine for her streetcar.

15 At about the same moment Lewis was writing in his log. "There'll be a short intermission while we bomb our target."

16 It was hot in the sun. Emiko saw a class-mate and greeted her. Together they moved back into the shade of a high concrete wall to chat. Emiko looked up at the sky and saw, far up in the cloudless blue, a single B-29.

17 It was exactly 8:10 a.m. The other people waiting for the streetcar saw it too and began to discuss it anxiously. Emiko felt scared. She felt that at all costs she must go on talking to her friend. Just as she was thinking this, there was a tremendous greenish-white flash in the sky. It was far brighter than the sun. Emiko afterwards remembered vaguely that there was a roaring or a rushing sound as well, but she was not sure, for just at that moment she lost consciousness.

18 "About 15 seconds after the flash," noted Lewis, 30,000 feet high and several miles away, "there were two very distinct slaps on the ship from the blast and the shock wave. That was all the physical effect we felt. We turned the ship so that we could observe the results."

19 When Emiko came to, she was lying on her face about forty feet away from where she had been standing. She was not aware of any pain. Her first thought was: "I'm alive!" She lifted her head slowly and looked about her. It was growing dark. The air was seething with dust and black smoke. There was a smell of burning. Emiko felt something trickle into her eyes, tasted it in her mouth. Gingerly she put a hand to her head, then looked at it. She saw with a shock that it was covered with blood.

20 She did not give a thought to Hideko. It did not occur to her that her sister who was in another part of the city could possibly have been in danger. Like most of the survivors, Emiko assumed she had been close to a direct hit by a conventional bomb. She thought it had fallen on the post-office next to the station. With a hurt child's panic, Emiko, streaming with blood from gashes in her scalp, ran blindly in search of her mother and father.

21 The people standing in front of the station had been burned to death instantly (a shadow had saved Emiko from the flash). The people inside the station had been crushed by falling masonry. Emiko heard their faint cries, saw hands scrabbling weakly from under the collapsed platform. All around her the maimed survivors were running and stumbling away from the roaring furnace that had been a city. She ran with them toward the mountains that ring the landward side of Hiroshima.

22 From the *Enola Gay*, the strangers from North America looked down at their handiwork. "There, in front of our eyes," wrote Lewis, "was without a doubt the greatest explosion man had ever witnessed. The city was nine-tenths covered with smoke of a boiling nature, which seemed to indicate buildings blowing up, and a large white cloud which in less than three minutes reached 30,000 feet, then went to at least 50,000 feet."

23 Far below, on the edge of this cauldron of smoke, at a distance of some 2,500 yards from the blast's epicentre, Emiko ran with the rest of the living. Some who could not run limped or dragged themselves along. Others were carried. Many, hideously burned, were screaming with pain; when they tripped they lay where they had fallen. There was a man whose face had been ripped open from mouth to ear, another whose forehead was a gaping wound. A young soldier was running with a foot-long splinter of bamboo protruding from one eye. But these, like Emiko, were the lightly wounded.

24 Some of the burned people had been literally roasted. Skin hung from their flesh like sodden tissue paper. They did not bleed but plasma dripped from their seared limbs.

25 The *Enola Gay*, mission completed, was returning to base. Lewis sought words to express his feelings, the feelings of all the crew. "I might say," he wrote, "I might say 'My God! What have we done?'"

26 Emiko ran. When she had reached the safety of the mountain she remembered that she still had her shoulder bag. There was a small first-aid kit in it and she applied ointment to her wounds and to a small cut in her left hand. She bandaged her head.

27 Emiko looked back at the city. It was a lake of fire. All around her the burned fugitives cried out in pain. Some were scorched on one side only. Others, naked and flayed, were burned all over. They were too many to help and most of them were dying. Emiko followed the walking wounded along a back road, still delirious, expecting suddenly to meet her father and mother.

28 The thousands dying by the roadside called feebly for help or water. Some of the more lightly injured were already walking in the other direction, back towards the flames. Others, with hardly any visible wounds, stopped, turned ashy pale, and died within minutes. No one knew then that they were victims of radiation.

29 Emiko reached the suburb of Nakayama.

30 Far off in the *Enola Gay,* Lewis, who had seen none of this, had been writing, "If I live a hundred years, I'll never get those few minutes out of my mind. Looking at Captain Parsons, why he is as confounded as the rest, and he is supposed to have known everything and expected this to happen...."

31 At Nakayama, Emiko stood in line at a depot where riceballs were being distributed. Though it distressed her that the badly maimed could hardly feed themselves, the child found she was hungry. It was about 6 p.m. now. A little farther on, at Gion, a farmer called her by name. She did not recognize him, but it seemed he came monthly to her home to collect manure. The farmer took Emiko by the hand, led her to his own house, where his wife bathed her and fed her a meal of white rice. Then the child continued on her way. She passed another town where there were hundreds of injured. The dead were being hauled away in trucks. Among the injured a woman of about forty-five was waving frantically and muttering to herself. Emiko brought this woman a little water in a pumpkin leaf. She felt guilty about it; the schoolgirls had been warned not to give water to the seriously wounded. Emiko comforted herself with the thought that the woman would die soon anyway.

At Koi, she found standing-room in a train. It was heading for 32 Otake with a full load of wounded. Many were put off at Ono, where there was a hospital; and two hours later the train rolled into Otake station. It was around 10 p.m.

A great crowd had gathered to look for their relations. It was a 33 nightmare, Emiko remembered years afterwards; people were calling their dear kinfolk by name, searching frantically. It was necessary to call them by name, since most were so disfigured as to be unrecognizable. Doctors in the town council offices stitched Emiko's head-wounds. The place was crowded with casualties lying on the floor. Many died as Emiko watched.

The town council authorities made a strange announcement. They 34 said a new and mysterious kind of bomb had fallen in Hiroshima. People were advised to stay away from the ruins.

Home at midnight, Emiko found her parents so happy to see her 35 that they could not even cry. They could only give thanks that she was safe. Then they asked, "Where is your sister?"

For ten long days, while Emiko walked daily one and a half miles 36 to have her wounds dressed with fresh gauze, her father searched the rubble of Hiroshima for his lost child. He could not have hoped to find her alive. All, as far as the eye could see, was a desolation of charred ashes and wreckage, relieved only by a few jagged ruins and by the seven estuarial rivers that flowed through the waste delta. The banks of these rivers were covered with the dead and in the rising tidal waters floated thousands of corpses. On one broad street in the Hakushima district the crowds who had been thronging there were all naked and scorched cadavers. Of thousands of others there was no trace at all. A fire several times hotter than the surface of the sun had turned them instantly to vapour.

On August 11 came the news that Nagasaki had suffered the same 37 fate as Hiroshima; it was whispered that Japan had attacked the United States mainland with similar mysterious weapons. With the lavish circumstantiality of rumour, it was said that two out of a fleet of six-engined trans-Pacific bombers had failed to return. But on August 15, speaking for the first time over the radio to his people, the Emperor Hirohito announced his country's surrender. Emiko heard him. No more bombs! she thought. No more fear! The family did not learn till June the following year that this very day young Tetsuro had been killed in action in Manchuria.

38 Emiko's wounds healed slowly. In mid-September they had closed with a thin layer of pinkish skin. There had been a shortage of antiseptics and Emiko was happy to be getting well. Her satisfaction was short-lived. Mysteriously she came down with diarrhoea and high fever. The fever continued for a month. Then one day she started to bleed from the gums, her mouth and throat become acutely inflamed, and her hair started to fall out. Through her delirium the child heard the doctors whisper by her pillow that she could not live. By now the doctors must have known that ionizing radiation caused such destruction of the blood's white cells that victims were left with little or no resistance against infection.

39 Yet Emiko recovered.

40 The wound on her hand, however, was particularly troublesome and did not heal for a long time.

41 As she got better, Emiko began to acquire some notion of the fearful scale of the disaster. Few of her friends and acquaintances were still alive. But no one knew precisely how many had died in Hiroshima. To this day the claims of various agencies conflict.

42 According to General Douglas MacArthur's headquarters, there were 78,150 dead and 13,083 missing. The United States Atomic Bomb Casualty Commission claims there were 79,000 dead. Both sets of figures are probably far too low. There's reason to believe that at the time of the surrender Japanese authorities lied about the number of survivors, exaggerating it to get extra medical supplies. The Japanese welfare ministry's figures of 260,000 dead and 163,263 missing may well be too high. But the very order of such discrepancies speaks volumes about the scale of the catastrophe. The dead were literally uncountable.

43 This appalling toll of human life had been exacted from a city that had been prepared for air attack in a state of full wartime readiness. All civil-defence services had been overwhelmed from the first moment and it was many hours before any sort of organized rescue and relief could be put into effect.

44 It's true that single raids using so-called conventional weapons on other cities such as Tokyo and Dresden inflicted far greater casualties. And that it could not matter much to a victim whether he was burnt alive by a fire-storm caused by phosphorus, or by napalm or by nuclear fission. Yet in the whole of human history so savage a massacre had never before been inflicted with a single blow. And modern thermonuclear weapons are upwards of 1,000 times more powerful and deadly than the Hiroshima bomb.

45 The white scar I saw on Emiko's small, fine-boned hand was a tiny metaphor, a faint but eloquent memento.

EXPLORATIONS:

Kildare Dobbs, *Reading the Time*
John Hershey, *Hiroshima*
Ernie Regehr and Simon Rosenblum, eds., *The Road to Peace*
John Whittier Treat, *Writing Ground Zero: Japanese Literature and the Atomic Bomb*
Paul W. Tibbets, *The Tibbets Story*
http://www.acepilots.com/usaaf_tibbets.html
http://www.csi.ad.jp/ABOMB
http://www.dannen.com/decision
http://www.lclark.edu/~history/HIROSHIMA
http://www.doug-long.com
http://www.dannen.com/hiroshima_links.html

STRUCTURE:

1. Identify Dobbs' THESIS STATEMENT, the principle from which his argument is *deduced.* In what very direct way does the rest of this selection teach us to apply that principle?
2. "The Scar" is mostly a *narrative,* in fact two parallel narratives. How do the stories of Emiko and of Captain Lewis complement each other? How does each focus differently on nuclear war?

3. Dobbs' argument is a short essay enclosing a long narrative. Where does each part join the next? And what is the strategy behind this plan?

STYLE:

1. In his log Captain Lewis writes "it's a very beautiful day" (par. 9), and in paragraph 11 Dobbs adds "It was a lovely morning." What effect do these pleasant words have in the context of the situation? What literary device underlies their power?
2. Captain Lewis writes in his log, "There'll be a short intermission while we bomb our target" (par. 15). Do these words seem peculiar? If so, why?
3. In referring to the first operational nuclear bomb as "Little Boy" (par. 7), what does Dobbs add to the force of his narrative?
4. Paragraphs 23, 24, 27 and 36 are filled with gruesome details that show the effects of "Little Boy." Does this help Dobbs' argument? Do these details spur the reader to oppose nuclear weapons? Or, in their dreadfulness, do they lead the reader to drop the subject and think of other things?
5. What qualifies the SYMBOL of Emiko's scar to close the essay?

ARGUMENTATION AND PERSUASION:

1. Dobbs' argument is *deductive*, based on his opening premise that "To think about thermonuclear war in the abstract is obscene. To think about any kind of warfare with less than the whole of our mind and imagination is obscene. This is the worst treason" (par. 3). Identify five passages in which he shuns abstraction to dwell on the CONCRETE and personal experience of nuclear war. Does he apply his own thesis by using "the whole of [his] mind and imagination"?
2. Point out three passages where Dobbs shows Captain Lewis' abstract view of nuclear war to be "obscene." Does the *contrast* between Lewis' bird's-eye view and Emiko's ground-level view develop Dobbs' premise?

3. Does Dobbs make his point mostly through *argumentation* or *persuasion*? To what extent does he *argue* through objective logic, fact and example? To what extent does he *persuade* through IRONY, loaded words, fright or other appeals to emotion?
4. In the closing, why does Dobbs shift from specific examples to generalizations and statistics (pars. 42–44)?

IDEAS FOR DISCUSSION AND WRITING:

1. Albert Einstein, discoverer of the mathematics behind the atomic bomb, said that if he had foreseen the results of his work, he would have chosen to be a shoemaker. Do you hold Einstein and the scientists who worked on "Little Boy" responsible for the carnage in Hiroshima? Or should the scientist pursue abstract truth and leave the application to others?
2. All the rest of his life, Paul Tibbets, who had piloted the *Enola Gay* on her deadly mission, believed he had done the right thing: dropping the atomic bomb on Japan to end the war and save the lives of American soldiers. Yet in 2007 when he died at age 92, he requested that his ashes be scattered on the Atlantic Ocean, so there would be no gravesite that would give protestors a place to demonstrate. How do you explain the PARADOX in his thinking?
3. The Cold War and the arms race between East and West are said to be over. Can we stop dreading nuclear weapons and war now? How dangerous is the new post-9/11 terrorism compared to the old arms race? Give *examples.*
4. In her book *A Matter of Survival: Canada in the 21st Century,* the Canadian economist Diane Francis states, "Already a global government has formed through the auspices of the United Nations and the G-7 process." Do you believe her? Would a true global government prevent war? To what extent could you see Canada functioning as the "police" of such a global government, through its military or peacekeeping missions?
5. **PROCESS IN WRITING:** *Politicians often state that one letter received from a citizen is worth a thousand votes. Decide whether you think Canada should spend more or less on its military. Now write to the Minister of*

Defence, arguing your point deductively. *Apply your premise to a specific example or examples, such as tanks, fighter planes, submarines, destroyers, military bases, the pay rate of personnel, etc. As you look over your "discovery draft," see whether you have specialized in either* argumentation *or* persuasion. *If your treatment seems too extreme, modify it in your second draft with a dose of the other approach, to produce a combined treatment like that of Dobbs. In your final draft edit for conciseness (the best letters to politicians are short). Finally, send your e-mail or letter (you need no stamp to mail a letter to any member of Parliament).*

Note: See also the Topics for Writing on the Online Learning Centre at www.mcgrawhill.ca/olc/conrad.

JOY KOGAWA

Grinning and Happy*

*With three published books of poetry to her credit—*The Splintered Moon *(1967),* A Choice of Dreams *(1974) and* Jericho Road *(1977)—Joy Kogawa had become a respected minor poet. But in 1981 she caused a sensation with her first novel.* Obasan *represented a new step for Kogawa as a writer and as a person: in it she explored her own past and one of the most serious injustices of Canadian history. Born in Vancouver in 1935, Kogawa was a child during the Second World War when the federal government classified Japanese-Canadians as "enemy aliens." Her parents' house in Vancouver was seized, and the family was moved first to a relocation camp in Slocan, B.C., then to the sugar-beet fields of southern Alberta, which are the setting of our selection from the novel. Our narrator is modelled after Kogawa herself, Stephen is the narrator's brother, Obasan is the narrator's silent and suffering aunt and "Aunt Emily" is modelled after Muriel Kitagawa, a Japanese-Canadian activist whose letters Kogawa studied in the National Archives in Ottawa. These same characters returned in* Naomi's Road *(1986), a children's adaptation of* Obasan*, then in Kogawa's 1992 sequel for adults* Itsuka*, about the struggle of Japanese-Canadians to gain redress for the wrongs described in* Obasan*. Her third novel,* The Rain Ascends *(1995), looked to new subject matter, the unmasking of a respected Protestant minister as a sexual abuser of children. Yet its themes echo those of* Obasan *and* Itsuka*, as the sins of the fathers are visited upon new generations. Then in 2000 appeared another book of poems,* A Song of Lilith*, and in 2003 her selected poems,* A Garden of Anchors*. Though her recent work is well regarded, it is still* Obasan *that places Kogawa among our major Canadian writers.*

*Editor's title.

1 There is a folder in Aunt Emily's package containing only one newspaper clipping and an index card with the words "Facts about evacuees in Alberta." The newspaper clipping has a photograph of one family, all smiles, standing around a pile of beets. The caption reads: "Grinning and Happy."

> 2 **Find Jap Evacuees Best Beet Workers**
> **Lethbridge, Alberta, Jan. 22.**
>
> 3 Japanese evacuees from British Columbia supplied the labour for 65% of Alberta's sugar beet acreage last year, Phil Baker, of Lethbridge, president of the Alberta Sugar Beet Growers Association, stated today.
>
> 4 "They played an important part in producing our all-time record crop of 363,000 tons of beets in 1945," he added.
>
> 5 Mr. Baker explained Japanese evacuees worked 19,500 acres of beets and German prisoners of war worked 5,000 acres. The labour for the remaining 5,500 acres of Alberta's 30,000 acres of sugar beets was provided by farmers and their families. Some of the heaviest beet yields last year came from farms employing Japanese evacuees.
>
> 6 Generally speaking, Japanese evacuees have developed into most efficient beet workers, many of them being better than the transient workers who cared for beets in southern Alberta before Pearl Harbor....

7 Facts about evacuees in Alberta? The fact is I never got used to it and I cannot, I cannot bear the memory. There are some nightmares from which there is no waking, only deeper and deeper sleep.

8 There is a word for it. Hardship. The hardship is so pervasive, so inescapable, so thorough it's a noose around my chest and I cannot move any more. All the oil in my joints has drained out and I have been invaded by dust and grit from the fields and mud is in my

bone marrow. I can't move any more. My fingernails are black from scratching the scorching day and there is no escape.

Aunt Emily, are you a surgeon cutting at my scalp with your fold- 9
ers and your filing cards and your insistence on knowing all? The memory drains down the sides of my face, but it isn't enough, is it? It's your hands in my abdomen, pulling the growth from the lining of my walls, but bring back the anaesthetist turn on the ether clamp down the gas mask bring on the chloroform when will this operation be over Aunt Em?

Is it so bad? 10

Yes. 11

Do I really mind? 12

Yes, I mind. I mind everything. Even the flies. The flies and flies 13
and flies from the cows in the barn and the manure pile—all the black flies that curtain the windows, and Obasan with a wad of toilet paper, spish, then with her bare hands as well, grabbing them and their shocking white eggs and the mosquitoes mixed there with the other insect corpses around the base of the gas lamp.

It's the chicken coop "house" we live in that I mind. The uninsu- 14
lated unbelievable thin-as-a-cotton-dress hovel never before inhabited in winter by human beings. In summer it's a heat trap, an incubator, a dry sauna from which there is no relief. In winter the icicles drip down the inside of the windows and the ice is thicker than bricks at the ledge. The only place that is warm is by the coal stove where we rotate like chickens on a spit and the feet are so cold they stop registering. We eat cloves of roasted garlic on winter nights to warm up.

It's the bedbugs and my having to sleep on the table to escape the
nightly attack, and the welts over our bodies. And all the swamp bugs 15
and the dust. It's Obasan uselessly packing all the cracks with rags. And the muddy water from the irrigation ditch which we strain and settle and boil, and the tiny carcasses of water creatures at the bottom of the cup. It's walking in winter to the reservoir and keeping the hole open with the axe and dragging up the water in pails and lugging it back and sometimes the water spills down your boots and your feet are red and itchy for days. And it's everybody taking a bath in the round galvanized tub, then Obasan washing clothes in the

water after and standing outside hanging the clothes in the freezing weather where everything instantly stiffens on the line.

16 Or it's standing in the beet field under the maddening sun, standing with my black head a sun-trap even though it's covered, and lying down in the ditch, faint, and the nausea in waves and the cold sweat, and getting up and tackling the next row. The whole field is an oven and there's not a tree within walking distance. We are tiny as insects crawling along the grill and there is no protection anywhere. The eyes are lidded against the dust and the air cracks the skin, the lips crack, Stephen's flutes crack and there is no energy to sing any more anyway.

17 It's standing in the field and staring out at the heat waves that waver and shimmer like see-through curtains over the brown clods and over the tiny distant bodies of Stephen and Uncle and Obasan miles away across the field day after day and not even wondering how this has come about.

18 There she is, Obasan, wearing Uncle's shirt over a pair of dark baggy trousers, her head covered by a straw hat that is held on by a white cloth tied under her chin. She is moving like a tiny earth cloud over the hard clay clods. Her hoe moves rhythmically up down up down, tiny as a toothpick. And over there, Uncle pauses to straighten his back, his hands on his hips. And Stephen farther behind, so tiny I can barely see him.

19 It's hard, Aunt Emily, with my hoe, the blade getting dull and mud-caked as I slash out the Canada thistle, dandelions, crab grass, and other nameless non-beet plants, then on my knees, pulling out the extra beets from the cluster, leaving just one to mature, then three hand spans to the next plant, whack whack, and down on my knees again, pull, flick flick, and on to the end of the long long row and the next and the next and it will never be done thinning and weeding and weeding and weeding. It's so hard and so hot that my tear glands burn out.

20 And then it's cold. The lumps of clay mud stick on my gumboots and weight my legs and the skin under the boots beneath the knees at the level of the calves grows red and hard and itchy from the flap flap of the boots and the fine hairs on my legs grow coarse there and ugly.

21 I mind growing ugly.

I mind the harvest time and the hands and the wrists bound in rags to keep the wrists from breaking open. I lift the heavy mud-clotted beets out of the ground with the hook like an eagle's beak, thick and heavy as a nail attached to the top of the sugar-beet knife. Thwack. Into the beet and yank from the shoulder till it's out of the ground dragging the surrounding mud with it. Then crack two beets together till most of the mud drops off and splat, the knife slices into the beet scalp and the green top is tossed into one pile, the beet heaved onto another, one more one more one more down the icy line. I cannot tell about this time, Aunt Emily. The body will not tell. 22

We are surrounded by a horizon of denim-blue sky with clouds clear as spilled milk that turn pink at sunset. Pink I hear is the colour of llama's milk. I wouldn't know. The clouds are the shape of our new prison walls—untouchable, impersonal, random. 23

There are no other people in the entire world. We work together all day. At night we eat and sleep. We hardly talk anymore. The boxes we brought from Slocan are not unpacked. The King George/Queen Elizabeth mugs stay muffled in the *Vancouver Daily Province.* The camera phone does not sing. Obasan wraps layers of cloth around her feet and her torn sweater hangs unmended over her sagging dress. 24

Down the miles we are obedient as machines in this odd ballet without accompaniment of flute or song. 25

"Grinning and happy" and all smiles standing around a pile of beets? That is one telling. It's not how it was. 26

EXPLORATIONS:

Joy Kogawa,
Obasan
Itsuka

Barry Broadfoot, *Years of Sorrow, Years of Shame: The Story of Japanese Canadians in World War II*

Ken Adachi, *The Enemy That Never Was: A History of the Japanese Canadians.*

Ann Sunahara, *The Politics of Racism: The Uprooting of Japanese Canadians During the Second World War*

Joy Kogawa (video, 1998, 45 min., Sleeping Giant Productions)
http://voices.cla.umn.edu/vg/Bios/entries/kogawa_joy_nakayama.html
http://www.brocku.ca/canadianwomenpoets/Kogawa.htm
http://quarles.unbc.ca/kbeeler_html/research/kog1.html
http://www.najc.ca
http://www.lib.washington.edu/subject/Canada/internment/intro.html

STRUCTURE:

1. Why does Kogawa "frame" her argument by citing the newspaper article in both her opening and closing?
2. How does the device of *contrast* help organize this selection?
3. What percentage of *examples* has Kogawa reached in the content of this selection? Is it enough? Do you use enough?
4. How important is *description* to the success of this passage? Give examples.
5. Most THESIS STATEMENTS are placed early in an argument. Why is Kogawa's put in the very last line?

STYLE:

1. Until *Obasan*, Kogawa was best known as a poet. What poetical qualities do you see in this sample of her PROSE?
2. To what extent does Kogawa communicate by SENSE IMAGES? Cite one case each of appeals to sight, hearing, touch, taste and smell.
3. The poet Kogawa fills her prose with FIGURES OF SPEECH. Point out three good SIMILES and three good METAPHORS.
4. In paragraphs 14 through 17, how many times does the contraction "it's" appear at or near the beginning of a sentence? Is the *repetition* accidental or deliberate? What is its effect?
5. How many words long is the first sentence of paragraph 19? How many times does it use the word "and"? Is this run-on sentence accidental or deliberate? What is its effect?

ARGUMENTATION AND PERSUASION:

1. As a member of a persecuted minority, Kogawa's narrator rejects a *deductive* stance; she shuns the official "telling" of the newspaper article, and instead produces her own eyewitness "telling." Point out at least ten pieces of evidence that lead *inductively* to her own conclusion that the newspaper's version of the truth is "not how it was."
2. Does Kogawa rely more on *argumentation* or on *persuasion*? To what extent does she communicate through reason, and to what extent through emotion?
3. Analyze Kogawa's tools of *persuasion*: point out at least five loaded words, five SENSE IMAGES and five FIGURES OF SPEECH that build emotion. Identify one case of deliberate repetition, and one of extreme sentence length, both of which build emotion. Does all this persuasion put you on guard? Or does it convince you?

IDEAS FOR DISCUSSION AND WRITING:

1. How often are you, like Kogawa's narrator, caught between two or more views of the truth? Cite a recent case. Did you act *deductively*, accepting a view already held by yourself or others, or did you move *inductively* to a new conclusion?
2. The narrator and her family are Canadian citizens of Japanese descent, removed by our federal government from the coast of British Columbia during the Second World War for fear they would betray Canada to enemy Japan. (Not a single case of such betrayal was ever found.) Many families were separated and their property taken. Attack or defend these official actions against citizens like Kogawa's fictional family. Have such acts occurred in Canada before? Since? Can you imagine them happening in future to any group you belong to?
3. During the war the Canadian government confiscated an island off British Columbia, compensating its Japanese-Canadian owner with $2000. Two generations later his granddaughter, a university student, estimated the worth of this property at $200 million. In 1988 the Canadian government officially apologized to

the Japanese-Canadians and offered each survivor of the epoch $21,000. Has the wrong been righted? Attack or defend our government's actions.

4. You are the student in question 3 above. Write to the prime minister, arguing either *deductively* or *inductively* that the island be restored to the heirs of its original owner. *Or* you are the present owner. Write to the prime minister, arguing either *deductively* or *inductively* that your island should not be seized and given to descendants of the man who once owned it.
5. **PROCESS IN WRITING:** *Name a group that you believe has been badly treated by Canadian society (for example, Native people, immigrants, the disabled, the elderly, farmers, AIDS victims, single parents, etc.). Take notes, then write an* inductive argument *giving the evidence that led to your belief. In a further draft, fine-tune the balance of* argumentation and persuasion. *Now share this version with a small group of classmates, and apply their best advice. Edit. Finally, read your good version aloud to the whole class, and be ready to defend your view.*

Note: See also the Topics for Writing on the Online Learning Centre at www.mcgrawhill.ca/olc/conrad.

RITA SCHINDLER

Thanks for Not Killing My Son

All we know about Rita Schindler is what she herself says in her letter. It was a student who noticed "Thanks for Not Killing My Son" in the "Have Your Say" feature of the December 30, 1990 Toronto Star. *He tore it out and brought it to his writing teacher, exclaiming what a fine argument it was. The teacher agreed. By the time the editor of this book tried to reach Ms. Schindler, though, the* Star *had discarded her address. None of the many Schindlers listed in the Toronto phone book knew her, and the hospital mentioned in her letter would not divulge information. As this new edition was being put together we tried again to find her, but could not. Finally, Access Canada, the Canadian Copyright Licensing Agency, gave permission to reprint the letter, as it can do in such cases. We sincerely believe that Ms. Schindler would want her eloquent and highly principled argument made available to more persons of her son's generation. If you happen to know her, please show her this book and ask her to contact the publisher, who will direct her to the agency office where her author's fee is waiting.*

1 I hope you will print my letter of gratitude to the strangers who have affected our lives.

2 Sometime between 1:30 p.m., Dec. 8, and 1 a.m., Dec. 9, a young man was viciously attacked—beaten and kicked unconscious for no apparent reason other than walking by you on a public sidewalk.

3 He was left lying in a pool of blood from an open head wound—in the Victoria Park-Terraview area. He was found around 1 a.m. and taken to Scarborough General Hospital where ironically his mother spent 48 hours in labor before giving him birth, 23 years earlier.

His mother is angry of course, but thankful for the following rea- 4
sons.

First of all—his eye socket was shattered and hemorrhaging but his 5
eyesight will not be affected. Thank you.

His ear canal was lacerated internally from a tremendous blow to the 6
side of his head. The cut could not be stitched and the bleeding was difficult to stop. But his eardrum seems to be undamaged—thank you.

He required numerous stitches to his forehead, temple and face but 7
your boots didn't knock one tooth out—thank you. His head was swollen almost twice its size—but Mom knew that his brain was intact—for he held her hand for six hours as he lay on a gurney, by the nurses station, I.V. in his arm—his head covered and crusted with dried blood—waiting for x-ray results and the surgeon to stitch him up.

So, thank you for this eyesight, his hearing and his hands which 8
you could have easily crushed.

His hands—human hands—the most intricately beautiful and 9
complex instruments of incredible mechanism—the result of billions of years of evolution—and you people used yours to beat another human being. Five guys and two girls to beat one person. Who do I thank? Did you know he was a talented young musician with a budding career—and that playing his keyboards and piano mean more to him than my words can say.

And when his friends were talking about revenge, I heard him say, 10
"No, I don't want someone else's mother to go through what mine has." That's who you were kicking in the head. And so—I thank you for not causing the most horrible and devastating thing that can happen to any parent—that is—the untimely tragic loss of a child—at any age.

You could have kicked him to death but you only left him to die, 11
thank you. A person found him and called for help.

I am his mother—and I have been given a second chance—thanks 12
to you.

I hope that someday you'll have children and love them as much as 13
I love mine—but I wouldn't wish on your child what you did to mine.

Rita Schindler 14
Scarborough 15

EXPLORATIONS:

William Golding, *Lord of the Flies*
Anthony Burgess, *A Clockwork Orange*
Dan Korem, *Suburban Gangs: The Affluent Rebels*
Frederick Mathews, *Youth Gangs on Youth Gangs*
www.bullying.org
www.cyberbullying.ca
http://www.cln.org/themes/youth_violence.html
http://www.wsd1.org/PC_LMS/pf/youthgangs.htm
http://www.ps-sp.gc.ca/prg/cp/bldngevd/2007-yg-2-en.asp
http://www.cbc.ca/news/background/bullying
http://www.cbc.ca/news/background/virk
http://en.wikipedia.org/wiki/Reena_Virk

STRUCTURE:

1. Schindler's argument is cast as a letter. For what *audience* is it meant? The youths who attacked her son? All the readers of the *Toronto Star*? How well does her "letter" work as an essay?
2. Schindler organizes her letter by examining in turn each injury inflicted on her son. Point out each. What proportion of the letter's content is given to these *examples*? Could the point have been made without them?
3. After all her ironic "thanking," Schindler ends more literally: "I wouldn't wish on your child what you did to mine." Is her closing weak because it drops the IRONY, or strong because it caps the point?

STYLE:

1. Six of Schindler's paragraphs have only one sentence. Give reasons. Is this style effective?
2. How CONCISE is this selection? Try to find a passage of deadwood that could have been cut.

3. How FORMAL or INFORMAL is Schindler's TONE? Give examples. Does the tone fit the content? Why or why not?

ARGUMENTATION AND PERSUASION:

1. "You could have kicked him to death but you only left him to die, thank you," writes the victim's mother in paragraph 11. Her letter of "thanks" is *persuasion* as strong as any in this book. Explain the IRONY of Schindler's "thanking" her son's attackers.
2. Find and explain at least ten more IRONIES in this selection.
3. The author might have called her son's attackers "thugs," "goons" or worse. Would this openly *persuasive* mode be more effective than the "thanks" she gives? Defend your answer with reasons.
4. In addition to *irony*, the introduction to this chapter lists *repetition*, *fright* and *climax* as techniques of persuasion. How does Schindler use each? Respond with examples.
5. Does Schindler make her point *deductively* (through an innate rejection of violence) or *inductively* (through the many examples she cites, leading to her point)? Can an argument go both ways at once? Would this be a failure of logic?

IDEAS FOR DISCUSSION AND WRITING:

1. Does Schindler attempt only to heap shame on her son's attackers, or do you also detect, for example in the closing, a desire for reconciliation?
2. When his friends desired revenge, the son said, "No, I don't want someone else's mother to go through what mine has" (par. 10). What would *you* have said? Defend your answer with reasons.
3. How much do techniques of nonviolent resisters such as Mahatma Gandhi and Martin Luther King have in common with the responses of Rita Schindler and her son? Is their way ultimately weaker or stronger than the way of those who defend themselves through violence? Give examples.
4. Think of a time when you witnessed bullying at school. Tell the story to the class. Was the incident resolved, and if so, how?

5. In 1997 Reena Virk, a 14-year-old student in Saanich, Vancouver Island, was brutally beaten by classmates, mostly girls, and left dead under a bridge. Review this event in the websites given in "Explorations," then give as many reasons as you can why this tragedy occurred. Now give as many ways as you can how this tragedy could have been avoided.
6. Is there violent crime at your school or campus? Give examples. Defend or attack the "zero tolerance" policy of some school boards that permanently expel students who commit violent offences. Are there other solutions?
7. Are public forums such as the letters to the editor column or blogs or Internet chatrooms good vehicles for promoting our own ideas? Do others actually read and heed what we say?
8. **PROCESS IN WRITING:** *Read the crime news in your newspaper or hear it on radio or TV. Choose one violent act that provokes your anger or concern. Consider how, like Rita Schindler, you can respond to it through* IRONY *to* persuade *your audience to take your side. Make notes, look them over, then write a rapid first draft of a letter to the perpetrator, or to the public, or to both. The next day look it over. Will it startle and persuade the* AUDIENCE *by meaning the opposite of what it says? (Remember Schindler's "thanking" the attackers, or in Chapter 8 Stephen Leacock's "advice" on how to live to be 200.) Is the ironic* TONE *consistent? Is the letter concise, like Schindler's? If not, revise. Finally, check the spelling and grammar. When you have produced your good draft, send it as a letter to the editor of the newspaper you read. Or post it with an appropriate discussion group on the Internet. Check either for responses. Collect them, then show them, with the original letter, to the class.*

Note: See also the Topics for Writing on the Online Learning Centre at www.mcgrawhill.ca/olc/conrad.

ROBERT CHRISTY

Life with Cerebral Palsy

In the essay that follows, from the February 5, 2001 Maclean's, *Robert ("Bob") Christy tells much of his life story. Here are a few more facts: In 1940 he was born to parents who, though he had cerebral palsy and stuttered, taught him to believe he was not disabled. He learned the lesson well, emerging as a lifelong optimist whose motto is "To Look Beyond What You See." In 1963 Christy earned a B.A. in commerce, economics and math from Queen's, and in 1965 an M.B.A. from the University of Toronto. Then during a successful 30-year career in the federal public service in Ottawa and Regina, he was a social policy researcher, analyst, advisor and writer. Now retired and a grandfather, Christy writes on issues of physical disability, while living with his wife Gail, who also has cerebral palsy and is an ordained minister in the United Church of Canada.*

Much of Christy's essay deals with a famous legal case. In 1993 Saskatchewan farmer Robert Latimer put his 12-year-old daughter Tracy, severely disabled and in pain from cerebral palsy, into the cab of his truck. He then filled the cab with exhaust fumes till she died. Always known by friends and neighbours as a loving father, Latimer said he did it to end her pain. The court cases that followed were widely covered in the news. In 1997 a judge granted Latimer a constitutional exemption in order to give him a sentence of only two years—with just one year to be served in jail. Supporters were overjoyed, while groups representing the disabled were enraged. A higher court then overturned the verdict, and in 2001 the Supreme Court of Canada upheld the second-degree murder charge with a life sentence and no chance of parole for ten years. However, day parole was finally granted in 2008. The debate continues: Who is right, the friends and neighbours who think Latimer did a kindness for Tracy, or opponents of mercy killing who guard the rights of the disabled?

1 My name is Bob, and I am living a wonderful life as a son, brother, husband, father, father-in-law and grandfather. I have studied at three post-secondary institutions, received bachelor's and master's degrees from two of Canada's top universities, and had a 30-year career with the federal government. But people may want to tell me what's best for me, because I have cerebral palsy. When I was young, I was popular in the community and at school, received high grades through working hard and exercising an agile mind, and did everything other kids my age did. Yet a close relative thought I should have been "destroyed at birth," because of my condition. I'm a raging extrovert, energized by people, and humorous when I am with them. Yet those who paid my salary put me into jobs away from the public eye, doing research and policy writing, refusing me the chance to do the things I could do best. When I didn't shine or meet the potential that those who knew me thought I should achieve, people could justifiably say: "What do you expect? He has cerebral palsy."

2 Among the many people I know from all walks of life are a professor, now dead, who taught in a major Canadian university, an Anglican priest and her spouse, a water resources economist who is listed in *Who's Who*, and my wife, a clergywoman who is one of the leaders of the largest Protestant denomination in Canada. We all have cerebral palsy. I've travelled, stood on the Great Wall in China and cruised down the Yangtze River, through the Three Gorges. I've been on safari, swum in the Indian Ocean and played golf in Kenya. I've walked the beaches of Trinidad, stood in the main square of Lima, driven a car in England, Scotland, Ireland (north and south) and Wales, and prayed at the Western Wall of the Second Temple in Jerusalem. I paid for it all myself, through writing contracts, even though I have cerebral palsy.

3 But now I cry. For the plight of Robert Latimer and his family, who will suffer for 10 long years because in their frustration, ignorance and—grudgingly, I'll say—love, they followed their own pigheadedness, apparently did not listen to the wisdom of others and did not grasp the help that was there for their daughter Tracy, whom he killed because he said he could not stand her pain.

4 I also weep for the lack of knowledge of people in our so-called high-literacy nation that think cerebral palsy hurts. It doesn't. What hurts is atrophy when muscles are not used: as the saying goes, use them or lose them. Physiotherapy and patterning help blood flow

and ease any pain. Another thing that hurts is the attitude of others. I weep for the many people who, in their ignorance, think Latimer did the "right thing"—who, think, perhaps, that murder, if committed in love to save someone from a "horrible life," is OK if it's a disabled person who dies. Would they feel that way if a person killed another out of love to save the "loved one" from a horrible life as a street person? And I cry for politicians who have forgotten the promises made in 1981, the International Year of Disabled Persons. They are the ones who could be easily tempted to listen to whoever makes the loudest noise, regardless of right or wrong.

But maybe I cry most of all for me; in spite of my cleverness, dili- 5
gence and successes now and in future, will I only be judged in a negative, non-flattering way as "Bob, the man with cerebral palsy"?

EXPLORATIONS:

Elaine Geralis, ed., *Children with Cerebral Palsy: A Parents' Guide*
http://www.cerebralpalsy.org
http://www.ofcp.on.ca/aboutcp.html
http://www.chninternational.com/default.html
http://www.cbc.ca/news/background/latimer/index.html
http://en.wikipedia.org/wiki/Euthanasia
http://www.hawking.org.uk/home/hindex.html
http://www.stevenfletcher.com/profile.php

STRUCTURE:

1. Why does Christy give his name, Bob, in both the opening and closing sentences? What are the effects?
2. Identify Christy's THESIS STATEMENT. Why is it placed towards the middle of the essay?
3. Paragraph 2 is stuffed with a series of quick and colourful *examples.* Are there enough? Is it possible to have too many? Does Christy? What are the effects?
4. Christy ends his argument with a question. Is it a real question? If not, what is its purpose?

STYLE:

1. In question 2 above, we looked at Christy's thesis statement, "But now I cry," which begins paragraph 3. Now identify every place in the rest of the essay where he writes "I cry" or "I weep." Is this *repetition* accidental or deliberate? What are its effects?
2. For what AUDIENCE do you believe Christy is writing? What challenges does he face in communicating with non-disabled readers? Point out everything he does to teach them the facts of his own condition.

ARGUMENTATION AND PERSUASION:

1. To what extent is "Life with Cerebral Palsy" *induction*, based on *examples* that lead to its author's points? Identify at least ten such examples.
2. Does Christy's essay also employ *deduction*, applying a general principle to specific cases?
3. Does Christy's essay work only through logical thought (*argumentation*) or do we also feel *persuasion*? We have already seen the large amount of evidence he presents to argue his case; now look for places where emotion is used as a tool to help us accept his views.

IDEAS FOR DISCUSSION AND WRITING:

1. In the introduction to this essay, review the case of Robert Latimer, who in 1993 killed his daughter Tracy to end her pain from cerebral palsy. Do you view this mercy killing as a crime? Did Latimer deserve the minimum ten-year prison sentence he received? Were disability organizations right in supporting this court decision, so that future disabled persons would be safer? Or do you view Latimer as a loving parent who did the best for his child, and then was unjustly punished? Defend your answers with reasons.
2. In paragraph 3, Christy "cries" for the Latimer family, despite his viewing Latimer's act as "murder." Does this attitude weaken or strengthen his overall argument?
3. One of the world's most brilliant physicists and astronomers, Stephen Hawking, is severely disabled by amyotrophic lateral

sclerosis. Visit his official home page at http://www.hawking.org.uk/home/hindex.html. Find out how he goes about his work despite his disability, then tell the class.

4. Are you disabled, or do you have a family member or friend who is? Report to the class on the challenges of the disability, and how to face them.
5. Stephen Fletcher had won Manitoba's kayaking championship, had canoed thousands of miles of northern rivers, and was working as an engineer. Then in a highway collision with a moose, he became a paraplegic. Visit his blog at http://www.stevenfletcher.com/profile.php, to read how Fletcher became an MP in the 2004 federal election, and Senior Health Critic for the Conservative Party. Report to the class on how he has achieved this success despite a severe physical disability.
6. In Canada we often see special facilities for the disabled: elevators, ramps, Braille signs in elevators, audible signals at traffic lights, seeing-eye dogs, etc. Is this enough? Do you have suggestions for what more might be done?
7. **PROCESS IN WRITING:** *Do an Internet search on Saskatchewan farmer Robert Latimer, and spend a couple of hours reading and taking notes (or printing materials) on his famous court case mentioned above. Now decide whether you support or condemn Latimer's act of mercy killing. Write a short outline of your argument, then do a quick discovery draft. Look it over. Is it mostly* deduction *(beginning with a principle you believe in strongly, then applied to make sense of the facts)? Or is it mostly* induction *(examining the facts of the case, then using them to arrive at an overall* THESIS STATEMENT*)? Examine also your* TONE*: Do you argue rationally, using mostly fact to support your* argumentation*? Or has this controversial topic made you emotional, so that you in turn use emotion as your main way to* persuade *the reader? At the top of the page, label your essay* DEDUCTION or INDUCTION, *and also label it* ARGUMENTATION or PERSUASION. *Now make sure your approach is consistent. Revise and polish. Finally, join with a small group of your classmates to share each other's papers and your reactions to them.*

Note: See also the Topics for Writing on the Online Learning Centre at www.mcgrawhill.ca/olc/conrad.

LT.-GEN. ROMÉO DALLAIRE, WITH MAJOR BRENT BEARDSLEY

*Cri de coeur**

Making peace can take more courage than making war. In 1993 the United Nations named Canadian Lieutenant-General Roméo Dallaire commander of an international peacekeeping force with a tough mandate: to stop an ethnic conflict in the tiny African country of Rwanda. (The career soldier from Quebec seemed a natural choice for operations in a French-speaking nation.) Out of old resentments stemming from the Belgian colonial era, the majority Hutus had begun a persecution of their former masters, the Tutsis. Dallaire saw genocide coming. He alerted the UN, the United States, France and other key players. He requested, then demanded, more troops and weapons. When the slaughters began in spring of 1994, he hounded the major UN countries to save the Tutsis—but they all declined to help, because they saw in Rwanda no strategic value and no oil. So Dallaire and his tiny force went into action: they moved thousands of Tutsis to safety behind the front lines of a rebel Tutsi force; they used moral suasion to defy the governing Hutus; and the apparently fearless General personally intimidated members of the government to obey terms of the peace treaty they had signed. But when the dust settled after 100 days of butchery, some 800,000 men, women and children had died. Dallaire blamed himself, and sank into depression. But over the next decade the world acknowledged its own guilt, and his heroism. Almost a dozen books, documentaries and feature films now tell the story (see "Explorations"). The best of these is Dallaire's own

**Cri de coeur*: Editor's title, in French meaning "a cry from the heart."

book Shake Hands with the Devil: The Failure of Humanity in Rwanda *(2003). Our selection is the book's introduction to this harrowing story. The memoir has become an international bestseller, and has been called the most important Canadian book of the decade. Though Dallaire himself seems not to believe it, these pages portray a true Canadian, and world, hero.*

It was an absolutely magnificent day in May 1994. The blue sky 1
was cloudless, and there was a whiff of breeze stirring the trees. It was hard to believe that in the past weeks an unimaginable evil had turned Rwanda's gentle green valleys and mist-capped hills into a stinking nightmare of rotting corpses. A nightmare we all had to negotiate every day. A nightmare that, as commander of the UN peacekeeping force in Rwanda, I could not help but feel deeply responsible for.

In relative terms, that day had been a good one. Under the pro- 2
tection of a limited and fragile ceasefire, my troops had successfully escorted about two hundred civilians—a few of the thousands who had sought refuge with us in Kigali, the capital of Rwanda—through many government- and militia-manned checkpoints to reach safety behind the Rwandese Patriotic Front (RPF) lines. We were seven weeks into the genocide, and the RPF, the disciplined rebel army (composed largely of the sons of Rwandan refugees who had lived over the border in camps in Uganda since being forced out of their homeland at independence), was making a curved sweep toward Kigali from the north, adding civil war to the chaos and butchery in the country.

Having delivered our precious cargo of innocent souls, we were 3
headed back to Kigali in a white UN Land Cruiser with my force commander pennant on the front hood and the blue UN flag on a staff attached to the right rear. My Ghanaian sharpshooter, armed with a new Canadian C-7 rifle, rode behind me, and my new Senegalese aide-de-camp, Captain Ndiaye, sat to my right. We were driving a particularly dangerous stretch of road, open to sniper fire. Most of the people in the surrounding villages had been slaughtered, the few survivors escaping with little more than the clothes on their backs. In a few short weeks, it had become a lonely and forlorn place.

Suddenly up ahead we saw a child wandering across the road. I 4
stopped the vehicle close to the little boy, worried about scaring him

off, but he was quite unfazed. He was about three years old, dressed in a filthy, torn T-shirt, the ragged remnants of underwear, little more than a loincloth, drooping from under his distended belly. He was caked in dirt, his hair white and matted with dust, and he was enveloped in a cloud of flies, which were greedily attacking the open sores that covered him. He stared at us silently, sucking on what I realized was a high-protein biscuit. Where had the boy found food in this wasteland?

5 I got out of the vehicle and walked toward him. Maybe it was the condition I was in, but to me this child had the face of an angel and eyes of pure innocence. I had seen so many children hacked to pieces that this small, whole, bewildered boy was a vision of hope. Surely he could not have survived all on his own? I motioned for my aide-de-camp to honk the horn, hoping to summon up his parents, but the sound echoed over the empty landscape, startling a few birds and little else. The boy remained transfixed. He did not speak or cry, just stood sucking on his biscuit and staring up at us with his huge, solemn eyes. Still hoping that he wasn't all alone, I sent my aide-de-camp and the sharpshooter to look for signs of life.

6 We were in a ravine lush with banana trees and bamboo shoots, which created a dense canopy of foliage. A long straggle of deserted huts stood on either side of the road. As I stood alone with the boy, I felt an anxious knot in my stomach: this would be a perfect place to stage an ambush. My colleagues returned, having found no one. Then a rustling in the undergrowth made us jump. I grabbed the boy and held him firmly to my side as we instinctively took up defensive positions around the vehicle and in the ditch. The bushes parted to reveal a well-armed RPF soldier about fifteen years old. He recognized my uniform and gave me a smart salute and introduced himself. He was part of an advance observation post in the nearby hills. I asked him who the boy was and whether there was anyone left alive in the village who could take care of him. The soldier answered that the boy had no name and no family but that he and his buddies were looking after him. That explained the biscuit but did nothing to allay my concerns over the security and health of the boy. I protested that the child needed proper care and that I could give it to him: we were protecting and supporting orphanages in Kigali where he would be

much better off. The soldier quietly insisted that the boy stay where he was, among his own people.

I continued to argue, but this child soldier was in no mood to dis- 7
cuss the situation and with haughty finality stated that his unit would care and provide for the child. I could feel my face flush with anger and frustration, but then noticed that the boy himself had slipped away while we had been arguing over him, and God only knew where he had gone. My aide-de-camp spotted him at the entrance to a hut a short distance away, clambering over a log that had fallen across the doorway. I ran after him, closely followed by my aide-de-camp and the RPF child soldier. By the time I had caught up to the boy, he had disappeared inside. The log in the doorway turned out to be the body of a man, obviously dead for some weeks, his flesh rotten with maggots and beginning to fall away from the bones.

As I stumbled over the body and into the hut, a swarm of flies 8
invaded my nose and mouth. It was so dark inside that at first I smelled rather than saw the horror that lay before me. The hut was a two-room affair, one room serving as a kitchen and living room and the other as a communal bedroom; two rough windows had been cut into the mud-and-stick wall. Very little light penetrated the gloom, but as my eyes became accustomed to the dark, I saw strewn around the living room in a rough circle the decayed bodies of a man, a woman and two children, stark white bone poking through the desiccated, leather-like covering that had once been skin. The little boy was crouched beside what was left of his mother, still sucking on his biscuit. I made my way over to him as slowly and quietly as I could and, lifting him into my arms, carried him out of the hut.

The warmth of his tiny body snuggled against mine filled me with 9
a peace and serenity that elevated me above the chaos. This child was alive yet terribly hungry, beautiful but covered in dirt, bewildered but not fearful. I made up my mind: this boy would be the fourth child in the Dallaire family. I couldn't save Rwanda, but I could save this child.

Before I had held this boy, I had agreed with the aid workers and 10
representatives of both the warring armies that I would not permit any exporting of Rwandan orphans to foreign places. When confronted by such requests from humanitarian organizations, I would argue that the money to move a hundred kids by plane to France

or Belgium could help build, staff and sustain Rwandan orphanages that could house three thousand children. This one boy eradicated all my arguments. I could see myself arriving at the terminal in Montreal like a latter-day St. Christopher° with the boy cradled in my arms, and my wife, Beth, there ready to embrace him.

11 That dream was abruptly destroyed when the young soldier, fast as a wolf, yanked the child from my arms and carried him directly into the bush. Not knowing how many members of his unit might already have their gunsights on us, we reluctantly climbed back into the Land Cruiser. As I slowly drove away, I had much on my mind.

12 By withdrawing, I had undoubtedly done the wise thing: I had avoided risking the lives of my two soldiers in what would have been a fruitless struggle over one small boy. But in that moment, it seemed to me that I had backed away from a fight for what was right, that this failure stood for all our failures in Rwanda.

13 Whatever happened to that beautiful child? Did he make it to an orphanage deep behind the RPF lines? Did he survive the following battles? Is he dead or is he now a child soldier himself, caught in the seemingly endless conflict that plagues his homeland?

14 That moment, when the boy, in the arms of a soldier young enough to be his brother, was swallowed whole by the forest, haunts me. It's a memory that never lets me forget how ineffective and irresponsible we were when we promised the Rwandans that we would establish an atmosphere of security that would allow them to achieve a lasting peace. It has been almost nine years since I left Rwanda, but as I write this, the sounds, smells and colours come flooding back in digital clarity. It's as if someone has sliced into my brain and grafted this horror called Rwanda frame by blood-soaked frame directly on my cortex. I could not forget even if I wanted to. For many of these years, I have yearned to return to Rwanda and disappear into the blue-green hills with my ghosts. A simple pilgrim seeking forgiveness and pardon. But as I slowly begin to piece my life back together, I know the time has come for me to make a more difficult pilgrimage: to travel back through all those terrible memories and retrieve my soul.

°St. Christopher: A fearless martyr of the third century, patron saint of travellers.

I did try to write this story soon after I came back from Rwanda in 15
September 1994, hoping to find some respite for myself in sorting out how my own role as Force Commander of UNAMIR interconnected with the international apathy, the complex political manoeuvres, the deep well of hatred and barbarity that resulted in a genocide in which over 800,000 people lost their lives. Instead, I plunged into a disastrous mental health spiral that led me to suicide attempts, a medical release from the Armed Forces, the diagnosis of post-traumatic stress disorder, and dozens upon dozens of therapy sessions and extensive medication, which still have a place in my daily life.

It took me seven years to finally have the desire, the willpower 16
and the stamina to begin to describe in detail the events of that year in Rwanda. To recount, from my insider's point of view, how a country moved from the promise of a certain peace to intrigue, the fomenting of racial hatred, assassinations, civil war and genocide. And how the international community, through an inept UN mandate and what can only be described as indifference, self-interest and racism, aided and abetted these crimes against humanity—how we all helped create the mess that has murdered and displaced millions and destabilized the whole central African region.

A growing library of books and articles is exploring the tragic 17
events in Rwanda from many angles: eyewitness accounts, media analyses, assaults on the actions of the American administration at the time, condemnations of the UN's apparent ineptitude. But even in the international and national inquiries launched in the wake of the genocide, the blame somehow slides away from the individual member nations of the UN, and in particular those influential countries with permanent representatives on the Security Council, such as the United States, France and the United Kingdom, who sat back and watched it all happen, who pulled their troops or didn't offer any troops in the first place. A few Belgian officers were brought to court to pay for the sins of Rwanda. When my sector commander in Kigali, Colonel Luc Marchal, was court-martialled in Brussels, the charges against him were clearly designed to deflect any responsibility away from the Belgian government for the deaths of the ten Belgian peacekeepers under my command. The judge eventually threw out all the charges, accepting the fact that Marchal had performed his

duties magnificently in a near-impossible situation. But the spotlight never turned to the reasons why he and the rest of the UNAMIR force were in such a dangerous situation in the first place.

18 It is time that I tell the story from where I stood—literally in the middle of the slaughter for weeks on end. A public account of my actions, my decisions and my failings during that most terrible year may be a crucial missing link for those attempting to understand the tragedy both intellectually and in their hearts. I know that I will never end my mourning for all those Rwandans who placed their faith in us, who thought the UN peacekeeping force was there to stop extremism, to stop the killings and help them through the perilous journey to a lasting peace. That mission, UNAMIR, failed. I know intimately the cost in human lives of the inflexible UN Security Council mandate, the pennypinching financial management of the mission, the UN red tape, the political manipulations and my own personal limitations. What I have come to realize as the root of it all, however, is the fundamental indifference of the world community to the plight of seven to eight million black Africans in a tiny country that had no strategic or resource value to any world power. An overpopulated little country that turned in on itself and destroyed its own people, as the world watched and yet could not manage to find the political will to intervene. Engraved still in my brain is the judgment of a small group of bureaucrats who came to "assess" the situation in the first weeks of the genocide: "We will recommend to our government not to intervene as the risks are high and all that is here are humans."

19 My story is not a strictly military account nor a clinical, academic study of the breakdown of Rwanda. It is not a simplistic indictment of the many failures of the UN as a force for peace in the world. It is not a story of heroes and villains, although such a work could easily be written. This book is a *cri de coeur* for the slaughtered thousands, a tribute to the souls hacked apart by machetes because of their supposed difference from those who sought to hang on to power. It is the story of a commander who, faced with a challenge that didn't fit the classic Cold War–era peacekeeper's rule book, failed to find an effective solution and witnessed, as if in punishment, the loss of some of his own troops, the attempted annihilation of an ethnicity, the butchery of children barely out of the womb, the stacking of

severed limbs like cordwood, the mounds of decomposing bodies being eaten by the sun.

This book is nothing more nor less than the account of a few humans who were entrusted with the role of helping others taste the fruits of peace. Instead, we watched as the devil took control of paradise on earth and fed on the blood of the people we were supposed to protect.

Explorations:

Lt.-Gen. Roméo Dallaire, with Major Brent Beardsley, *Shake Hands with the Devil: The Failure of Humanity in Rwanda*
Gerald Caplan, *Rwanda: The Preventable Genocide*
Barbara Coloroso, *Extraordinary Evil: A Brief History of Genocide*
Gil Courtemanche, *A Sunday at the Pool in Kigali* (novel)
Joseph Conrad, *Heart of Darkness* (novella)
Hotel Rwanda (feature film, 2004)
Ghosts of Rwanda (PBS documentary)
The Last Just Man (documentary film, 2002)
Shake Hands with the Devil: The Journey of Roméo Dallaire (documentary film, 2005)
Shake Hands with the Devil (feature film, starring Roy Dupuis, 2007)
http://en.wikipedia.org/wiki/Rom%E9o_Dallaire#Early_life_and_education
http://www.thirdworldtraveler.com/Heroes/Gen_Romeo_Dallaire.html
http://tanadineen.com/COLUMNIST/Columns/Dallaire.htm
http://www.pbs.org/wgbh/pages/frontline/shows/ghosts/interviews/dallaire.html

Structure:

1. Read the opening paragraph aloud. How does Dallaire prepare us for his topic, in telling of the "absolutely magnificent day," the "gentle green valleys" and the "mist-capped hills" of Rwanda?

2. The logic of *cause and effect* plays a large part in Dallaire's argument. Point out five examples of it in these pages.
3. To what extent is "*Cri de coeur*" a *narrative*?
4. In not fighting over "one small boy," the general follows military good sense. But he goes on to say, "in that moment, it seemed to me that I had backed away from a fight for what was right, that this failure stood for all our failures in Rwanda" (12). Point out all the ways in which this selection is an *analogy* to larger things.

STYLE:

1. The author's first language is French. Apart from the term *cri de coeur*, chosen from paragraph 19 as our title, do you see any effects of this fact on his style?
2. Read paragraphs 7–8 aloud, if you can. What overall technique lies behind their power to evoke horror?

ARGUMENTATION AND PERSUASION:

1. Examine the logic of this selection. Is it mostly *deduction* (extending a principle to explain individual cases) or *induction* (letting examples lead to a point)?
2. To what extent does the General's *cri de coeur* ("cry from the heart") use emotion, or *persuasion*, to make its points? Give examples. And to what extent does it work through logic, or *argumentation*? Can it draw on both at once?

IDEAS FOR DISCUSSION AND WRITING:

1. After an 11-year-old boy found his 5-year-old sister near the corpses of their parents, he said, "I will hunt the killers to the end of the world. I will kill their children when I grow up. I know the killers; even 70 years from now, I will remember how they and their children look" (*The Ottawa Citizen*, July 13, 2000). What conclusions would you draw from this *example*?
2. As this book was going to press, ten years after the events in Rwanda, another genocide had begun in the Sudan, a country with almost no central government and with no Roméo Dallaires

to intervene. Give your suggestions as to how this continuing tragedy can be ended.

3. After contemplating the downward spiral of his own mental health, the General concludes, "It is time that I tell the story from where I stood" (18). Why did it take nine years for him to put it on paper? Do you believe that writing and sharing his "story" has brought him peace? Canadian novelist Sylvia Fraser once said "Writing is healing." Do your own acts of writing lead your own conflicts toward peace?
4. At one hopeless point during the conflict, Dallaire was asked "What in the hell are you doing here? Why are you staying?" He replied, "If I can save one life, then it's worth it." "Yeah, but there are tens of thousands being slaughtered every day." The General concluded, "Then maybe if I could be a witness, maybe I'll have a chance to tell everything that we've been seeing." Now tell of the time you, too, were a "witness," and what it accomplished.
5. In her 2007 book *Extraordinary Evil: A Brief History of Genocide,* Barbara Coloroso, who writes widely on the problem of bullying in schools, states that genocide is "the most extreme form of bullying." Describe to the class the worst example of bullying that you personally have seen or experienced in school, and point out any similarities you detect between it and the tragedy Dallaire describes in his book.
6. **PROCESS IN WRITING:** *Like Roméo Dallaire, use* persuasion *to "tell the story" of the worst conflict you have ever been in. First close your eyes and remember the situation or incident, then freewrite for several minutes. Look over these notes and work the best of them into a rapid first draft. Be sure to state your THESIS STATEMENT, the overall main point. Later review the 11 devices of* persuasion *listed on pages 349–351 of our chapter introduction, and add them wherever they will strengthen your message. Add SENSE IMAGES, as Dallaire has, to bring the scene alive. Add TRANSITIONS (such as "then," "next" and "finally") to speed the* narrative, *and add logic signals to sharpen your thoughts. Finally, edit for STYLE and correctness, then read the piece aloud, with feeling, to the class. Later consider whether this act of writing has brought you peace.*

Note: See also the Topics for Writing on the Online Learning Centre at www.mcgrawhill.ca/olc/conrad.

GLOSSARY

abstract Theoretical, relying more on GENERALIZATION than on facts and examples. Abstract writing may lack interest and force, because it is hard to understand and the ideas are hard to apply. *See also* the opposite of abstract, CONCRETE.

allegory In poetry or PROSE, a passage or an entire work that has two levels of meaning: literal and symbolic (*see* SYMBOL). Like a parable, an allegory draws such numerous or striking parallels between its literal subject and its implied subject that, without ever stating "the moral of the story," it leads us to perceive a moral or philosophical truth. An allegory, though, is longer and more complex than a parable. It also differs from an analogy in that it does not openly identify and compare the two subjects.

allusion An indirect reference to a passage in literature or scripture, to an event, a person, or anything else familiar to the reader. An allusion is a device of compression in language, for in a few words it summons up the meaning of the thing to which it refers, and applies that meaning to the subject at hand. Critics of big government, for example, often *allude* to Big Brother, the personification of governmental tyranny in George Orwell's novel *1984*.

anecdote A short account of an interesting incident. An anecdote can be a joke or a true story about others or oneself, and is often used as an example to introduce an essay, close an essay or illustrate points within an essay.

audience The reader or readers. One of the essayist's crucial tasks is to match the level and strategy of an argument to the needs and qualities of the particular audience that will read it. *See* the section "Who is my audience?" in this book's introductory essay, "The Act of Writing," p. 100.

bias words Terms that, either subtly or openly, encourage strong value judgements. SUBJECTIVE language is a vital ingredient of much good writing, especially in description and in persuasion; to avoid it completely is difficult and often undesirable. The important thing is to avoid blatantly loaded language in an essay: terms like "jerk," "slob," "cretin," "geezer," "Hogtown," "Newfie," "tree hugger" or "neocon" will inflame an uncritical reader and offend a critical one. Note that many bias words are also SLANG.

cliché A worn-out expression that takes the place of original thought: "sadder but wiser," "bite the bullet," "hustle and bustle," 'been there, done that," "the bottom line," and "no pain, no gain." All clichés were once fresh, but like last year's fad in clothing or music, have lost their appeal and may even annoy.

climax In an essay, the point where the argument reaches its culmination, its point of greatest intensity or importance. The closing of an essay is normally a climax; if it is not, it may give the impression of trailing feebly off into nothingness.

colloquial Speech-like. Colloquial expressions like "cop," "guy," "kid," "nitty gritty" and "okay" are often used in conversation but are usually avoided in essays, especially FORMAL essays. Though lively, colloquialisms can be inexact: "guy," for example, can refer to a rope as well as a person, and "kid" can refer to a goat as well as a child. *See also* SLANG.

conciseness The art of conveying the most meaning in the fewest words. A concise essay does not explain its topic less fully than a wordy one; it just uses words more efficiently. Concise writers get straight to the point and stay on topic. They are well enough organized to avoid repeating themselves. They give CONCRETE examples rather than pages of ABSTRACT argument. They use a short word unless a long one is more exact. And most concise writers, to achieve these goals, revise extensively.

concrete Factual and specific, relying more on examples than on abstract theory. Concrete language makes writing more forceful, interesting and convincing by recreating vividly for the reader what the writer has experienced or thought. SENSE IMAGES, ANECDOTES, FIGURES OF SPEECH and CONCISENESS all play a part in concrete language and are usually lacking in its opposite, ABSTRACT language.

deduction A kind of logic that accepts a general principle as true, then uses it to explain a specific case or cases. *See* "Deduction," p. 346, and its opposite, "Induction," p. 347.

dialogue The quoted conversation of two or more people. Normally a new paragraph begins with each change of speaker, to avoid confusion as to who says what. A bit of dialogue can lend colour to an essay, but heavy use of it is normally reserved for fiction and drama.

economy See CONCISENESS.

epigram A short, clever, and often wise saying. The best-known epigrams are proverbs, such as "What can't be cured must be endured" and "To know all is to forgive all."

epigraph A short introductory quotation prefixed to an essay or other piece of writing.

essay Derived from the French term *essai*, meaning a "try" or "attempt," the word "essay" refers to a short composition in which a point is made, usually through analysis and example. While most essays are alike in being limited to one topic, they may vary widely in other ways. The *formal essay*, for example, is objective and stylistically dignified, while the *familiar essay* is subjective, anecdotal and sometimes colloquial.

euphemism A polite expression that softens or even hides the truth: "pass away" for "die," "senior citizens" for "old people," "low-income neighbourhood" for "slum," "gosh darn" for "God damn," "perspire" for "sweat," "terminate" for "kill," and "de-hire" or "select out" for "fire." Euphemisms have become more and more common in uses ranging from personal kindness to advertising to political repression.

fable A tale, usually about animals, that teaches a moral truth or lesson meant for humans. Examples range from the classical Greek fables of Aesop about animals such as the tortoise and the hare, to modern fables such as Basil Johnston's selection in this book, "Modern Cannibals of the Wilds."

fiction Imaginative literature written in PROSE. Consisting mainly of novels and short stories, fiction uses invented characters and plots to create a dramatic story. Most ESSAYS, by contrast, rely on literal fact and analysis to create an argument. There is of course an area of overlap: some fiction is very factual and some essays are very imaginative.

figures of speech Descriptive and often poetic devices in which meaning is concentrated and heightened, usually through comparisons:

A. **Simile**: A figure of speech in which one thing is said to be *like* another. ("With its high buildings on all sides, Bay Street is like a canyon.")
B. **Metaphor:** A figure of speech, literally false but poetically true, in which one thing is said to *be* another. ("Bay Street is a canyon walled by cliffs of concrete.")

C. **Hyperbole**: Exaggeration. ("The office buildings rise miles above the city.")

D. **Personification**: A figure of speech in which a non-human object is described as human. ("At night the empty buildings stare from their windows at the street.")

formal Formal writing is deliberate and dignified. It avoids partial sentences, most contractions, colloquial expressions and slang. Instead its vocabulary is standard and its sentences are often long and qualified with dependent clauses. It follows accepted rules of grammar and principles of style. *See also* INFORMAL.

generalization A broad statement of overall principle, as opposed to an explanation using specific examples. Although an essay needs generalizations, especially in places such as the THESIS STATEMENT and the CONCLUSION, most arguments that lack concrete examples are dull and difficult to understand.

hyperbole *See* FIGURES OF SPEECH.

image In literature, a mental picture triggered by words. Because they strongly stimulate thought and feeling, yet take little space, well-chosen images are vital ingredients of writing that is CONCRETE and has CONCISENESS. *See also* SENSE IMAGES.

induction A kind of logic that derives a general principle from the evidence of specific examples. *See* "Induction," p. 347, and its opposite, "Deduction," p. 346.

informal Informal writing resembles speech and, in fact, is often a representation of speech in writing. It may contain partial sentences, many short sentences, contractions, COLLOQUIAL expressions and sometimes SLANG. *See also* its opposite, FORMAL. Academic essays avoid almost all informal language.

irony A manner of expression in which a statement that seems literally to mean one thing actually means another. "Wonderful!" is a literal remark when said by a dinner guest enjoying the pie, but an ironic complaint when said by a driver who has backed into a tree. In a larger sense, *irony of situation* is a contrast between what is expected to happen and what does happen. It is this that creates our interest in the national leader who is impeached, the orphan who becomes a millionaire or the evangelist convicted of tax fraud. Irony is a powerful tool of argument and especially of SATIRE.

jargon Technical language or language that seeks to impress by *appearing* difficult or technical. Specialized terms can hardly be avoided in technical explanations: How could two electricians discuss a radio without words like "capacitor," "diode" and "transistor"? But these same words may need defining when put in an essay for the general reader. Other jargon uses technical-sounding or otherwise difficult words to seem important. An honest essayist will try to avoid "input," "output," "feedback," "interface," "knowledgeable," "parameters" and other ugly words of this sort when writing for the general reader.

juxtaposition The deliberate placing together of two or more thoughts, IMAGES or other elements that emphasize each other, usually by contrast.

metaphor *See* FIGURES OF SPEECH.

neologism A newly invented word. Some new terms are accepted into our standard vocabulary. For example, the word "laser" quickly became standard because we needed it to label a new and important invention. Most newly minted words are nuisances, though, meaningless to the many readers who do not know them.

objective The opposite of SUBJECTIVE. In objective writing the author relies more on hard evidence and logical proof than on intuitions, prejudices or interpretations.

onomatopoeia A poetical device in which language sounds like what it means. Some onomatopoetic words, such as "boom," "bang" and "crash," are obvious sound effects; others, such as "slither," "ooze" and "clatter," are more subtle. Onomatopoeia can be achieved not only through word choice but also through larger aspects of style. A series of short sentences, for example, gives an impression of tenseness and rapidity.

paradox A statement that seems illogical but that in some unexpected way may be true. The Bible is full of paradoxes, as in "Blessed are the meek, for they shall inherit the earth."

personification *See* FIGURES OF SPEECH.

prose Spoken or written language without the metrical structure that characterizes poetry. Conversations, letters, short stories, novels and essays are all prose.

pun A play on words. A pun is based either on two meanings of one word or on two words that sound alike but have different meanings. Often called the lowest form of humour, the pun is the basis of many jokes. (Why did the fly fly? Because the spider spider.)

quotation The words of one person reproduced exactly in the writing or speech of another person. A well-chosen quotation can add force to an argument by conveying the opinion of an authority or by presenting an idea in words so exact or memorable that they could hardly be improved upon. Quotations should be reproduced exactly, placed in quotation marks and attributed to their source. In writing research papers, there are whole systems of presenting and documenting quotations.

reduction to absurdity A technique of SATIRE in which the subject is belittled through being portrayed as absurd. A favourite device of humorists, such as Stephen Leacock.

sarcasm Scornful and contemptuous criticism, from the Greek word *sarkazein* ("to tear flesh").

satire Humorous criticism meant to improve an individual or society by exposing abuses. In TONE, satire can range from light humour to bitter criticism. Its main tools are wit, IRONY, exaggeration and sometimes SARCASM and ridicule.

sense images Descriptive appeals to one or more of the reader's five senses: sight, hearing, touch, taste and smell. Sense images are vital in helping the reader to experience, at second hand, what the writer has lived in person. CONCRETE language has many sense images; ABSTRACT language does not.

simile *See* FIGURES OF SPEECH.

slang Racy, unconventional language, often limited to a certain time, place or group. Slang is the extreme of colloquial language, terminology used in conversation but hardly ever in an ESSAY except for dialogue or special effects. One reason to avoid a slang term is that not everyone will know it: expressions like "swell," "square" and "far out" have fallen out of use, while expressions like "bug juice," "croaker," "jointman" and "rounder" are known to only one group—in this case, prison inmates. *See also* COLLOQUIAL.

stereotype An established mental image of something. Most stereotypes are of people and are based on their sex, race, colour, size or shape, economic or social class, or profession. Jokes about mothers-in-law, "Newfies," absent-minded professors, woman drivers or short people are all examples of stereotyping. While they may provoke humour, stereotypes are anything but harmless: they prevent recognition of people's individuality and they encourage prejudices which, at their extreme, can result in persecution like that of the Jews in Nazi Germany.

style In general, the *way* something is written, as opposed to *what* it is written about. Style is to some extent a matter of TONE—light or serious, INFORMAL or FORMAL, ironic or literal. It is also a matter of technique. Word choice, FIGURES OF SPEECH, level of CONCISENESS and characteristics of sentence structure and paragraphing are all ingredients of style. Although a writer should pay close attention to these matters, the idea that one deliberately seeks out "a style" is a mistake that only encourages imitation. An individual style emerges naturally as the sum of the writer's temperament, skills and experience.

subjective The opposite of OBJECTIVE. In subjective writing the author relies more on intuitions, prejudices or interpretations than on hard evidence and logical proof.

symbol One thing that stands for another, as in a flag representing a country, the crescent representing Islam or a logo representing a company. Symbols in word form appear frequently in poetry, drama, fiction and also essays.

thesis statement The sentence or sentences, usually in the introduction, that first state the main point and restrict the focus of an essay.

tone The manner of a writer toward the subject and reader. The tone of an essay can be light or serious, INFORMAL or FORMAL, ironic or literal. Tone is often determined by subject matter; for example, an essay about parties is likely to be lighter and less formal than one about funerals. An innovative writer, though, might reverse these treatments to give each of the essays an ironic tone. The identity of the reader also influences tone. An essay for specialists to read in a technical journal will tend to be more OBJECTIVE and serious than one written for the general reader. The main point for the writer is to choose the tone most appropriate to a particular essay and audience, then maintain it throughout.

transition A word, phrase, sentence or paragraph that moves the reader from one part of the essay to the next. Transitions, even ones as short as "next," "then," "as a result," "on the other hand," "in conclusion" or "finally," are crucial not only to speeding the argument along, but also to pointing out its logic.